Learning to be a Person in Society

Learning is a lifelong process and we are the result of our own learning. But how exactly do we learn to be a person through living? In this book, Peter Jarvis draws together all the aspects of becoming a person into the framework of learning. Considering the ongoing 'nature versus nurture' debate over how we become people, Jarvis's study of nurture – what learning is primarily about – builds on a detailed recognition of our genetic inheritance and evolutionary reality. It demonstrates the ways in which we become social human beings: internalising, accommodating and rejecting the culture to which we are exposed (both directly and through electronic mediation) while growing and developing as human beings and people.

As learning theory moves away from traditional, single-discipline approaches it is possible to place the person at the centre of all thinking about learning, by emphasising a multidisciplinary approach. This wide-ranging study draws on established research from a number of disciplines into the complexities that make us who we are. It will appeal to a wide variety of audiences: those involved in all fields of education, the study of learning and development, human resource development, psychology, theology and the caring professions.

Peter Jarvis is an internationally renowned expert in the fields of lifelong learning, adult and continuing education and is founding editor of the *International Journal of Lifelong Education* (Taylor & Francis). He is Professor of Continuing Education at the University of Surrey (where he was formerly the head of the Department of Educational Studies) and is a former Adjunct Professor in the Department of Adult Education, University of Georgia, USA. He also holds honorary visiting professorships at City University (UK), Pecs University (Hungary) and Tianjin Radio and Television University (China), and is Special Professor at the University of Nottingham. Peter is a prolific author, whose recent publications include: *The Routledge International Handbook of Lifelong Learning*; *Democracy, Lifelong Learning and the Learning Society*; and *Globalization, Lifelong Learning and the Learning Society* (winner of the 2008 Cyril O. Houle World Award for Outstanding Literature in Adult Education).

Learning to be a Person
in Society

Peter Jarvis

Routledge
Taylor & Francis Group

LONDON AND NEW YORK

First published 2009
by Routledge
2 Park Square, Milton Park, Abingdon, Oxon, OX14 4RN

Simultaneously published in the USA and Canada
by Routledge
270 Madison Avenue, New York, NY 10016

Routledge is an imprint of the Taylor & Francis Group, an informa business

© 2009 Peter Jarvis

Typeset in Sabon by Prepress Projects Ltd, Perth, UK
Printed and bound in Great Britain by CPI Antony Rowe,
Chippenham, Wiltshire

British Library Cataloguing in Publication Data
A catalogue record for this book is available from the British Library

Library of Congress Cataloging in Publication Data
Jarvis, Peter, 1937-
Learning to be a person in society / Peter Jarvis.
p. cm.
Includes bibliographical references.
1. Educational sociology. 2. Learning, Psychology of. 3. Experiential learning.
4. Self-culture. I. Title.
LC191.J375 2009
303.3'2--dc22   2009001035

ISBN10: 0–415–41902–6 (hbk)
ISBN10: 0–415–41903–4 (pbk)

ISBN13: 978–0–415–41902–4 (hbk)
ISBN13: 978–0–415–41903–1 (pbk)

August 10, 2009

To Liam and Ryan, and Martin and their parents, from whom I have learned more than they could have possibly taught me

Contents

Preface

This book is truly about lifelong learning rather than using the concept to discuss just one element of the topic. This book seeks to present a much more comprehensive picture – it is genuinely about lifelong learning – starting with learning in the womb and recognising the significance of disengagement in old age. The book is not confined to a single disciplinary perspective although the significance and the contribution of individual disciplines are implicitly recognised throughout.

Conceptually, then, lifelong learning has been a confused concept with a wide variety of usages, from 'learning from cradle to grave' to a simpler 'work life learning', which in practice made it a synonym for adult vocational education. Examine any of the European Commission's policy documents on lifelong learning and see how they omitted whole areas of lifelong learning. But it has not only been a confused concept: it has had a confused practice. In the European Commission, for instance, 'Higher Education' and 'Education and Training' have never been included in lifelong learning and it was only when the Commission brought out a report on 'Adult Learning' that senior citizens were included in the learning debate. The same divisions have been retained with academia – few adult educators attended conferences on children's learning, and vice versa, even though in many instances the actual subject was common to both of them. Most books on lifelong learning have actually been restricted to adult learning – but this one seeks to rectify this.

The first six chapters of the book set the scene by clarifying some of the major concepts: Chapter 1 recognises that learning is not only individual but social and that it is also about evolution and the development of the brain. It is recognised that there is a need for serious studies about the relationship between brain science and learning, and between evolution and learning. Chapter 2 recognises that learning occurs in a societal context and Chapter 3 explores early childhood learning – for the 'child is the father of the man': all learning theories need to understand this. In Chapter 4 it is recognised that a great deal of our learning comes from and is affected by early childhood learning and that this occurs within practical living probably more than in formal educational situations. Chapter 5 explores the idea of human experience which underlies all human living and learning but is rarely discussed in experiential learning books, and in the final chapter of the first section, Chapter 6, it is recognised that there is no intrinsic meaning to creation but that we, as human beings, have evolved in such a way as to seek meaning to our existence and so we endeavour to impose meaning upon creation – this is the beginning of both science and religion.

The second section of the book seeks to combine the disciplines and the diverse studies in different aspects of human learning in 10 brief chapters. It examines experiencing and perception; thinking, knowledge and belief; feeling, doing and interacting; valuing and positioning in society. Each of these chapters points us to the holism of human learning as it examines recent research in each topic. Finally, the last two chapters point us to becoming and being – towards a philosophy of learning – so that we can see not only that throughout our lives we are always learning and in this sense becoming, but that at every point in time we are a being – a person. We are truly learning to be persons in society – learning to be ourselves.

The book points the way to further studies in a number of areas including teaching, philosophy of learning and even the science of learning. It is not an end-product but a stage in the process of seeking to understand human learning and even humanity a little better. In this sense, it is as much a practical book as it is a theoretical one.

No book like this can be written without the help and support of colleagues, friends and family. The book is dedicated to my family, from whom I have learned so much about learning, and although I have not named my wife, Maureen, she has been one of my most important teachers throughout my life – she has also been most understanding during the time that I have been writing it. As I have been privileged to travel around the world lecturing on lifelong learning, I have learned so much from colleagues in different countries and different cultures – I am most grateful to them. However, I gave drafts of the early chapters to two colleagues, Della Freeth of City University and Bernard Jensen of the Danish Pedagogical University, and their kindly critical comments made me reorientate the whole book – to them I am especially grateful. I am also grateful to Bernard because he suggested that I read a number of books that at the time I did not know, and I hope that he will see from the text how influential those suggestions have been.

Nevertheless, the book is the outcome of my own studies. I am responsible for its errors, but the main reason for writing it was that I cherish the fond hope that it might prove useful in helping others to learn: it is written for teachers practising the art of helping others to learn, for students who wish to know more about human learning and for the general reader who seeks to understand a little more about the human person.

Peter Jarvis
Thatcham
31 December 2008

Section I

Laying the foundations

Chapter 1

A person in society

Of course, everyone becomes a person in society: we cannot stop this. And, so, why write a book about learning to be a person in society? Perhaps this is an obvious question, but the answer is much more difficult – it does not just happen by birth or by chance; we actually learn to become the people we are. I learn to be me! You learn to be you! But we do not just learn to be us during our schooling. Learning is much broader than education – learning is a lifelong process and we are the result of our own learning. It is this that we are going to try to understand in this book. And, so, in this first chapter we are going to examine some of the fundamental concepts underlying this complex social process, and we will see that this is both a psychological and a sociological study of learning, although it must necessarily incorporate philosophical aspects since learning is, in one sense, a humanistic process. The approach of any one discipline to learning is insufficient for our understanding of learning to be a person in society but we will rely very heavily on psychological studies, especially of early childhood.

This first chapter seeks to clarify the concepts and examine the implications of our thinking – it has three parts: the first part looks at the concept of the person, the second at society and the third at the person in society.

Part 1: The concept of the person

In the contemporary world, one which has experienced the genetic revolution in the past quarter of a century, we do well to ask 'What is the person?', 'What makes us human?'. It is incontrovertible that we human beings are members of the ape family – DNA research has demonstrated just how much we are members of this family, and so the question is 'What makes us human?'. Are we only great apes (Dunbar, 2007)? Dunbar, amongst many others, argues that the fundamental difference is 'the theory of mind' – 'the capacity to imagine another individual's mind states' (Dunbar, 2007: 40). First-order intentionality is the term used to cover these mind states, and Dunbar (ibid.: 41) suggests that there is no evidence to suggest that any animals apart from chimpanzees (and perhaps other of the great apes) have a theory of mind. If they do so, he suggests that the level to which they have evolved is about the same level as children aged four or five years. But human beings have more sophisticated levels of intentionality; the human mind, he suggests, has been in existence for only about 200,000 years – a short time when we consider that our last common ancestor with the apes probably lived about five and a half million years ago. This is a very similar position to that taken by Tomasello (1999: 55), who writes:

> We have at most only 6 million years, but more likely only one-quarter of a million years, to create uniquely human cognition, and this is simply not sufficient, under any plausible evolutionary scenario, for genetic variation and natural selection to have created many different and independent uniquely human modules.

Tomasello (ibid.: 54) argues that human cultural inheritance rests on twin pillars:

> sociogenesis, by means of which most cultural artefacts and practices are created, and cultural learning, by means of which these creations and the human intentions and perspectives that lie behind them are internalized by developing youngsters.

And so we can see that from within an evolutionary framework, it is still meaningful to enquire about the nature of personhood since we may locate ourselves as being at the pinnacle of the process of evolution whilst still acknowledging that we are by our genetic inheritance members of the ape family, but discussion about the nature of the person has to leave the evolutionary perspective and begin to look at the phenomenon from a more humanistic perspective.

The person, like society, has a common-sense usage, but in order to clarify our thinking we do need to explore the several meanings of the term. It is perhaps significant that the term 'person' does not occur in the index of Rogers' (1961) classic *On Becoming a Person*, although he does discuss 'personal constructs' and has a whole section on the philosophy of the person from a therapist's perception. This illustrates the position from which Rogers is approaching this topic and, although therapy throws considerable light on the subject, not all individuals become persons as a result of therapy. But we will also find a lot more from Rogers in his *Freedom to Learn* studies (Rogers, 1983; Rogers and Freiberg, 1994); even here his main focus is therapeutic although he claims that the goal of learning and therapy is to be 'a fully functioning person'. This is clearly the end-product of his therapeutic process, but it is also the aim of many psychological studies and policy statements on learning. Other psychologists have tried in a variety of ways to capture the complexity of becoming a fully functioning person: for instance, Maslow's (1968) famous hierarchy of needs – physiological, safety, love and belonging, self-esteem and self-actualisation – illustrates this position.

McAdams' (2001) full study of the person, to which we will make reference from time to time throughout this book, tells us more about the personality traits and characteristics than it does about the concept of the person itself. Haslam's (2007) introduction to personality is also referred to throughout this book. Apter (1989) suggests that the person has distinctness, continuity and autonomy. MacMurray (1979 [1961]: 27), however, suggests that 'the term "person" fulfils the same function from the standpoint of the agent as the term "self" does in traditional philosophy, which thinks from the standpoint of the subject'. But we do use the word in a variety of different ways, as *Collins English Dictionary* shows:

- an individual human being;
- the body of a human being, e.g. 'on his/her person';
- a grammatical category, e.g. singular or plural;
- an individual having certain rights and obligations in law;
- a being characterised by personality, consciousness, rationality, morality and self-awareness;
- a role or guise;
- actually present, e.g. in person.

Almost all of these usages are open to considerable debate, and we will return to these shortly. However, when we consult a philosophical dictionary (Speake, 1984) we are confronted with a short discussion which points us to Locke's work. Locke wrote that a person is:

> A thinking intelligent being that has reason and reflection and can consider itself as itself, the same thinking thing in different times and places; which it does only by that consciousness which is inseparable from thinking and, as it seems to me, essential to it: it is impossible for anyone to perceive without perceiving that he does perceive. When we see, hear, small, taste, feel meditate or will anything, we know that we do so. Thus it is always to our present sensations and perceptions, and by this everyone is to himself that which he calls a *self*: it is not being considered in this case whether the same *self* be continued in the same or diverse substances.
>
> (Locke, 1947: 180, italics in original)

Immediately we are confronted with the concept of 'self' here. This is a term to which we will return but, following MacMurray, I see 'self' as the nearest equivalent to the person in relation to this study. One other feature that emerges immediately is that the self may be 'of the mind' but whether

it is of 'the brain' is more controversial. Indeed, we have to note immediately that there is a controversy about the nature of the person as body
and mind, in which the self is a construct of the mind, and so on. It is an
unresolved debate, but the position adopted here is that the self is learned,
as is the mind, and that there is a very complex relationship between body/
brain and mind. Indeed, I agree with Feser (2006: 211) when he concludes
that 'Descartes' basic contention that the mind is irreducible to the brain
or body has not been refuted'. But we can at least begin to see that even a
simple term such as 'person' is open to much more debate than is apparent
on the surface.

It is significant in all these formulations that the ability to do – to act,
create and relate – is hardly present in this discussion although many contemporary scholars see this at the heart of our humanity. Arendt (1958)
opens her classic work on the human condition by discussing *viva activa*,
in which she says there are three dimensions – labour, work and action.
Labour is the basic human condition – it is the bodily processes; work corresponds to the unnaturalness of the human condition – it is the artificial
world of production; action is the activity that goes on between people,
especially the political elements that enable people to live together – it
is relating. In a similar way, Archer (2000: 154–90) sees the practical as
pivotal in her arguments about being human. Doing is at the heart of being
human, but creating is the process of building our world and making it a
better place for us all to live: we all need to become experts in doing and
creating – we should not be content with mere competencies – in our contribution to the world. Consequently, we need to include this dimension in
any understanding that we have of the person – the ego.

For the moment let us accept that the person is an individual capable
of doing, thinking and sensing in a wide variety of ways. I will return to
this discussion at the end of this work. However, the person is not fully
formed at birth – what I am arguing here is that the person is learned in the
process of human living and, therefore, the self only emerges out of this
process and so unlike many experientialists the self is a problematic in this
process. Newman (2008: 288) comments that 'most experiential learning
starts with the self as a given' and, although his assertion might have some
validity, it is not true for all experiential learning theorists and so it is a
pity that he did not widen the scope of his investigation and start with
consciousness. But there is another problem: most experiential learning
theories start with the adult whereas, in this book, we start with the fetus!
The person is individual, and it is important from the outset of this study
to recognise that the Enlightenment focused on the individual to such an
extent that it became central to a great deal of our thinking; however, in
this contemporary society, modernity is regarded being as flawed (Gray,
1995; Jarvis, 2008) and so the focus of our study can no longer be on
the isolated individual because the person lives in relationship. Individuals
emerge out of relationship.

Part 2: The concept of society

Margaret Thatcher, when she was prime minister of the UK, famously exclaimed that 'there is no such thing as society'. Of course, if she was looking for an empirical reality, such as a house, or even a world, then she was perfectly correct. But there are many things that cannot be reified, such as light, a black hole, and so on. Society is another such concept: it cannot be reified but that does not mean that it does not exist, and so it is now necessary for us to explore the complexities of this common concept in precisely the same way as we have for person. This will form the first part of this section and in the second we will examine the concept of culture, which has been regarded in the past as something that is society-wide.

Society

Once more *Collins English Dictionary* provides a starting point:

* the totality of relationships among organised groups of human beings or animals;
* a system of human organisation generating distinctive cultural patterns and institutions;
* a system of human beings with reference to its social and economic organisation;
* those with whom one has companionship;
* an organised group of people associating for some specific purpose;
* a privileged class of people;
* the social life of such a privileged class;
* companionship;
* a small community of plants within a larger association.

These are very general descriptions of forms of human relationship and organisation. A sociological dictionary suggests that sociologists, while accepting the above definitions, also treat it as in some ways equivalent to the nation state (Abercrombie *et al.*, 2000), which in the light of globalisation and other social processes has ceased to be a simple, single political entity. Globalisation is a theme that has occupied many books (Jarvis, 2007a) but it is not the processes of recent globalisation or global culture that are the major issues for our purposes: it is the nature of the culture of a society that is significant, and we can see that there is now no 'pure' single racial or ethnic culture even if there was in the past. We are confronted with a global society through the media, and in most areas in which we live there are representatives of a number of ethnic groups, so that the more general dictionary definitions might reflect the reality of the society in which many, if not most, people live. It is a multicultural society and in the West it is a society that is dominated by the culture of modernity.

Although the nation state has lost the idea of sovereign independence, governments still have certain forms of jurisdiction over specific territories, and these countries are organised regionally and locally; they have forms of governance over the population irrespective of the different people's ethnic origins. In this sense, society is now separated from the idea of a single culture and people live in their own 'life-worlds', which is the term some sociologists prefer to convey the idea of the person in society; however, before we discuss this idea we need to look at the concept of culture.

Culture

Like the first two concepts that we have examined, culture is a word common to everyday life and so once again we will start by looking at *Collins English Dictionary*'s definitions:

- the total of the inherited ideas, beliefs, values and knowledge, which constitutes the shared basis of social action;
- the shared traditions which are transmitted and reinforced by members of a social group;
- a particular civilisation;
- the artistic and social pursuits, expressions and tastes valued by a society;
- the enlightenment or refinement resulting from these pursuits;
- the cultivation of plants;
- the experimental growth of micro-organisms . . .

(There are several other usages given in the dictionary – all referring to topics that do not concern this study, such as agriculture.)

Once again, this is not a reifiable concept although there is a tendency to treat it as a thing. It is about practices and beliefs and values, and so on. When we turn to the sociological dictionary (Abercrombie *et al.*, 2000) we find a more complex discussion, but one essential to our study. Culture is:

- contrasted with the biological – the non-biological aspects of human society;
- contrasted with nature – it is to do with civilisation rather than barbarism;
- contrasted with structure – it is the social cement which keeps the institutions of society intact;
- contrasted with the material – it is the realm of beliefs etc. influenced by society's substructure;
- a way of life – each society had a common culture;
- contrasts between ways of life – high and popular culture, with the former being elitist.

The widest of these definitions contrasts culture to the biological and so we will adopt this wide definition here – culture is 'the word we give to . . . (the) world of images, stories, objects and ways of acting to which we have recourse in our struggle to exist. But culture is not what determines the acting, or the need to act. These are existential imperatives' (Jackson, 2005: 103). The obvious point to make here is that the person is a combination of these broad perspectives – both biological and cultural – and the study of both is important for us if we are to begin to understand human learning. Gehlen (1988: 29) reached a similar conclusion from an anthropological perspective years earlier when he wrote (italics in original):

> In order to survive, he [humankind] must master and recreate nature, and for this reason man must *experience* the world. He acts because he is unspecialized and deprived of a natural environment to which he is adapted. The epitome of nature restructured to serve his needs is called *culture* and the culture world is the human world . . . Culture, therefore, is 'second nature' – man's restructured nature.

But unlike the animals, humans may have minimal instincts although they have many predispositions and inclinations as a result of their evolution and their learning in the womb and so they have to learn this second nature and pass it on from generation to generation, so that children's education is often seen as transmitting the most worthwhile knowledge from one generation to the succeeding one. In this sense, education is 'from above' since the dominant forces in the older generation decide what should be included in the curriculum – one way of viewing curriculum is that it is a selection from culture. However, culture does not remain a static phenomenon, and Wexler (2006: 185) suggests historically culture would have remained rudimentary until the advent of a developed language. Tomasello (1999: 5) has argued:

> Basically none of the most complex human artefacts or practices – including tool industries, symbolic communication, and social institutions – were invented once and for all at a single moment by any one individual or group of individuals. Rather, what happened was that some individual or group first invented a primitive version of the artefact or practice, and then some later user or users made a modification or 'improvement,' that others then adopted perhaps without change for many generations, at which point some other individual or group of individuals made another modification, which was then learned and used by others, and so on over historical time in what has sometimes been dubbed 'the ratchet effect'.

Hence, culture has undergone a process of cumulative evolution but, although it differs between East and West, it remains all the knowledge, skills, attitudes, beliefs, values and emotions that we, as human beings, have added to our biological base and which we externalise as a result of our learning. Culture is a social phenomenon; it is what we as a society, or a people, share and which enables us to live as society. In order for a society to survive, it is necessary that we should each learn our own culture and appreciate the cultures of others. Learning, then, becomes necessary for the survival of societies and in the process we, as human beings, learn to be.

But culture differs from country to country, although some of the main cultural differences are between those which stem from the Judeo-Greek–European heritage countries, i.e. Western civilisation, and those that emanate from Confucian heritage countries, i.e. Eastern civilisation. Nisbett (2003: xv) notes that before he started his studies into comparative cultures he had assumed universality and hard-wiring of the brain, and so he was very surprised when there were major differences between countries and that individuals could be trained: his studies led to the significant conclusion: 'Human cognition is not everywhere the same' (ibid.: xvii) and these cultural groupings have significant differences. This conclusion is also echoed by Donald (2001: 274), when he suggests that language 'is a collective product and must have evolved as a group adaptation in the context of mimetic, expressive culture'. Such conclusions are fundamentally significant for learning theory.

Culture, then, is society-wide or at least social group- or ethnic group-wide, so that we can talk of British culture, American culture, Chinese culture, and so on, but they are no longer 'pure' because as a result of migration, the media, travel, and so on, the cultures of the world are dissipated and fused together in different ways in different parts of each country. Globalisation and rapid social change have affected the nature of society, and most societies are now multicultural. We all live in multicultural life-worlds that are gradually reflecting the locality, so that there is a certain myth about the unity of culture, which is the danger of reification to which we alluded above. Archer (1988) calls this the myth of cultural integration, and she goes on to show why she considers it a myth, although we may individually and subjectively integrate those cultures to which we are exposed through our learning processes – but we integrate them into our own biographies. We are aware of the fact that because of industrialisation, globalisation, migration, and so on, cultural homogeneity is probably restricted to pre-industrial peoples and small rural communities. Consequently, a number of different cultures exist in most urban societies in the West that are now regarded as multicultural and this phenomenon is exacerbated by the media. This might well result in some persons not acquiring the same sense of security, sense of community membership and self-identity as people did in previous generations, which, in turn, has given rise to identity crisis, what Giddens (1991) refers to as 'existential anxiety'.

It is also necessary to recognise that within complex societies there are different lifestyles, patterns of social living, organisations and so on, so that it is common practice to refer to the cultures of subgroups or sections of society as subcultures. Consequently, we can talk of the subculture of the school or the subculture of the work organisation, and so on, and now we can begin to see why sociologists have so many different perspectives on culture.

Part 3: The person in society

People no longer live in a single cultural society: they live in life-worlds which consist of a unique combination of cultural practices, depending on where people live and on their social position – amongst other things. Society is a combination of systems and life-worlds and the life-world is multicultural. In his discussions of the life-world, Habermas (1987: 117, italics in original) suggests that:

> No matter whether one starts with Mead from basic concepts of social interaction or with Durkheim from basic concepts of collective representation, in either case society is conceived from the perspective of acting subjects as the *lifeworld of the social group*. In contrast, from the observer's perspective as someone not involved society can be conceived only as a *system of actions* such that each action has a functional significance according to its contribution to the maintenance of the system.

Habermas argues that societies can be conceived as both system and life-worlds, but from the learners' perspective we can take the first part of this quote although we would want to add that the life-world and the society are not the same phenomenon. Society consists of many overlapping and intersecting life-worlds and we all construct our own life-worlds.

> The life-world is something to be mastered according to my particular interests. I project my plans into the life-world, and it resists the realization of my goals, in terms of which some things become feasible to me and others do not. From the outset, however, I find in my life-world fellow men who appear not merely as organisms but rather as bodies endowed with consciousness, as men 'like me'. A fellow-man's behaviour is not, if you will, a spatiotemporal event, but rather action 'like mine'.
>
> (Schutz and Luckmann, 1974: 15)

Our life-worlds are about practical living in the everyday and so our learning is about action in a pragmatic manner in order to achieve certain goals and behaviours. In this sense, most of our everyday learning is action learning – learning theoretical knowledge occurs at specified times, such as attending educational institutions, devoting time to reading and writing, and so on: it is about primary rather than secondary experience. For the most part we are dealing with practical knowledge and utilising our own experience (remembered biographical learning – we will return to the topic of experience in Chapter 5), and so it is not hard to see why the learning of the elders was in bygone generations regarded as wisdom. Our life-world is one with which we are familiar and so our behaviour can be taken for granted. As Schutz and Luckmann (ibid.: 7) write:

> I trust that the world as it has been known by me up until now will continue further and that consequently the stock of knowledge obtained from my fellow-men and formed from my own experiences will continue to preserve its fundamental validity . . . From this assumption follows the further one: that I can repeat my past successful acts. So long as the structure of the world can be taken as constant, as long as my previous experience is valid, my ability to act upon the world in this and that manner remains in principle preserved. As Husserl has shown, the further ideality of the 'I can always do it again' is developed correlative of the ideality of the 'and so forth'.

In a sense, we are 'at home' in our life-world and we learn to take pleasure in it: we can take our world for granted and it is perceived to be true because we are in harmony with it and our internal and external worlds are congruent and we are also at one with the individuals in our life-world – our personal community, as it were. There is a sense of unity and harmony – solidarity, if you like. But as we develop this personal community changes: as we go through our various socialisation processes, so our horizons change and expand. Our life-world is not a static phenomenon and is dependent upon our own biography and our own learning. Our life-world is dependent upon our use of appropriate language and culture, and our own learning and as we change from one situation to another, so we find we move from one domain to another. As Habermas (1987: 125) puts it:

> Participants find the relations between the objective, social and subjective worlds already preinterpreted. When they go beyond the horizon of a given situation, they cannot step into a void; they find themselves right away in another, now actualized, yet *preinterpreted* domain of what is culturally taken for granted. In everyday communicative practice there are no completely unfamiliar situations. Every new situation appears in a lifeworld composed of a cultural stock of knowledge that is 'always already' familiar.

In these familiar situations, we learn to fit in and we adjust our behaviour accordingly in relationship to those others with whom we interact and, as we have already pointed out, there is often an element of power in this interaction. This adjustment is a form of learning – incidental and often unintended and unrecognised as learning, since we are involved in imitation of others in the life-world, trial and error and discovery learning when we cannot copy others, and so on. Additionally, we recognise that our subjective life-world is actually an intersubjective one, and for as long as we function within familiar territory we can take our world for granted – that is habitualise it – and we can share the meanings we give situations with those with whom we interact, but we may not always agree with each other although we will understand from where each is coming.

It is clear that we live in life-worlds which are social and so we are faced with the question of individuality – a concept with which a great deal of thinking in the West has started. Individuality was not a new concept at the time of the Enlightenment and was probably first discussed in the writings of the Hebrew prophet, Jeremiah, in the seventh century before Christ when he wrote about individual responsibility:

> The fathers have eaten sour grapes, and the children's teeth are set on edge.
> But every one shall die for his own sin; every man who eats sour grapes, his teeth shall be set on edge.
>
> (Jeremiah 31:29–30)

Individuals are responsible for their own actions: this is one of the earliest references in literature to individual responsibility. People are free to act in their own self-interests or in wider interests despite the group, but they have to take responsibility for their actions rather than putting that responsibility on the group. And although individual responsibility is significant, we find that Aristotle, amongst many others, is well aware of the influence of the group upon individual behaviour (see Nussbaum, 1986). Clearly, individual responsibility is important as we think about learning to be persons in society; the issue at this moment is the mere fact of and significance of the individual in the group. But the group is more significant to the individual than the Enlightenment allowed.

In order to prove existence, Descartes started with the individual – *I think, therefore I am*. In contrast, existentialists reverse this assertion since existence is assumed and never needs to be proven. This means that the Cartesian dictum is unnecessary – but this does not automatically exclude some form of dualist arguments about the relationship between the mind and the body. I am! But what does existence actually mean? I know I am, and I do not need to prove it to myself. Because I am, I think. Maquarrie (1973: 125) writes:

But what does it mean to say, 'I am'? 'I am' is the same as 'I exist'; but 'I exist', in turn, is equivalent to 'I-am-in-the-world', or again 'I-am-with-others'. So the premise of the argument is not anything so abstract as 'I think' or even 'I am' if it is understood in some isolated sense. The premise is the immediately rich and complex reality, 'I-am-with-others-in the world'.

But Bergson (1998 [1911]: 7) makes another vitally important point:

> for a conscious being to exist is to change, to change is to mature, to mature is to go on creating oneself endlessly.

Existence, then, is never unchanging and for human beings it is always social; we live and move and have our being in a social context. We will argue throughout this volume that learning is the driving force of human change through which the human essence emerges and is nurtured. But, also, 'I-am-in-the-world' and 'I-am-with-others' are different phenomena: in the former, we are in the wider world but the latter can refer to our life-world (see Luckmann, 1983; Habermas, 1987; Williamson, 1998). But we know that we are in the world because we act, as MacMurray (1979 [1961]: 17) argued, 'We know existence by participating in existence', or, as Husserl said, 'I live *in* my Acts' (cited in Schutz, 1972: 51). I am, therefore I act, but also I act, therefore I am. But action is rarely meaningless, so that underlying action is intention and meaning but, paradoxically we have to learn meaning.

Social living is not only doing: it is meeting. Buber (1958: 17) wrote that 'all real living is meeting'. He goes on to conclude that this meeting is a present phenomenon between *I* and *Thou*. But he (ibid.: 22) goes even further to claim that, 'In the beginning is relationship', and it is 'through the *Thou* that the man becomes *I*'. The significance of the other is clearly seen in child psychology, in which we learn that the baby's brain grows and develops after birth. Gerhardt (2004: 43) explains the significance of the relationship to this process:

> Lots of positive experiences early on produce brains with more neural connections – more richly networked brains. We have all our neurons at birth, and we don't need to grow any more, but what we do need is to connect them up and make them work for us. With more connections, there is better performance and more ability to use particular areas of the brain.

Without the group, there can be no person. It is not that we live in society but that we are part of society – we are a part of society by class, age, gender, occupation and so on. It is we who are born in society and we become ourselves as a result of social living, and through our social living we contribute to the growth and development of other persons. This intrinsic connection between the person and the group, in which each member is bonded to some extent or another with other members of the group, is one of the main reasons for the paradox of the individual in the group, to which we will return later. Although the group is intrinsic to our growth, once we are grown then we assume our own individual responsibility and can decide whether we wish to continue to play our role in the group or whether, for one reason or another, we wish to step outside of it.

However, the fact that the person is always part of society/group/family does not end the study of locating the person in society since we have become more aware that in this globalised world each society is part of a larger entity – humanity itself. Humanity has a long history as palaeontologists and evolutionary psychologists, amongst others, have demonstrated to us. Humanity has evolved and as part of that evolution we have changed and developed to become the human beings that we now are. And so, we could depict the place of the ego in the wider society as in Figure 1.1. The upward arrows depict the process of time through which we have evolved, and in this sense we can now begin to locate one of the major contemporary debates – to what extent has humankind evolved so as to change the nature of culture? Do individuals have built into their brains (hard-wired) all the results of evolution so that the part that culture and learning play is significantly less than we originally thought? Clearly, this is the beginning of a long and drawn-out debate that I do not want to explore in depth here, although to fail to discuss it even briefly would do a disservice to our quest in this study. At the same time, not to recognise its significance also does a disservice.

Haslam (2007: 89–94) provides a clear introduction to the discussion when he suggests that both neurobiology and behavioural genetics offer

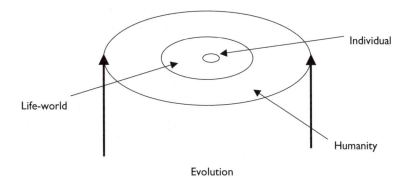

Evolution

Figure 1.1 The social individual within humankind.

important perspectives upon personality: 'neurobiology tells us about the brain processes that give rise to behaviour and its variations, and behavioural genetics tells us about the inherited structures that give rise to these brain processes' (ibid.: 89–90). Evolution is the natural process that operates on the genetic variation. Haslam (ibid.: 90) makes the point that 'evolution works in a slow, blind, and trial-and-error manner to improve the "design" of the biological species, ensuring that its genes underpin an array of functional adaptations'. At the same time, while the evolutionary process is not producing a standardised species, cultural differences into which we are socialised highlight the differences in us as persons: Haslam (ibid.: 94) suggests that 'most of the non-genetic contributions to personality are due to "non-shared environment": influences that are distinctive to individuals rather than shared within families'. Blakemore and Frith (2005: 186–7) show that, when we learn, our individual brains change and that this plasticity is not limited to childhood. Once we accept that the brain changes, it is possible to suggest the possibility of genetic change in the individual learner, which can then be transmitted to the next generation, but such genetic changes have not yet been demonstrated. In this sense, we can see that human learning still finds an important place within the wider spectrum of study which is beginning to be called 'the science of learning'.

From the outset, it is important to note that few, if any, scholars would deny that evolution has occurred, but few have tried to explain it as fully as Dawkins (1976, 2006) has (see also Dennett, 1995, 2006). Dawkins would argue that evolution has played an extremely large part, and in order to summarise this position I am using Blackmore (2007) as one reference to Dawkins, but see also Dawkins (2006: 222–34). Following Dawkins, she starts by pointing out that fundamental to all human evolution is a process of imitation in which information is copied with variation and selection and that this is what Dawkins (1976) calls the 'replicator'. We shall return to imitative learning as fundamental to human growth and development below. For Dawkins the most familiar replicator is the gene, which survives as other bodies die in the process of time. The fact that the genes that successfully copy and survive have succeeded so that they will be copied and proliferate is why they are called 'selfish' by Dawkins. However, he wanted to break away from the idea of genes and so he called them 'memes' – 'units of cultural inheritance' (ibid.: 222), which he (ibid.: 92) suggested included 'tunes, ideas, catch-phrases, clothes, fashions, ways of making pots or building arches'. The literal meaning of meme is 'that which is imitated', and we will see in the work of Tomasello (1999) a totally different and, I believe, a more realistic approach to mimesis, or mimetics. Memes, if they exist, are what are copied, whereas what we learn by ourselves are not memes – nor are any of our primary experiences. Conceptually memes are at the heart of some theories of the evolutionary process and are its driving force because the learning that is built into the meme is now part of the evolutionary process – it is part of our hard-wiring. Blackmore (2007: 12) summarises this position:

> This is really a general argument about the design of human nature. Whichever direction memetic evolution happened to take in the past, we humans would become better able to copy the memes that were successful – whether those words, music, paintings, rituals or anything else. Our modern brains therefore carry the traces of our past memetic evolution.

Evolution is clearly basic to our thinking, but the problem lies in the extent to which hard-wiring occurs and whether there is evidence for the existence of memes – and if not we need to understand more about the processes of hard-wiring. Fundamentally, memetics is a reductionist theory that needs a lot more hard scientific research to prove its point, and so this study turns to the manner in which Tomasello deals with imitation. Significantly, Blakemore and Frith (2005), while recognising the significance of genes to learning, make no mention of memes in their study of the learning brain. Nelson (2007: 44) also makes the point that no genes have been identified that influence human behaviour and also points out that genetic behaviourists separate the gene from the environment in a manner that does not lead to a clear understanding of human development. The similarity between memetics and mimesis is that they both point to a fundamental understanding of imitation although they have different ways of viewing it. Theorists of early childhood learning, then, start with imitation. Children imitate from birth and Tomasello (1999: 52) regards children between the ages of one and three years as 'imitation machines'. This imitation occurs in the intimate relationships that occur in the early life of a child; Tomasello (ibid.: 55) does not reject an evolutionary perspective but he wants to produce a dual perspective on human development:

> We have at most only 6 million years, but much more likely only one-quarter of a million years, to create uniquely human cognition, and this is simply not sufficient, under any plausible evolutionary scenario, for genetic variation and natural selection to have created many and different uniquely human cognitive modules.

He (p. 54) does accept that many of the skills possessed by all the primates, including human beings, are the result of the evolutionary processes. Other scholars, such as Donald (2001), reach similar conclusions, although Blackmore (2007: 7), wrongly and without evidence in my opinion, accuses Donald of rejecting the whole of the argument out of fear. Tomasello's dual position is attractive since it allows us both to accept the validity of the evolutionary argument but also to recognise that evolution is a slower process than that of individual learning – even imitative learning – and so culture also plays a dominant part in human development.

Conclusion

From the above discussion, we can see that each of the major terms is contentious and we have laid the foundations here to understand what it means to learn to become persons in society. All of the major concepts are inter-related and intertwined, yet there are fundamental differences about the place of culture and therefore learning in the process of becoming human persons. We have briefly reviewed this debate, although the relationship between evolution and learning calls for a more in-depth study. Whereas imitation is at the heart of this process, the memetic theory appears reductionist and speculative – more speculative than the theories it tries to replace. We are now, therefore, in a better position to explore a basic theory of human learning.

Chapter 2

Learning in society

In the previous chapter we demonstrated that society is a fundamental necessity to human growth and development of the person and so any theory of learning must recognise the paradox of its being an individual process that takes place in the context of the wider society and that it is one that is greatly influenced by that society. Consequently, we will begin this chapter with an examination of the way that the wider society influences learning and thereafter we will look at the learning processes themselves. Much of this material has appeared in other books of mine although never within a framework such as this.

Part I: The influence of the wider society

This part falls into two subsections: the first examines the idea of interpersonal relationship and the second depicts individuals being socialised into the subculture of their life-worlds.

Individuals in relationship

As we argued in the last chapter, relationship is at the heart of human living. We are not born as individuals – we were all born at the end of a cord, attached physically to our mothers, and only when the cord is severed do we become separate entities, although still totally dependent on our mothers and significant others. It is, then, in interpersonal relationships and through communication that we begin to acquire (learn) culture, although in the first instance the culture is usually that of our parents' life-world. Culture is all that is added to 'bare life' (Agamben, 1995) in the process of our becoming human, or in the ideas that we used in Chapter 1 '(the) world of images, stories, objects and ways of acting to which we have recourse in our struggle to exist' (Jackson, 2005: 103). As we grow and develop, we both contribute to it and transmit it to others in our relationships: this is the nature of the person in the world.

The life-world is not a static phenomenon – it changes over time in relation to the changes in the wider world in which its members exist and changes in the individual's involvement in it, and so we cannot depict a simple relationship with it in respect of learning. The person exists in a 'flow of time' within the life-world, but there are at least three forms of relationship within the life-world that need to be considered, which also relate to the present and the future. In the present, there are two ways in which people act with the external world – through relationship with other individuals (I–Thou) and through an awareness of phenomena (things, events, and so on – I–It) (Buber, 1958). Even so, there is also an envisaged relationship with the world, which occurs when individuals think about the future while they are still in the present; they have desires, intentions, and so on. In a similar manner, we can think about the past, or about an idea – we can contemplate, muse and so on, and thus relate to ourselves. This reflecting upon our past results in our own awareness of our life history and educational biography (Dominice, 2000). These may be depicted in the following way:

Person to person	I ↔ Thou
Person to phenomenon (thing/event/memory)	I → It
Person to a future phenomenon	I → Envisaged Thou/It
Person to self	I ↔ Me

The double arrows represent a two-way relationship and these unbroken ones indicate that there is harmony between our biography and our experience of the Other. This relationship is an interpersonal one so that when we are in agreement with those with whom we interact there is a sense of harmony between us. But we also relate to ourselves, and when we are happy with the situation we have this same sense of harmony. We are in harmony with our knowledge of the world in which we are acting, but also with the emotions that we share – when we know that we can repeat our past successful acts, we feel 'at ease' in the world. It should be noted here that this sense of being in harmony means that fundamental both to the learning process and to life itself is an 'in-built' conservatism. But there are times when this harmony does not occur and we then experience disjuncture – this can happen when we come across a situation in which we are not sure how to act, or even when we experience a 'magic moment' that just stops us in our tracks. It is something out of the normal – abnormal or supranormal – and it gives rise to astonishment, wonder or some other emotion. It is at times like this that we become aware of our world. We will explore disjuncture more fully in a later chapter, but we can see immediately that it relates to consciousness and awareness, and I want to keep these two concepts separate throughout this study. In addition, there is an emotive dimension to disjuncture – 'unease' may be one way to describe it.

There is a sense in which the I ↔ Me relationship also occurs to some degree in the first three, although in the fourth one, unlike the others, it might also be an end in itself. This is reflection, but we want to suggest towards the end of the study that we need to extend this idea and suggest that it is fundamental to our being. At the same time, it is at the heart of desire, like and dislike, and other emotions that result in planning, thinking and, maybe, action. It is here, in the memories of previous experiences, that I interact with myself and learn and grow – it is reflection.

Additionally, during these processes there is an almost hidden element – time. Being-in-the-world automatically implies existence in time as well as space, and that it is impossible to step outside of either. Time is a contentious phenomenon – it is something that knows no boundaries and in which there is always emergence of newness – a sense of becoming. We are always becoming, but learning is an element in our being – it is always a present process. Time is, in a sense, external to us and is a flow of ever-changing reality which Bergson (1998, 1999, 2004; see also Lacey, 1989) called *durée*. However, we are not always conscious of its passing and when, suddenly, we become aware of it, we often exclaim 'How time flies'. Nevertheless, there are instances when we are thinking about the future and we have the opposite experience of time: 'Isn't time dragging?' When time drags we become very aware of the world in which we live, and this is important to our understanding of our own experience. When time flies, our biography is in harmony with our situation and we may not consciously learn. However, the experience of time is also related to our biological and social age – since children probably experience the passing of time as something slower than do the elderly. While we are acting in the world, we are not aware of the world beyond our actions, although our body continues to age through the ravages of time. However, frequently we are confronted with novel situations in this rapidly changing world, so that we cannot remain in harmony with the world and it is almost as if time stops and we experience the present situation (Oakeshott, 1933). It is this moment, when time seems to stop, that I have called disjuncture. Disjuncture occurs when our biographical repertoire is no longer sufficient to cope automatically with our perception of the situation so that our unthinking harmony with our world is disturbed and we feel unease. We have a tension with our environment. We become very conscious of our situation in the world. Indeed, we either problematise it or have it problematised for us. Potential disjunctural situations can be depicted thus:

Person to person	I ←//→ Thou
Person to phenomenon (thing/event/memory)	I –//→ It
Person to a future phenomenon	I –//→ Envisaged Thou or It
Person to self	I ←//→ Me

This awareness is not only a segment of our life-world upon which we focus, it is also an event or an episode in time; it is an experience – we will discuss the nature of experience in Chapter 5 and again in Chapter 7. We need to distinguish this meaning of the word 'experience' from that of total experience or life history, and we do so here by calling it *an experience* – an event or an episode. Neither occurs at a fixed moment in time: they may be short and immediate (event) or occur over a given period of time (episode). This is the elusive present. Now we think, feel and maybe do something about the outside world. We are aware of our world and have a sense of consciousness about it. The interaction between 'I' and 'the world', however, is itself a multifaceted phenomenon. For instance, our experience of the world varies in intensity, in formality and in mode. It can, amongst others, be spoken, written or non-verbal communication; formal, non-formal or informal interaction; emotionally, sensitive or cold; oral or silent; visual; tactile; something we like or approve of or vice versa; and so on. The sensations we have of the world are what are also transformed. It is about the whole person.

It is at the intersection of us and our world that we are presented with the opportunities to learn. Nevertheless, the world is also changing rapidly; our life in the world continues but through frequent changes and continuity has become instability and frequent, if not constant, disjuncture. We are constantly exposed to learning opportunities – either we learn from others with whom we interact, we learn as a result of reflection or by trial and error.

Individuals within their subcultures

People who live in very similar situations, speak the same language and often the same dialect and have similar experiences to each other know very similar stories, react to situations in similar ways, and so forth. They have similar cultural attributes, so that it is possible to generalise and talk of the (sub)culture of a life-world. Since no two people are exactly alike despite our evolutionary history, since they have had different experiences throughout their lives, their similarities are more than just superficial: they are similar enough for us often to be able to categorise them and place them in similar situations, such as working-class Liverpool, professional in the West Midlands, an American from the Deep South, a traveller from Japan, and so on. It is this similarity that enables us to talk about the culture of an area. It is also this similarity that can result in the concept being reified and treated as a thing but, like the concept of society itself, culture is abstract and generalised. One of the problems of generalisation, however, is that it distils out those particular and individual features that we all have that make up our personalities and so we use the idea of personality traits here to emphasise our individuality as a result of our learning. In Figure

2.1 we 'objectify' culture, rather than reify it in order to depict it: we must emphasise that culture is not an object but, in the sense that it is being used here, it is a 'generalised Thou'. Consequently, we take the arrows from the I–Thou relationship and separate them in order to demonstrate what happens in interaction within the group, or subculture.

In Figure 2.1, the arc represents the all-encompassing culture into which we are born and live. In primitive society it was possible to describe this as a single culture, but now this all-encompassing culture is what might also be described as multicultural. Culture is a problematic concept, and merely describing it as all-encompassing does not obviate the problem since it is not even the same phenomenon for all people in the same area – for instance young people growing up in UK retain their ethnic cultures, even though they also acquire a sense of 'Britishness', and others a sense of being a Muslim, and so on. This is also true for America and for every other country. We all have our own cultures and our own life-worlds.

Culture is far from being an entirely cognitive phenomenon – it is about our actions and our emotions: we can witness the different dimensions of the culture carried by people in social interaction. We learn appropriate behaviours and emotions in the cultural setting – what is approved and disapproved, liked and disliked, and so on. We learn what to do and what not to do, what to like and what not to like. Emotions are complex phenomena (Turner and Stets, 2005) and will be discussed in greater detail later in this book (Chapter 12), but suffice to say here that they are a mixture of the biological, personal and social.

From the time of our birth we are exposed to the culture of our subgroup and we learn from it through interpersonal communication, but in this world of mass media we are also exposed to a non-personal communication process, and from the earliest moment that we are exposed to television we are more affected by the external pressures upon us than we are able to affect that external world. We are socialised into it: we will discuss socialisation in greater depth in subsequent chapters, but it is

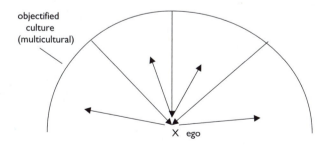

Figure 2.1 The internalisation of culture.

necessary to understand from the outset that socialisation does not mean that we become clones of those whom we imitate – our learning is much more sophisticated than that although there is a great deal of similarity which gives us our sense of our ethnic or religious identity, and so on. The clone is a biological copy, but since we are exposed to many different cultural stimuli we develop our own individuality: the point is that we are learning just through being exposed to other people and to the mass media. In our early days we have little or no control over the communications that we receive, and often we may not always be conscious of them or the effect that they have on us. At the same time, we have experiences from which we learn, and these communicative relationships are crucial to our growth and development as individual persons – as we have already argued, relationships precede individuality, although since the time of the Enlightenment we have wrongly started with the individual and individualism: in Buber's words, 'In the beginning is relationship'.

Part 2: Learning

There are many different theories of learning; we have already met some of the most fundamental in this chapter. We learn through being exposed to stimuli which we seek to remember; we learn through imitation of others' sounds or actions; we learn through our own discovery in the situation that we are in; and so on. These are the most fundamental ways of learning. Often we are conscious of the situation in which we are recipients of these stimuli, but there are many times when we are exposed to stimuli of which we are not conscious and so learning becomes a much more complicated process. It is this complexity which causes problems for our understanding of the concept and processes of learning.

In my own writing (Jarvis, 2006) I have included the idea that we learn from 'the perceived content' of our experiences, but the word 'perceived' has caused a number of problems, not because perception is not important but because it implies that everything in the processes of learning that we internalise is perceived. This creates problems with pre-conscious learning and tacit knowledge – concepts that we will discuss more fully in the following chapters. But, briefly, if we can learn pre-consciously then we may not have perceived what we have internalised. Consequently, I now adapt the definition that I used in my trilogy (Jarvis, 2006: 134) but omitting the word 'perceived'.

However, ever since I last discussed the concept of meaning (Jarvis, 1992), I have assumed that by spelling out 'knowledge, skill, attitudes, values, emotions, beliefs and the senses' in my definition I had captured the idea of meaning, but as I have continued to research and reflect upon the processes of learning I no longer feel that I can assume that meaning is contained in all of these different aspects of living; therefore I cannot omit it from the definition and so I have made a second adaptation since my last book on learning.

Learning is now defined as:

> The combination of processes throughout a lifetime whereby the whole person – body (genetic, physical and biological) and mind (knowledge, skills, attitudes, values, emotions, meaning, beliefs and senses) – experiences social situations, the content of which is then transformed cognitively, emotively or practically (or through any combination) and integrated into the individual person's biography resulting in a continually changing (or more experienced) person.

In a sense we are constructing our own biography whenever we learn – whilst we live our biography is an unfinished product constantly undergoing change and development – either through experiences that we self-initiate or else through experiences which are initiated by others. We are always learning to be persons in society, and here we are confronted by paradox – the person is always complete whenever we consider a person whom we know but we also know that the person is never complete. For as long as we can learn from conscious experiences people are and are always becoming and we develop our personalities in different ways.

Depending upon our personality we may respond to experiences in very different ways – Haslam (2007: 26–8) suggests that there are five major axes along which we develop personality traits and these are quite individualistic: extraversion, agreeableness, conscientiousness, neuroticism and openness to experience. Each has its polar opposite and each develops with our learning but each will affect the way that we respond to experiences and continue to learn. Clearly, those with a high curious personality trait are likely to be more receptive to learning experiences than someone who is careless and irresponsible, and so on. Although it is not our intention to pursue personality trait theory far in this study, we can see that it is important in helping us to understand the way that individuals respond differently to their experiences and how some are more likely to learn from them than are other people.

Nevertheless, we learn in a variety of different ways, but always from the experience of living: this is the existential element in learning. Learning is always about 'being' and 'becoming': it is ontological and it occurs within the context of the life-world, although we must never forget that this actually occurs within the wider theoretical framework of evolved humanity and that these influences do play their part in our everyday life and learning. Learning also always occurs within time, even though we may not always be aware of its passing.

In fact, there are a few very basic processes through which we go when we learn: remembering, imitating, adapting, experimenting and reinforcing. They reflect our earliest experiences and are so common that they need little discussion. At the same time, they are basic to our human being in the world.

Remembering

The act of recall is trying to bring back to our consciousness an experience which we have had previously. We know that memory occurs in neural networks in the brain and that different types of memory are stored in different locations in the brain (Gardner, 1983; Donald, 2001), but Donald maintains that brains are programmed by culture. This, I feel, is reifying culture. Memory is programmed by the sensory inputs that come from human interaction and we know that the recall is never precisely accurate and always depends on our original internalising of the experiences. Nevertheless, memory is at the heart of our thinking about identity since we recall past experiences and relate them to current ones.

Imitating

Once more this depends on human relationships: this is regarded by scholars of all persuasions as crucial to human development. Copying what we see and what we experience is basic to our human being. Dawkins (1976: 15) considers this as genetic. He calls it a replicator and he feels that any theory of the origin of life must have fundamental properties, namely self-replicating genetic entities (ibid.: 269). However, Tomasello (1999), who regards children as 'imitation machines', thinks that there is just insufficient evidence for this genetic perspective. He (ibid.: 83) claims 'that imitative learning . . . represents infants' initial entry into the cultural world around them'. It is in the differing interpretations of culture that these two perspectives are antithetical and it seems to me at this point in time that the memetic theory of Dawkins still lacks sufficient proof to displace the traditional understanding of culture and learning.

Adapting

If we are faced with a situation which is not quite the same as a previous one, we learn to adapt our behaviour, almost unthinkingly, in order to fit into the expectations of the life-world. Adaptation involves a slight adjustment in our behaviour which does not always demand that we rethink our theoretical perspective about the situation itself: it is a behavioural response and the cognitive element may be little more than an awareness that we have of the changed situation.

Experimenting

This is the traditional trial and error approach to learning. If we do not know the answer to a problem, we try out likely solutions until one fits. We can see children using this approach in play. But it is a 'scientific' method in as much as it seeks evidence that the solution utilised explains the problem.

Reinforcing

This has two versions: in classical conditioning (Pavlov, 1927) the learner learns to associate the presentation of a reward with a stimulus that occurs fractionally before it, whereas in operant condition (Skinner, 1968) the response is shaped by the reward so that, for every action that approximates or achieves the desired outcome, the learner receives a reward. Psychologically we know that these work in certain situations and, although they contribute to an understanding of learning, they do not exhaust our knowledge of the subject.

At the same time, these five approaches to learning are quite basic to humanity and are amongst the most commonly practised in everyday living. But in themselves they do not exhaust the whole of the learning processes. I (Jarvis, 2008: 6) have tried to do this as a much more complex set of processes depicted in Figure 2.2. We need to follow this figure through each point so that we can begin to appreciate the complexity of the processes of learning that it contains.

Time

The horizontal arrows at the top of the figure depict time – but we often live through time and presume on our life-world and apparently are not learning. For as long as this occurs we are not conscious of having an experience: in a sense we are not changing nor are we changing the world. For as long as we can presume upon the world, we do not consciously affect it, nor do we consciously learn, but this is an issue for learning – we may be internalising some information unconsciously. It is only when, for various reasons, we cannot presume upon the world that we are forced to question it: Why? What for? How? These are the questions that a young child asks at about the age of four years – ones that parents and teachers often dread – and yet they are the indicators of the need to learn. We continue to have these experiences throughout our lives, and how far we pursue answers to the questions depends to some extent on our personalities and how curious we are. It is at moments like this that we become conscious of time – it is almost as if time stands still and we become aware of the present.

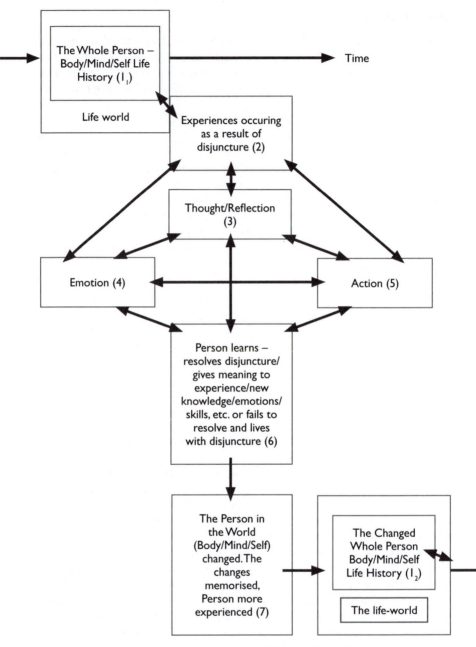

Figure 2.2 The transformation of the person through learning.

Person

We explored the concept of the person in the last chapter and we pointed to the significance of intentionality, which in Tomasello's dual inheritance model of our past is important. In common with the apes, we experience both sociogenesis and cultural learning, which have a common cognitive dimension; however, human cognition has developed very rapidly – more rapidly than evolution would allow. This has enabled us to learn culturally, and we learn the subculture of our social world.

Life-world

As we learn the subculture of the society into which we are born, so we construct our own life-world: we feel at home in this environment and we can take the world for granted, as we saw in Chapter 1. However, the social world is not like a machine that operates in an unchanging manner. Because it is a world of human beings who can behave unpredictably, and one in which social change is very rapid, we are constantly faced with unknown situations upon which we cannot presume and thus which we are not sure how to cope with – it is this that I have called disjuncture.

Disjuncture

Disjuncture is a complex phenomenon. It is best described as the gap between what we expect to perceive when we have an experience of the world as a result of our previous learning, and, therefore, our biography, and that with which we are actually confronted. The complexity of this experience may be depicted as shown in Figure 2.3.

Coincidence is when there is no conscious experience because we can presume upon the world. Divergence is when there is a slight difference and we can adjust our behaviour to respond to the situation without changing our understanding of the world (our theory/meaning). Separation is when there is a larger gap between the two, and this is where the questioning begins and where our conscious learning starts. Distinction is when the gap is so wide that we know that in order to bridge it we have to undertake a great deal of learning, e.g. by taking a course of study – or the gap eventually grows so wide that we know that we can never bring the two parts together, which may be a meaningless or a very meaningful experience. We will discuss this later in the book. Conscious disjuncture begins at the point of separation – we are aware of the situation and we consciously experience the world, but we do this cognitively, emotively and practically. Disjuncture occurs in all three dimensions of experience, and is often a combination, although sometimes it occurs in a single dimension.

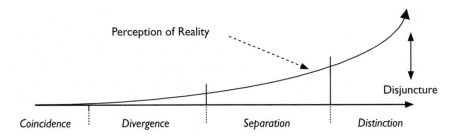

Figure 2.3   Disjuncture – the distance between perception of the reality and individual biography.

Experience

Experience is when we are conscious of the world, are aware of the specific situation and know that we are having an experience, even if we do not actually acknowledge it at the time. We are recipients of stimuli that originate externally to us but which we internalise through our senses and we become aware of the situation and focus upon it. These stimuli may be regarded as primary experiences – i.e. we experience them directly – or mediated or secondary experiences in which we are told about something by a mediator, a teacher or by the media themselves – but we learn only from the internalised experience. However, these experiences can occur at any time in our lives and in any place – so that we not only learn in educational institutions, we learn at work, at home, in the community and so on. We discuss this concept in greater depth in Chapters 5 and 7.

Thinking, feeling, doing

We deal with our experience by memorising it, thinking about it, feeling it or doing something about it, and so on. These processes are discussed fully in the second section of this book. The outcome of the processes is that we learn about the content of the experience and/or we learn more about ourselves even though we are unable to learn from the content of the experience. As a result we become changed individuals as we see in box 7 of Figure 2.2. Then the process begins all over again, or, indeed, two or more processes might be going on simultaneously and so in Figure 2.2 we show that the process is ongoing. Learning is an ontological process.

Conclusion

We can see just how complex learning is when we try to trace the routes through Figure 2.2: we get rote learning, reflective learning (analytical, critical and creative), surface and deep learning, emotional learning, learning about beliefs, values and attitudes – and we get both action learning and skills learning, and so on. The significant thing about this or any learning theory is that they all stem from our experience in the world – even though the actual experience of internalising information may not always be conscious. Learning, then, is an individual process that occurs within a social framework which begins in the womb and certainly before birth.

Chapter 3

Learning in early childhood

Early childhood is the time when the human being first experiences society and undergoes a tremendous amount of learning, and so I have included a brief chapter about early childhood in order to lay the foundations for the remainder of the book. This is probably the period in life (the first three years) when the most learning actually occurs, and so it is necessary when we consider lifelong learning to recognise this – adult educators should consider this period in seeking to understand adult learning but, likewise, childhood educators should, I think, also look at the whole of life. In this chapter we will meet many of the issues with which we will be confronted later in the book since early childhood learning underlies a great deal of our later living. The chapter is divided into five sections – the primacy of relationship, learning and the senses, play, language and socialisation – and it will conclude with a brief discussion on the first years.

Part 1: The primacy of relationship

Enlightenment thought emphasised the individual, reflecting the West's Judeo-Christian and Greek heritage, although it apparently jettisoned a great deal of the former, whereas Eastern thought has always emphasised the harmony of the whole and the individual's place within it. There have, however, always been thinkers from the Judeo-Christian heritage who have placed relationship at the forefront of their thinking, but they have not achieved the prominence that perhaps they have merited. In the following paragraphs we will focus on some of these.

Paradoxically, if we try to start with the individual in the beginning of life, we fail to find the individual – since from the moment of our conception we are totally contained within our mother's womb. From that time there is life and relationship but there is no knowable individuality in the womb itself, so that Martin Buber (1958) could rightly claim that in the beginning is relationship. From the outset of our lives we are dependent upon our mothers, but this relationship appears to be much more complex than originally imagined. In research with monkeys, for instance, Harlow and Mears (1979; cited in Wexler, 2006) concluded that even the provision of milk was not the end in itself for the mother's provision but that the provision of milk fosters the mother–child relationship and it is this relationship that is important for the child's future development. During these interactions children learn both awareness and attention. Donald (2001) makes a significant point about this relationship in the light of the current debates about the existence of consciousness when he asks how the relationship between mother and child can continue when all the cells from each body (mother's and child's) change over time but the relationship remains.

Significantly, it is in this relationship that bonding between mother and child occurs, and this is the beginning of a relationship of love, to which we will return when we discuss questions of universal ethic (Chapter 15). However, there is another aspect of this relationship that is important, because the child learns to trust the mother for the provision of food and drink. Trust and therefore a sense of faith emerges in this relationship – another aspect of human living to which we will return when we look at believing and the growth of faith. All of these vital elements of human living are learned pre-consciously.

We are interconnected with other people from the outset of our own lives; from the earliest moments after birth, young babies seek and experience relationship with their parents – so-called 'protoconversations' (Tomasello, 1999: 59), in which young children mimic the behaviour of their carers. Imitation is a fundamental method of learning throughout life, and it begins almost with the onset of life outside the womb. But as we grow our sphere of relationship broadens: I relate to other people – both face to face and later through other media; I relate to the external natural world; but I also relate to my previous experiences, my memories of those experiences, and so on, so that I relate to myself. In Buber's terms, the interpersonal living relationship is *I–Thou* whereas we have *I–It* and *I–Me* relationships, as we saw in the previous chapter. Whereas I, as learner, learn through all the relationships, the first (*I–Thou*) is a living personal relationship. Indeed, Buber actually calls the *I–Thou* relationship a primary word – a unity. And it is significant that many years later Ogden (1986: 171; cited in Wexler, 2006: 124) actually says that 'It is . . . the mother–infant that is the unit of psychological development'. Nevertheless, every experience must just precede our awareness of it by nanoseconds, although we feel that it is completely simultaneous and in the present: this I will call here the 'experienced present'. The third relationship is different – *I–Me* – but in it there is a sense in which my memories, my life history and so on appear objective in the self. In this sense it is also an *I–It* relationship since it is only through objectification of my own life that I can understand myself, and I do this in the present. This three-way relationship is simultaneous and it can transcend immediate time. Buber actually adds a fourth relationship – one with spiritual beings – but I have no intention of entering this contentious subject here as it would lead us away from our central theme, although we will examine learning both spirituality and religion in this book. Buber (1958: 51) goes on to claim the following:

> Individuality makes its appearance by being differentiated from other individualities. A person makes his appearance by entering a relationship with other persons.

In a similar manner another philosopher, MacMurray (1979 [1961]: 91), captured the emerging individual·in relationship:

> the development of the individual person is the development of his individual relation to the Other. Personal individuality is not an original given fact. It is achieved through the progressive differentiation of the original unity of the 'You and I'.

Children discover their individuality only by progressively differentiating themselves from their mothers and their families. The reason for this, MacMurray adduces, is because we are accustomed to start with the ideas of reflection rather than those that come from action but, as he argues, persons are agents so that we have to start with action. We will also make this point very clearly when we discuss learning and everyday life. Significantly, however, this is also the issue between situation and understanding and the reverse process of moving from understanding to situation.

Relationship precedes individuality and in this sense there is a primacy of relationship.

But that primacy is even more significant in the conception and growth of the fetus and also the development of the brain in the earliest months after birth. The fetus's senses function as they develop in the womb, so that pre-conscious and pre-cognitive learning occur weeks before birth. Tremlin writes:

> As early as the first trimester of a pregnancy, the fetus already possesses centers of balance and motion that respond to the mother's own movements. At the halfway point of gestation a fetus can hear. Sight remains severely muted; unlike the sense of hearing, there are few external stimuli in the uterus. But by the seventh month the eyelids are open and the fetus can see by diffused light coming through the abdominal wall. Taste, too, is working as the fetus takes in the amniotic fluid. In addition to these basic functions of sense and motor control, there is also clear evidence that the brain is busy *learning* in the womb. One example utilizes the fetus' well-developed sense of hearing. Clever experiments that chart the rhythm sucks on a rubber nipple reveal

preferences for a mother's voice and other patterns of sound heard in the womb.

(Tremlin, 2006: 51, italics in original)

I well recall teaching an adult class in Alaska when we were discussing pre-conscious learning and a pregnant First Nation woman told the class that her people taught mothers-to-be to talk to their babies in the womb. Fetuses learn by sense experience in the womb in a pre-conscious and pre-cognitive manner but the status of that learning is less clear. Are the outcomes knowledge or tacit or potential knowledge? Do they predetermine the outcomes of future learning or do they merely influence them?

Indeed, it might well be claimed that the universality of the drum beat reflects the pre-conscious learning of the mother's heart beat learned pre-consciously in the womb. However, Dennett (1999; cited in Blackmore, 2007: 11) used a similar example of the heart beat but from a much more speculative basis, which he admits, when he suggested that:

One day one of our distant hominid ancestors sitting on a fallen log happened to start banging on it with a stick – *boom boom, boom*. For *no good reason at all*. This was just idle diddling . . . mere nervous fidgeting, but the repetitive sound striking his ears just happened to feel to him a slight improvement on silence . . . Now introduce some other ancestors who happen to see and hear this drummer. They might . . . again *for no reason,* find their imitator-circuits tickled into action.

Pre-conscious learning is a much more rational reason for understanding the universality of the beat in music than Dennett's speculations and, even if his speculation has some basis, then he has still not accounted for the reason why *boom, boom, boom* is nicer than silence. Although I will argue that imitation is at the heart of early human learning, I feel that learning – especially pre-conscious learning from our own biology – is much less speculative than Dennett's conjecturing. Part of the fetus's growth process is incorporating experiences into itself in some way. We know the same from people's experiences of favourite or disliked tastes since they correspond to the mothers' experiences while the fetus was still in the womb, and so on.

Moreover, this process does not stop at birth, since the brain in which those 'learnings' are stored is not completely formed at birth:

the orbitofrontal cortex, which is so much about being human, develops almost entirely post-natally. This part of the brain develops after birth and doesn't begin to mature to toddlerhood.

There is nothing automatic about this. Instead, the kind of brain that each baby develops is the brain that comes out of his or her particular experiences with people. It is very 'experience dependent' (Gerhardt, 2004: 37–8).

As Gerhardt goes on to note, it is hard to consider a baby developing a social dimension without being in relationship with others, and so the child enters the cultural environment early in its development, depends on significant others and learns relationship through experience. Consequently, we can see the significance of relationship at the outset of life and we can also see why there is a propensity to accept what we are told, or, in Gadamer's (1976) terms, we can see the significance of tradition and prejudice. Indeed, research has shown that we cannot live in isolation: in a well-known experiment at McGill University in the 1950s students were paid to spend time in complete isolation: despite the payment none lasted for 72 hours and many needed psychological help – we all need outside stimulation, or, in other words, relationship.

But it is in relationships that our learning begins and, as Gerhardt indicates, this process of learning aids and abets the growth of the brain after birth – but it is social learning, and the part of the brain that is growing is the social brain. The person, then, is always in society, and we also start learning the emotions very early in our lives – indeed, some of them are hard-wired and we have to learn how to control them! As we pointed out in the previous chapter, we do have experiences from the time of birth and we learn to memorise from sensations: Donald (2001: 75) suggests that memorising sensation is the basis of consciousness itself and that we learn consciousness in this same process. It can thus be seen that consciousness itself has evolved through learning and remembering and this same process is evident in our human development. It is the expanding brain that provides us with the opportunity of broadened experience from which we can continue to learn. Indeed, we are freed from the immediate experience and able to memorise past experiences. The basis of our learning is awareness itself – the act of experiencing – although it is attention that focuses our learning in a conscious manner.

In bringing this section to a close, we can see that we have been confronted here with the idea of pre-conscious learning: a form of learning that I first discussed in *Adult Learning in the Social Context* (Jarvis, 1987). There are, however, at least three forms of pre-conscious learning:

- One is that which occurs while the fetus is in the womb – in this case it seems that it occurs through the physical connections between mother and fetus that might, in some way, programme the brain before the birth of the mind but the outcomes of which become apparent in later conscious experiences in the person.

- A second form occurs when we have experiences the content of which we internalise, although we are concentrating and aware of specific aspects of it rather than others. Yet the other aspects of the event or episode are also internalised and are also retained in the mind although we are unaware of it – some of these aspects might be activated by subsequent experiences so that we can recall them and learn from them. If this activation does not occur fairly soon after the initial experiences the memory trace may be lost. We have all had experiences of this type when we have internalised something that has occurred in our immediate experience.
- Through the processes of social living we are constantly adjusting our behaviour to respond to the divergent elements of disjuncture and not necessarily adjusting our theories of behaviour or meaning, and we gradually gain expertise or even wisdom without realising that it has occurred, although others may recognise it in us.

It is quite possible to explain pre-conscious learning through a careful analysis of how the brain functions. The traditional view has been that the sensory organs transmit their messages to the thalamus and then to the neocortex and from there to the limbic brain. But Goleman (1995: 18), referring to the work of LeDoux informs us that:

> there is a smaller bundle of neurons that leads directly from the tha-lamus to the amygdala, in addition to those going through the larger path of neurons to the cortex. This smaller and shorter pathway – something like a neural back alley – allows the amygdala to receive some direct input from the senses and start a response *before* they are fully registered by the neo-cortex.

LeDoux discovered that the emotional system can act independently of the neocortex or that emotional reactions do not require conscious par-ticipation. Once we accept that this pathway exists, we can understand the possibility of learning pre-consciously. Goleman (1995: 20) goes on the indicate that 'in the first few milliseconds of our perceiving something we not only unconsciously comprehend what it is but decide whether we like it or not'. In this sense we can see that certain of our emotions, per-haps our primary ones, precede rationality. But it is not only emotions but perception itself that occurs in these first milliseconds, and it is here that pre-conscious learning is to be found.

We will return to the idea of pre-conscious learning many times in this book, but it is one of the most fundamental forms of learning in the process of becoming a person starting not quite with life itself but from before birth and continuing through much of life itself after birth.

Part 2: Learning and the senses

It is clear from the above that our initial learning is from the senses and has a biological dimension to it, but it will become evident that we do not consider the idea that human beings are entirely driven by their genetic make-up (Dawkins, 1976) to be a valid proposition despite its continuing popularity as it does not produce sufficient evidence to displace child development theories (see Nelson, 2007). This does not mean that evolution should be rejected: it should not, although we need to recognise the extent of the debate when we look at human learning.

Whilst in the uterus, the fetus is already acquiring information (learning) through the senses. This process continues throughout the whole of life, but it is more complex after we have left the womb and as we grow and develop. In all experiencing and learning, the process begins with the bodily processes of sight, smell, sound, taste and touch. In itself each sense experience is meaningless, and so we need to give it meaning and name it, but this is a later process. When we can do this, and recall it, then we can begin to take our sense experiences for granted and yet still have cognitive disjunctures, but in many instances our disjuncture can begin with any of these sensations. We will all, no doubt, recall that game in which we have to guess the nature of an object from a picture taken from an unusual angle, or when we are asked to feel something that we cannot see, and say what it is. These games build on the idea of disjuncture – we cannot take the taste, touch, sight and so on for granted. Children probably have more disjunctural experiences that stem from sense experience than adults since they do not have the cognitive apparatus to give meaning to them in the first instance. It is only as we grow that we gain the knowledge necessary to cope with them.

Initially, babies have experiences, or sensations, that they do not know, and in the first instance they memorise these – and so the brain stores these sensations as early memories. But from the very earliest of days they have to distinguish between its memories and new sensations – both sensations of different phenomena and, even more difficult, sensations of the same phenomenon. Hence, they have to distinguish between the new experience and the memory of the past sensations of the same phenomenon, and this lies at the initial stages of conscious awareness. Learning, then, is memory, and memory is the reconstruction of earlier experiences. In this sense we learn to be conscious, as we suggested earlier in this chapter, but our experiences are meaningless and we have to learn to become conscious through a process of constructing and reconstructing our experiences. Indeed, for the child in its earliest of days, meaning almost certainly does not exist. Children have sense experiences that they cannot explain and so they live in ignorance, a phenomenon of which they may be unaware in the first instance. However, as they mature so they begin to give meaning to those initial sensations of sight, smell, sound, taste and touch, and their learning moves from the senses to the cognitions and the knowledge they learn from the sensations is conveyed in language and so later learning occurs primarily in the cognitive domain and the sense experiences are relegated to a secondary position. Consequently, as we mature, the more our learning assumes a cognitive dimension, but there are still times when we have a sense experience that we cannot explain in language – a disjunctural experience – and so we are forced to revert to the senses until we can give it meaning. In a way this was the problem that the American adult educator and populariser of the concept of andragogy, Malcolm Knowles (1970, 1980), tried to deal with when he wrote his book on *The Modern Practice of Adult Education* – the first edition he subtitled *Andragogy versus Pedagogy*, but as a result of the ensuing academic debate the revised edition was subtitled *From Pedagogy to Andragogy*. Yet he never really resolved his problem and the reason was probably because he did not distinguish learning from the senses and the emotions from learning from the cognitions, and so he was unable to clarify any relationship between children's learning and adult learning (Jarvis, 2007a). Adults continue to learn though the senses as well as through cognition and children learn cognitively from very early in their lives.

In the first instance, we can say that the initial stimulus is learned and remembered but it has no meaning: it is an S–R (stimulus–response) form of learning but there is a 'logic of meaning' underlying all experiences that later has to be satisfied. But this cannot really happen until children have acquired the capability of language. Once remembered, there is one sense in which these sensations can be taken for granted, but until we can give meaning to experiences there is another sense which forbids our taking it for granted. At the same time, there is an ongoing process of deciding whether we like or dislike the sensation which we have – and so we are learning feelings and attitudes at the same time. This process is often conscious but sometimes it is a pre-conscious experience and we decide the next time we have that sensation whether we like it or not: here, once again we can begin to see the significance of pre-conscious learning.

Once we have developed a cognitive dimension to our learning there is a sense in which the bodily aspects of learning, the senses, appear to lose a great deal of their significance. The dominance of the cognitive is natural, but the loss of the significance of the sense itself is dangerous to our humanity, and it is for this reason that we need to be slow and to be attentive to our experiences (Crawford, 2005) in order to learn the most from them. All learning begins with the sensations – even a sound or the sight of a symbol – and so we this form of learning can be depicted by Figure 3.1, which is but a simplified version of our more complex model of learning. Nevertheless, it is a model of learning from primary experience.

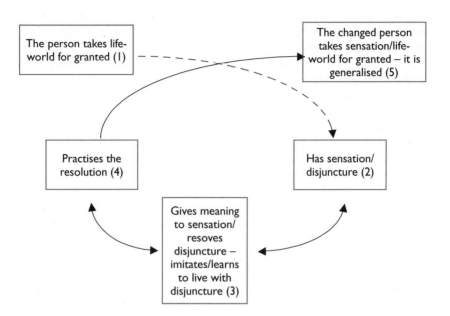

Figure 3.1 The transformation of the senses: learning from primary experience.

In Figure 3.1, we see that the disjuncture is caused by an inability to take the sensation for granted – this may be because the sense experience is new or because it is unrecognised, as well as because we cannot give it meaning (box 2) – we will discuss the concept of meaning quite fully in a later chapter. However, the arrow to box 2 is dotted because in early childhood the disjuncture is caused not because the sensation is destroying a previously taken for granted situation, but because it is providing a completely new developmental experience. Before the acquisition of language, or at least the understanding of language, the ascription of meaning is restricted, although other language forms, such as music and shape, can also give possible meanings for the trained mind, e.g. the artist or the musician. However, this is the children's dilemma: they have to learn to give it a meaning that is their own or they adopt (imitate) the meaning given by their wider society. Subjective meaning is important, but as we grow that subjective meaning has to relate to an objective meaning that lies outside the children themselves; this is to be found in culture, which is carried by other people and which we all learn through interaction. Over time and repeated experiences, children learn that the same experience that they have memorised can be given a generalised meaning, one which is usually embedded in culture and transmitted through interaction with significant others.

The double arrows between boxes 2 and 3 and between boxes 3 and 4 indicate that the learning is trial and error, or experimental and self-directed, in as much as in the first instance the meaning fits the sensation (box 3) and, in the second, the meaning is accepted by the social group (box 4). Acceptance by the group does not mean that it is correct – only that it is socially acceptable. If the children's subjective meaning is acceptable in as much as the people with whom they interact and upon whom they practise their answer do not contradict them in some way, then they can assume it to be socially correct even though it may not be technically correct. If not, then they are faced with a new learning situation later in their lives. As they continue to practise it, so they are able to universalise it and take it for granted, until the next time that a disjunctural situation occurs. Kolb (1984) actually includes generalisation in his learning cycle, but my research suggests that generalisation occurs not immediately following a new learning experience, but only after the resolution to disjuncture has been tried out on several occasions. If children do not resolve the dilemma, then they revert to box 2 and try again, so that the arrows between boxes 2 and 3 and between boxes 3 and 4 are not unidirectional, illustrating that there is a process of trial and error learning at both stages. At the point of taking our sensations for granted, which is the basis of habitual behaviour, they move to the next phase – as we will see when we discuss meaning itself rather than the sensation. Adults and older children are more likely than young children to experience disjuncture in the cognitive domain and to take the sensation stage for granted.

Nevertheless, those theorists who want to reduce everything to sensory experience actually claim that consciousness is 'empty of meaning' (Donald, 2001: 35), and by this approach they question the whole basis of learning theory and even human existence (see Bruner's (1990) criticism of this approach). But, Pinker (1999) admits, we cannot build an autonomous robot and even Donald (2001: 135–7), who wants to discover how meaning evolved in the evolutionary process, is forced to admit that its physical basis is not yet understood. At the heart of human learning is the acquisition of meaning through interaction and cultural experience and all the studies of learning and thinking psychology and the social sciences are implicitly questioned by those who place all their bets on evolution alone. By way of contrast, other scholars who play down the significance of consciousness do so because they see it as a cultural invention perpetuated through language, but even this position is open to considerable criticism, as we will see in the following pages.

Part 3: Learning in play

Play is not just the aimless passing of time with or by children: 'simply running around without purpose or rules is boring and does not appeal to children' (Vygotsky, 1978: 103); it is incorrect to regard play as action without purpose. There is a clear development in the way children play, and the age of about three years is when the transition takes place (Vygotsky, 1978: 93, 97; Nelson, 2007: 99–100). Before the age of three, play serves several functions in the child's world, as summarised by Nelson (2007: 101–2):

> In summary, these various action modes – imitation, gesture, object and event play, category sorting – allow toddlers to represent their meanings, their knowledge of things and how they function in events in the child's world. The representations are external, 'in the world' and available for reviewing. They are also available for others who engage with the child and who may attempt to interpret or to share the child's meaning . . . they are social steps towards shared meanings that become more precise as language enters more fully into the picture.

But thereafter Vygotsky (ibid.: 93) sees play as enabling children to create imaginary situations in which unrealisable desires can be realised. But these situations are zones of proximal development because in play children always behave beyond their average age. He claims that imagination is a new psychological process which is not present in the initial consciousness of children and it is at the heart of our understanding of play. However, play produces rules of behaviour in the situation, and children are sticklers for keeping to the rules, and so play helps children develop their imagination and learn rules and self-control. But imagination is not an end in itself:

> Creating an imaginary situation can be regarded as a means of developing abstract thought. The corresponding development of rules leads to actions on the basis of which the division between work and play becomes possible.
>
> (ibid.: 103–4)

It is during this time that the division between visual situations and the visual field, i.e. between situations of thought and real situations, occurs. It is this that led the political philosopher Kingwell (2000: 68–74) to think that the universalism of imagination could be the alternative to Kant's universalism of rationality. He (ibid.: 68) defines it as 'the capacity to see beyond the materials given'. It is a sense of challenging our own personal experience and empathising with us: it is the opportunity to imagine a different and better world than the one in which we live, and in this sense it is at the heart of both empathy and desire. Kingwell also reminds us that this same imagination can lead to sadism, and so it is not intrinsically universally good. He (ibid.: 73) concludes that 'Imaginative connections remind us, as nothing else can, that we are, as citizens embedded in cultures, neither entirely free nor entirely imprisoned'.

Play, then, is crucial to children's development, but during it we develop our imagination and learn to make and keep rules, we learn self-control and it assists us in the development of abstract thought. Imagination helps us empathise with ourselves and helps us have a vision of a better world.

Part 4: Learning language

There have been many volumes written on language learning (e.g. Vygotsky, 1978, *inter alia*) and we have no intention of trying to rehearse all of these treatises here, but crucial to language learning is relationship, which Tomasello (1999) expands to the idea of joint attentional scenes that develop when infants are about nine months old – that is when infants begin to tune in to the activities of adults which are not expressly directed towards them and they begin to understand the other as an intentional agent, like themselves. Infants at this age begin to reproduce adults' intentional behaviour through imitation. Tomasello is clear that there is no evidence for hard-wiring in these situations. Tomasello (1999: 82) claims that:

> Imitative learning of this type thus relies fundamentally on infants' tendency to identify with adults, present from an early age, and in their ability to distinguish in the actions of others the underlying goal and the different means that might be chosen to achieve it, present from nine months.

It is in these joint attentional scenes that children begin to use symbols since 'sounds become language for young children when and only when they understand that the adult is making that sound with the intention that they attend to something' (Tomasello, 1999: 101). Children then seek to imitate that sound and relate it to the type of situation in which they learned it – they recognise it as a shared symbol. The more time that children spend with their mothers between 12 and 18 months, the greater their vocabulary is likely to be because of it, and this results in a greater consciousness of the world in which the child lives.

What is clear from this discussion is that language does not precede culture but rather its development is dependent upon culture. Donald (2001: 279–80) suggests that there are several good reasons why we should start with culture in understanding language: it is consistent with our understanding of the evolving hominid brain; enculturation itself might account for a qualitative shift in human cognition; it accounts for imitative learning; it explains why language does not self-install in isolated individuals; and it gives us a means for referring language outside of itself.

Fundamentally, then, we see that language is learned in relationship through imitation and so it reflects the subculture of the child's life-world. In this sense, we can see that through various mechanisms children are socialised into their cultures and that, although we do not mirror them, there is sufficient of the image remaining for us to be located within the wide sphere.

Part 5: Socialisation

We are socialised into the culture of our life-world; as we have seen from the above discussion, socialisation is itself a series of learning processes. Berger and Luckmann (1966: 150) define primary socialisation as 'the first socialization an individual undergoes in childhood through which he becomes a member of society'. Secondary socialisation is the internalisation of institutional or institutionally based subworlds, and those who transmit the subculture are institutional functionaries and the relationship is specified by formal organisational procedures. The people with whom we interact are those functionaries – it is about relationship. Thereafter, the informal processes of acquiring that subculture continue through the everyday processes of social living and working. This means that the principles, practices and language of specific roles are learned and internalised. They (ibid.: 160) maintain that the biological limitations of humanity become decreasingly important as this process continues, but we would maintain here that both the biological and the genetic are more than they were to Berger and Luckmann. This is, of course, a return to the historic nature–nurture debate, but recent advances in brain research and evolutionary psychology mean that we have to take this work into consideration in our studies of human learning.

From birth onwards, a conscious awareness of the wider world gradually develops, and this is a learning process, but it is not all conscious learning: a great deal of pre-conscious learning still occurs, as we have already seen. It has been shown above that it is through relationship with significant others that a great deal of this learning happens, but in the contemporary world of the media it is not entirely possible to isolate the personal from the impersonal media transmissions to which we are all exposed, so that the dominant ideologies are also acquired early in life (see Jarvis, 2008).

However, what is also learned in this process is quite fundamental to the development of the person, and significant others play an important role in this process.

> The significant others who mediate the world to him modify it in the course of mediating it. They select aspects of it in accordance with their own location in the social structure, and also by virtue of their individual biographically rooted idiosyncrasies. The social world is 'filtered' to the individual through this double selectivity.
>
> (Berger and Luckmann, 1966: 151)

Berger and Luckmann are, however, too rational in their approach, since we often hear parents say 'I don't know where (s)he learned that!' We are aware that children copy adult behaviour in joint attentional situations, and the adults may not even be aware of precisely what the children are learning: in this sense the children's learning is unintended. In the same way, what is transmitted verbally may not just reflect the social position of the significant others, it may also have resulted from the children's pre-conscious learning, and so on. What it clear is that Berger and Luckmann are correct in recognising that the social world that children learn about and participate in is actually slightly different from that of their significant others: it changes through transmission itself, and it changes again as children grow and externalise and enter into dialogue with others. This is all part of the lifelong learning process.

The significant others all treat the children in accord with their perception of the child's place in the world, that is in relation to the social location of their parents, and so on. There is no doubt a sense of conformity about this. Children begin to internalise their modified version of the social world of the significant others, and in this process of internalisation they identify with its familiarity; herein we find elements of pleasure formation. They then begin to identify with the individuals who are significant others – a relationship is born. Children recognise themselves by the way that those with whom they have identified treat them in a similar manner – they begin to identify themselves. Children learn a social identity long before they learn an individual one – this is a stage in the process. But significantly, this is an incidental process and one in which the growing sense of consciousness plays its part: it would be wrong to claim that it is all pre-conscious learning but it would be just as false to regard it all as a conscious process – consciousness emerges in the process itself.

As we grow, so our world of interaction broadens and we learn from a greater variety of people; we are also more exposed to the media and so we get an even broader, if not a global, view from quite early in our lives. This is secondary socialisation – when we learn in the school and also in leisure groups and organisations. Some scholars think that there is a third socialisation process – into work. However, this may well be regarded as an unnecessary distinction and so for heuristic purposes we will deal with them together here. This form of socialisation occurs for the remainder of our lives – it is usually the informal and non-formal learning processes that occur when we, as adults, join organisations so that when we start work in a new organisation there is first the formal induction and this is followed by the informal processes of 'learning the ropes' and becoming a member of the organisation. In fact, this is what Lave and Wenger (1991) describe in their book *Situated Learning* when they look at the process of individuals moving from the periphery of an organisation towards its centre. The organisation's subculture is learned by the initiates: socialisation is part of the process of lifelong learning and it continues late into lives as older people join new organisations, such as Universities of the Third Age, after their retirement from work.

Socialisation, in all its forms, is the process whereby we internalise the exterior world and make it our own, but we are not merely reproductions of a past generation since there are so many extraneous factors, such as the media and people from other faiths and cultures with whom we interact and from whom we learn, which results in the fact that, although there are many similarities between us, there are also differences. At least two things emerge from this discussion: (1) there are two realities, one which is internal and the other which is external, although the former is not a perfect reflection of the latter so that we are imperfect reproductions of our culture and of the persons with whom we interact; and (2) we are also individuals. Bourdieu (1992: 127–8), commenting upon the first of these, writes:

> Social reality exists, so to speak, twice, in things and in minds, in fields and in habitus, outside and inside of agents. And when habitus encounters a social world of which it is the produce it is like a 'fish in water': it does not feel the weight of the water, and it takes the world about itself for granted . . . It is because this world has produced me, because it has produced the categories of thought that I apply to it, that it appears to me as self-evident.

The idea of two realities, an internal and an external, is very significant for our understanding of the learning process. During the course of our everyday lives, the increasing congruence of these two realities brings us pleasure whereas incongruence can be unpleasant – it is disjunctural. However, we rarely reflect on the fact, or even recognise, that we are learning pleasure and displeasure in a pre-conscious manner in the course of everyday living.

That we have internalised our culture means that we are likely to reproduce it, in the same way as we ourselves are imperfect reproductions. Imperfect reproduction allows for the development of individuality, but individuality must follow relationship. Nevertheless, this also raises quite significant questions about where we should begin our study of the person in society – with the individual or with the group? Indeed, it is the question that separates Western and Eastern thought to a considerable degree since the former begins with the individual and the latter with the field or context. With the development of individuality, we can see the paradox of human being emerge, since it is individuals who are enabled both to enter into relationship and to create new ones. Existence, therefore, demands both the social and the individual – both group and person simultaneously.

Concluding discussion

The idea that 'the child is father of the man' can be seen clearly in this chapter: much of what is learned in these early years remains with us throughout our lives. All of this learning gives children the opportunity of coping with the exigencies of their lives and as they grow and learn even more so they gain a greater confidence to respond to the situations in which they find themselves – but we must not forget that we are already genetic and biological beings from the outset and so all these learning experiences are themselves affecting the predispositions with which we are born. Nevertheless, these years are an important springboard, and so we might ask, 'Are we predetermined as a result of early years learning?'. Clearly, we have seen that parts of the brain are developed and 'wired up' during these years and we learn language, play, attitudes and desires, and so on, as a result of these experiences. In many ways we are being programmed by our learning in a social context – but it is only adding to the complex brain with which we are born and building the mind which comes as a result of our learning. From now on we are confronted with a major philosophical problem – to what extent are the brain and the mind separated? – and here we enter the debate about the nature of the mind (see Dennett, 1991; Chalmers, 1996; Donald, 2001; Maslin, 2001; Feser, 2005; *inter alia*), but our programming is not totally predetermining since we do have the capacity to learn to act against our predispositions and inclinations, although we do so in a situation which might not be described as a level playing field. Nevertheless, we can see that we may not actually be as free as we wish or even as free as we think we are. In some ways this programming has restricted our freedom – but this is another philosophical debate that demands to be discussed more fully in a philosophical study of learning.

However, one thing has become quite clear from this discussion of the early years, and that is that meaning and intentionality are already present in the child from early years and so it is necessary for us to examine the concept of meaning but, before we do this, we need to look at the way in which we continue to learn in everyday life.

Chapter 4

Practical living

As we have seen from the opening chapters, we have already started to learn from before the time of our birth, and this continues into our early years. Initially this learning is pre-conscious and pre-cognitive and through both our biological evolution and our development in the womb we bring to our lives predispositions that will affect our future learning: at birth we are by no means *tabula rasa*. Not only do we have predispositions – both learned and genetic – we are born into a world which has its own cultural history so that its people have devised their own answers to the problems generated by the fact that existence, the cosmos, and even being itself, have no in-built meaning. In other words, its cultures are responses to the problems that our predecessors faced at different times in their history, and it is this into which we are socialised and through which we build our own universe of meaning. However, this process occurs in the processes of living in society – a society that is changing very rapidly and it has made learning endemic! Bauman (2005: 1) opens his book *Liquid Life* in the following manner:

> Conditions of action and strategies designed to respond to them age quickly and become obsolete before the actors have chance to learn them properly.

Consequently, we live in a state of change all the time and that means that, unless we disengage from social living, we are constantly having potential learning experiences throughout the whole of our lives, and so we examine both action and the situation in this brief chapter.

Part 1: Action

Already we can begin to distinguish between the human condition and human nature: the human condition is 'life itself, natality and mortality, worldliness, plurality, and the earth [which] can never "explain" what we are or answer the question of who we are for the simple reason that they never condition us absolutely' (Arendt 1958: 11). Hence, we can already see two meanings to the word 'meaning': on the one hand, it is the meaning given to our experiences and, on the other, it is the meaning given to existence itself (see Chapter 6 for a discussion of meaning). Both of these are cultural phenomena. Later we will meet other meanings of this term, such as the meaning of phenomena, events, words, sentences, intentions, and so on. Human nature, however, also has at least two connotations – it is what we become as a result of our birth and learning. In a sense, there is a duality in human nature – that which is general to the human species and that which is specific to the individual. It will be recalled from earlier chapters, for instance, that, as a result of our early experiences, the neocortex of each individual is wired completely differently as a result of the patterns and networks of neurons that develop in our early years of life and which help form our perceptions of external reality. The building of our brain occurs, in part, as a result of those early learning experiences and continues at a slower rate as we age. It is, therefore, important to recognise that this process may well be different between the East and the West, and that we should not assume that we all undergo similar processes of wiring the neocortex.

Throughout these early chapters we have recognised the significance of relationship. Human living is about living in relationship with others and, in this sense, it is the 'living' rather than the 'learning' or the 'thinking' that has primacy to our being; this is not to say that thinking is not equally important, only that thinking occurs as a result of our living and not living as a result of our thinking. Arendt (1958) sees this as *Vita Activa* as opposed to *Vita Contemplativa* and, therefore, the importance of the worlds of labour and other forms of action, such as fabrication. In a different argument Archer (2000: 121–4) reaches a similar conclusion talking of the primacy of practice and she suggests that there are three pointers in this direction:

- Our embodiment.
- We all have transactions with reality from the first day of our lives.
- Our particular species-being has endowed us with various potentials, their development being socially contingent.

Husserl (cited in Schutz, 1967: 51) emphasised this when he wrote that 'I live *in* my Acts'. In precisely the same manner, Ricoeur, to whom we make reference later in this study, also starts with action:

Ricoeur wants his thought to be rooted in the concreteness of human experience; everything must relate back, in one way or another, to human action.

(Lowe, introduction to Ricoeur, 1986: x)

To be rooted in human experience is at the heart of our living. When we are taught we can learn *knowledge what* and even *knowledge how*, but this is as far as we can go. It is generalised information, and even if I learn it and make it my knowledge it is still insufficient. *Knowledge how* does not equip me to do anything – it is still in the cognitive domain. If I taught you how to play a game of cards, you still cannot play it until you have the cards in your hands and the experience of playing the game: this is the primary experience from which you learn. Now we learn from that experience and eventually we are *able to play*, but we also learn from that experience a different form of *knowledge how* and even *knowledge that* – now it is the subjective, personal knowledge learned from primary experience – it is our knowledge. But these forms of knowledge we may learn incidentally, or even pre-consciously in the process of doing. Since there is no conceptual relationship between the knowledge learned in secondary experience and *being able to* – we can learn that only by doing and having done and so we have learned our own knowledge – it has never been information or data and it only becomes data or information if we try to teach another. However, as we pointed out previously, once we do this, we are confronted with at least two insurmountable problems. First, once we try to put our experience into words, we can only speak from memory and, however immediate the memory, it is not the present, nor can we convey the sense of emotion contained in the experience or the learning that ensued. Second, experts in card playing may know all the rules but a great deal of their expertise lies not in rule-knowing but in the tacit knowledge of reading persons, situations or even the stage in the game. Tacit knowledge, as Polanyi (1967) showed us, is also an intrinsic part of our knowing, but it is one that we find difficult, if not impossible, to articulate.

In a different approach to practice, we find that Argyris and Schön (1974) start their study of 'theory in practice' from theory and apply it to practice; we will return to their work later. Their approach to theory needs careful and critical examination in the light of our understanding of learning, biography and behaviour: as a result of our previous learning and what we have learned to take for granted, it could be said that we develop a philosophy of behaviour and, as such, this could be conceived as a theory of action. In this sense, we develop implicit theories of action – tacit theories – so that it is impossible to divorce completely theory and practice and, in this sense, the claim would be true for Arendt, Archer and Ricoeur.

Unlike some of the of the early Enlightenment thinkers and those since that time who have embraced Enlightenment thinking, I feel – in common with a number of contemporary thinkers – that it is significant that we develop our understanding of human learning with and in practice, although laboratory experiments, and so on, may complement our understanding of practice. There is also a tacit theory in practical action itself and a more developed theory follows thereafter (see also Jarvis, 1999). This conclusion is important not only for our understanding of learning but also for our approaches to teaching. Significantly, it is in accord with Aristotle's formulation of practical wisdom when he emphasised that:

> What has been said is confirmed by the fact that while young men become geometricians and mathematicians and wise in matters like these, it is thought that a young man of practical wisdom cannot be found. The cause is that such wisdom is concerned not only with universals but with particulars, which become familiar from experience, but a young man has no experience, for it is length of time that gives experience.
>
> (Aristotle, 1925: VI.8, 148)

Theoretical subjects, then, might, but need not, be studied best by young people, but the practical business of living is something that can be mastered only by experienced people since it requires experience rather than scientific theory. We will return to the idea of agency in Chapter 13 when we look at doing.

Part 2: The situation

Much of our learning – even in everyday life – occurs in quite specific situations in our life-world, and it is necessary to recognise that our perception of the situation in which we are will affect our understanding of the event or its contents. In other words, we will see things culturally and individually as a result of our previous learning experiences, the memories of which are stored in our biographical history, and our biological history, which expands with age. Age is a major feature in our situation since we perceive the world differently as we age and so we are confronted with another basis for lifelong learning. But it is not only our biographical history that determines the way in which we perceive our situation; in every situation 'the ontological structure of the world is imposed upon me' (Schutz and Luckmann, 1974: 114). It is, for instance, a common experience to see people change their perceptions of a situation at work when they are promoted to a management position from that of an ordinary worker, when people age and retire, and so on. Learning is a personal, subjective construction of reality but it is also cultural. This may best be demonstrated by Witkin's (Witkin 1971) theory of field dependence: Nisbett (2005: 96–7) showed that Asian people are more field dependent than are Westerners. Consequently, they perceive situations and even causality differently, so that we can conclude that, generally speaking, perceptions of reality will differ between societies and cultures – although Nesbitt found that in some instances Western women approximated more closely to the Eastern perspective than did Eastern men. Therefore, there is a third element in this process, which is the phenomenological one, since it depends on the fact that where we are located socially will partially determine how we perceive a situation. However, even this is slightly oversimple because, if we are bicultural, our perception might be determined by the cultural framework within which we are functioning at that time. In my own experience of working in Hong Kong, one of the participants in a workshop which I facilitated was able to act in a Western manner, which accorded with her own experiences of being at university in Canada, when she was acting like a Western student and being the rapporteur for her group and speaking in English, but the following evening when she was not required to perform this role and she thought and acted as a Chinese student she was unable to speak out in the group and question the proceedings: she explained to me afterwards about why she was unable to play a Western student-type role on the second evening.

Generally we treat our situation as a fairly static phenomenon but we do have to recognise that the social structures of our life-world do change, often quite rapidly, and when they do all our taken-for-grantednesses and habits of daily living are destroyed and we have to discover new patterns for our lives. This is, in fact, a form of learning by doing. Aslanian and Brickell (1980) discovered that life transition is a major factor in people returning to studying – as it is to learning in general. The removal of social structures frees up individuals to do and learn new things. In the same manner, Lave and Wenger (1991) showed how we learn from and in our situation, which, in organisations, is a changing one as we become social-ised into the organisation within which we are learning.

Perhaps the easiest way to depict the learning situations of everyday life is in Figure 4.1, in which it is recognised that both intended and unintended

Type of learning

	Intended	Incidental
Formal	A	D
Non-formal	B	E
Informal	C	F

Type of situation

Figure 4.1 Possible learning situations.

learning can occur in the same situation, whether it is formal, non-formal or informal.

We can now illustrate the type of learning that might occur in each of these six different learning situations.

- Box A is *formal education and training* that occurs in an educational institution and any other bureaucratic organisation devoted to education and training.
- Box B can refer to the ongoing nature of learning that occurs in places such as the work place, community, and so on. Sometimes the learner is actually mentored in these situations.
- Box C is both *learning in everyday life* and *self-directed learning*. It is the type of learning that we undertake when we decide to teach ourselves a computer program, and so on. It can be individual learning or part of a group project.
- Box D refers to that *incidental learning* that occurs in formal situations, not always educational, but which the planners of the learning experience do not intend. For example, the realisation that the instructor is not really as knowledgeable as we thought, or that the room is badly designed, or that teacher does not really treat me as an autonomous individual, and so on.
- Box E also refers to *incidental learning* situations in non-formal learning episodes.
- Box F refers to *everyday learning*, which is probably the most common situation of all, especially in rapidly changing societies. In these we find ourselves in new situations and we have to learn how to cope – by thinking on our feet about our next action, and so on (Heller, 1984). If we fail to respond to this situation quickly, we usually have to plan our learning and then the situation moves to box C.

It is only in box A that we are expected to learn through secondary experience, which usually starts with a theoretical perspective – a legacy of the Enlightenment – although there are many other situations in which it occurs. However, the degree of formality is not the only variable in the subcultures of social situations that might affect either the type of learning or the behavioural outcomes of such learning: the politics and culture of the social context, the social position of both learners and teachers (leaders, managers, and so on) and even the status given to the knowledge being acquired will be amongst the factors that affect the type of experience from which the learners learn.

Understanding the situation, then, is a subjective but complex process, and in our everyday life we are quite likely to take for granted our social situation and even our perceptions of it. Indeed, we are mistakenly likely to regard them as objective.

Conclusion

It is in the situation that we have experiences in by and through which we learn, so that, before we look at the actual processes themselves, we do need to look carefully at the concept of experience itself.

Chapter 5

Experience

To say that we learn from experience is a truism, so why has the idea of experiential learning developed into such a popular area of learning theory? Perhaps the answer to this is that educationalists have taken for granted the idea that we learn cognitively and usually in formal settings, such as schools and in pedagogic processes. Once it was recognised that practice is more basic to learning than cognitive theorising, so the idea of experiential learning became more popular. Knowles's (1980) work on andragogy in the USA in the 1960s and 1970s led a great number of practitioners to utilise his thinking and his techniques – which were largely the traditional adult education ones. Andragogy, therefore, led to a considerable growth in thinking about experiential learning. But it also came to reinforce the idea that vocational learners had to spend some time in a placement during their occupational preparation and, eventually, this led to the rediscovery of apprenticeship models of vocational training. But an interesting paradox emerged – whereas experience became a common and taken-for-granted concept in the educational vocabulary, philosophers have always claimed that the concept of experience is one of the most difficult in the philosophical vocabulary (Oakeshott, 1933: 9). Knowles (1980), however, referred to it in only one way – that of our personal biography. The experience we bring to learning is fundamental to adult learning, and so anthologies of experiential learning (e.g. Weil and McGill, 1989) were more concerned with practice and early major studies (Boud *et al.*, 1983; Schön, 1983) were more concerned with reflection on practice – the cognitive – than with theorising about this complex concept. For others, the term 'experience' was only a focus (Marton *et al.*, 1984) rather a basis for dealing with the philosophical niceties of the concept, and these points remained true even for some later studies that examined experiential learning (Fraser, 1995). But the foundations were being laid in education for a move towards a more philosophical approach (Jarvis, 1992; Marton and Booth, 1997). In my most recent book on learning I tackled this topic more fully (Jarvis, 2006: 70–86) and this chapter is a development of the material that I put into that chapter: there is obviously some overlap with it, but there is also a lot of new material.

Fundamentally, there are two forms of experience: primary and secondary. If I were to describe my recent teaching experience in different parts of the world, you would be having a secondary experience – you would be hearing my words but not experiencing either the place in the world about which I was talking or my teaching there. In precisely the same way, if I were to teach you about my theory of globalisation (Jarvis, 2007b), you would be having a secondary experience, as you would if I were to discuss any theory with you because theory is secondary experience – it is information mediated to one person via another even though that information may be the other's own knowledge, although this does not have to be the case. In such experiences, we can learn *knowledge what* and even *knowledge how*, but this is as far as we can go. It is generalised information and, even if we learn it and make it our knowledge, it is still insufficient. *Knowledge how* does not equip us to do anything – it is still knowledge. However, if I taught you how to play the card game Whist, you still cannot play it until you have the cards in your hands and the experience of playing the game: this is primary experience. Now we learn from that experience and we are *able to play*, but we also learn from that experience a different form of *knowledge how* and even *knowledge that* – now it is the subjective, personal knowledge learned from primary experience – it is our knowledge. There is no conceptual relationship between the *knowledge learned* in secondary experience and *being able to* – we can learn that only by doing, and having done so we have learned our own knowledge – it has never been information or data and it becomes data or information only if we try to teach another person our knowledge. However, once we do this, we are confronted with at least two insurmountable problems. First, once we try to put our experience into words, we can only speak from memory and, however immediate the memory, we cannot convey the sense of emotion contained in the experience or the learning that ensued. Second, experts in card playing, for instance, may know all the rules of the game but a great deal of their expertise lies not in rule-knowing but in the tacit knowledge of reading persons, situations or even the strategic stage in the game. Tacit knowledge, as Polanyi (1967) showed us, is also an intrinsic part of our knowing but it is one which we find difficult, if not impossible, to articulate. He gives the example of a face in a crowd – we can recognise it but we find it impossible to describe it accurately. But Freud also taught us about the significance of the unconscious, and later in this chapter we will explore the pre-conscious, so that experience is broader than even awareness itself but not broader than experience as consciousness: perhaps 'conscious experience is not all there is to the mind' (Chalmers, 1996: 11).

At the heart of this is that all the forms of knowledge are learned – from either primary or secondary experience. It is from the experience that we learn, but, as we are beginning to see, when we use the word 'experience' in experiential learning and education we are usually referring to a practicum rather than this rather complex notion of experience *per se*.

Experience has many different meanings, and we learn from each of these manifestations that we call experiences. In this chapter I am going to explore just a few of these notions and seek to understand how each affects out understanding of learning. We will explore experience as consciousness, biography, episode/event, expertise (skill and wisdom), and we will conclude with two other conceptual difficulties about experience that point us to future deliberations. And so the question needs to be posed: precisely what do we mean by this profoundly difficult concept the meaning of which we tend to take for granted? *Collins English Dictionary* (1979) offers seven diverse interpretations:

- direct personal participation;
- a particular incident;
- accumulated knowledge;
- impact made on an individual by culture;
- totality of a person's thoughts, emotions, perceptions, encounters;
- to participate in;
- to be moved emotionally.

In contrast, a philosophical dictionary (Speake, 1984) is more concerned with the distinction between philosophical empiricism and philosophical rationalism: the former is about a person's cognitive dealings with the external world and the latter is more concerned with the subjectivity or privacy of our perceptions of the world and that we can claim little beyond these. It will probably have become obvious from our previous discussions that we are suggesting that learning is individual and totally private although it can occur in a public place: it is subjective since we learn from our own experience of external reality, even though individuals with similar backgrounds and in common situations may appear to have group experiences from which they learn together. Our individual learning, however, must find social outcomes to be meaningful, or even testable, although much learning is not testable in the crude way that education has often endeavoured to test it!

So how, then, do we define experience? To offer a simple definition in response to the question would be unwise: rather we will examine the concept from a variety of perspectives that recognise this complexity and which relate to the processes of human learning. We will examine the idea of experience as consciousness, biography, episode/event, expertise (skill and wisdom). I want to conclude with two other conceptual difficulties about experience.

Part I: Experience as consciousness

Understanding learning from experience means that we look at a wide range of disciplines across the whole lifespan and learning cannot be understood in any other way since this is a human activity of which cognition is but one part. Chalmers (1996: 11–16) suggests that there are two forms of conscious experience:

- Phenomenological – the mind as conscious experience and as a consciously experienced mental state in which we feel in certain ways.
- Psychological – the mind as a causal basis of behaviour.

He regards these two approaches as close to each other since many kinds of psychological states can be associated with phenomenological states, and so on – but they do not coincide, and in some ways this distinction relates to the I–Me situation discussed previously and to which we will return towards the end of this book.

Soon after birth we do have experiences and we learn to memorise from sensations; Donald (2001: 75) suggests that memorising sensation is the basis of consciousness itself and that we learn consciousness as we learn and remember. But the significant thing about consciousness is that we need to be conscious of something – we need to experience external reality in some way. Consciousness is a bridge between the bare life within a human being (Agamben, 1995) – this is a concept that is even more basic than the idea that existentialists call Being – and external reality itself, but it needs external stimulation to generate awareness and also for it to remain stable. This latter fact was clearly demonstrated in an experiment at McGill University, which we described previously, in which some students were paid a financial reward to do nothing – in fact to be denied sensory perception for as long as they could. None lasted longer than three days before giving up, and even then some were temporarily mentally harmed: consciousness requires external stimuli – or experiences – in order to be consciousness. In other words, we need both people with whom to interact and the cultural experience that such interaction produces. We become ourselves in such a cultural environment: ultimately we are not individuals but individuals-in-groups and in social situations. This relationship is something of an entity in itself and, as we have already argued, following Buber (1958), that relationship is something with which we start life.

However, we may not be born with conscious awareness, as we all recognise when we see a newborn baby; we learn it by experience, and like its evolution, it grows and develops in each of us. Following Donald (2001: 178–200), there appear to be three evolutionary dimensions of consciousness:

- *Selective binding.* Binding is the process whereby we link together phenomena to produce a perceptual unity and it is only through consciousness that we can be aware of the external world.
- *Short-term memory.* This dimension follows from the previous one in as much as any binding requires a short-term memory in order to hold the whole together and, as the brain evolves, the focus changes from the binding mechanism to give the brain power to be free from the immediate context. In this freedom lies the capacity to develop human learning.
- *Intermediate and long-term governance.* This builds on the previous two stages and expands the range of experience which forms the basis of our continued learning: it was during this stage of our evolution that the pre-frontal cortex and other regions of the tertiary cortex expanded, and this process occurred as a result of social interaction and the growth of culture.

It can thus be seen that consciousness itself has evolved through learning and remembering, and this same process is evident in our human development: it is the expanding brain that provides us with the opportunity of broadened experience from which we can continue to learn. Indeed, we are freed from the immediate experience and able to memorise past experiences. The basis of our learning is awareness itself – the act of experiencing – although it is attention that focuses our learning in a conscious manner. However, such conscious awareness is perhaps best recognised in language itself. When we can speak about an experience we are fully conscious of it, but once we actually speak about it we change its nature as Eliade (see Ricoeur, 1995: 48–55) explains, calling this phenomenon hierophantic when he writes about religious experience. I will return to this later in this chapter.

Bare life, then, is embodied and through the senses exposed to external stimuli, or *qualia*, which are processed through the brain. A more narrow use of this term *qualia* includes the idea of quality in sensory experience, such as colour, an approach that is favoured by some researchers (e.g. Rose, 2006), whereas others employ it more broadly to refer to all sensory experiences. However, the McGill experiment showed that we, humans, need much more than just consciousness to survive as normal human beings – we need experiences that are based in an external context about which we can become aware, or to which we can pay attention. This distinction is important – we are no doubt more aware of a wider context when we focus our attention, so that we can say that at one level we have an experience of the phenomenon to which we attend but we are often conscious of a wider reality. Consequently, there are degrees of awareness – some are at the heart of our concentration whereas others are at the periphery of our focus of attention, and in such skills as speed-reading we actually learn from our periphery as well as from the focus of our attention. From my own experience of getting people to write down their own learning experiences, it is clear that a great deal of learning in everyday life occurs at the periphery of our conscious awareness and even in our pre-consciousness. In these situations much of our knowledge is tacit. Our tacit knowledge is also reflected in a phenomenon that Marton and Booth (1997: 99–100) call appresentation, that is when we complete an incomplete experience by recalling knowledge that has been internalised without our full conscious awareness of it from an earlier experience.

Consciousness, however, spans all the levels of awareness, but it is expanded by language and ultimately by all other means of storing knowledge. What Crawford (2005) called attentive experiencing is significant here since it concentrates the mind on a specific phenomenon. In a sense, attentive experiencing is the type of awareness that occurs in in-depth thought, concentration or religious contemplation: in-depth learning that occurs as a result of our being more aware of the significance and content of that experience. The more that we attend to our experiences, the more we see in them and the more we learn from them: 'paying attention' is important to our conscious experience and is one of the most significant factors in learning. Significantly, in this rapidly moving world where people seem to have little time for anything a new movement is beginning – the slow movement (Honore, 2004) – which seeks to offer a challenge to the speed of the world and points us to the need for more attention to be given to the nature of experience. Thus, at one end of the spectrum we can have experiences of which we are not conscious because they happen so speedily but which require a further conscious experience to bring them to our conscious awareness, and at the other end of the spectrum we focus upon concentration, from which we gain a greater insight into our experience since we are more conscious of it and learn more from it.

However, we are confronted at this stage with the work of Freud, who pointed us to the unconscious mind, and Polanyi (1967), who highlighted tacit knowledge, and by my own research into learning, in which I discuss the significance of the pre-conscious in learning. Indeed, we can actually now see how the pre-conscious experience occurs, which is important in our thinking both about perception and about learning. Goleman (1995: 17–20) reports on work by LeDoux (1996), who shows that:

> sensory signals from the ear and eye travel first in the brain to the thalamus and then – across a single synapse – to the amygdala; a second signal is routed to the neo-cortex – the thinking brain. This branching allows the amygdala to begin to respond *before* the neo-cortex which mulls information through several levels of brain circuits before it fully perceives and finally initiates a more finely tailored response.

Consequently, those early information signals allow a pre-conscious response to sensations and, therefore, we are enabled to have pre-conscious experiences that also lead to pre-conscious learning.

Recently, as I noted earlier, I detected a conceptual anomaly in my own work: in my definition of learning in Chapter 1, I included the phrase 'the perceived content of which', which implies that what gets into my mind is something of which I am aware – but I have also written about pre-conscious learning, which suggests that things get into my mind about which I am not aware. There is no doubt that we all have pre-conscious experiences which get imprinted, as it were, in the brain – when the bodily sensations are transmitted to the brain and the network of neurons reconfigured in some small or large way. But, conceptually, does learning stop at the point when we are not aware of the initial stimulus? From my own observations and experience, it seems that pre-conscious learning happens in two stages. We can experience events although we are not aware of every facet of what we have internalised, but the whole event has been experienced and stored in the brain pre-consciously. A subsequent experience acts as a stimulus, the response to which is to call to conscious awareness an aspect of a previous experience of which we had not been conscious before and from which we can now learn. This is the fuzzy boundary of experience and, therefore, the fuzzy boundary of learning, but the actual learning still requires conscious awareness although the experience from which we learn need not be conscious at the time when we experience it.

Experience, then, is wider than conscious awareness but it cannot be wider than being itself – but the pre-conscious is clearly a significant aspect of our biography.

Part 2: Experience as biography

In my own definition of learning, which was discussed in Chapter 1, I suggest that the outcome of every learning event is built into our biographies, although these need not only be our cognitions (see OECD, 2007a), as our definition makes clear. In this sense we are learned persons, but we see from the discussion in the first part of this chapter that memory itself has evolved and that memory itself frees us from the immediate experience and yet in a complex manner it is a working memory that enables us to recall past experiences as and when they become relevant. Consequently, when we exclaim: 'In all my experience . . . ' we are really talking of all the learning events that have made us what we are at that moment in time. Biography is the sum of those experiences from which we have learned and we are the product of those experiences. It is no accident that the influential Faure Report (1972) was called *Learning to Be*.

Our biographies are our understanding about ourselves as we pass through time. Time, however, forms a major problem when we consider experience; Rose (2006: 394) remarks that more 'needs to be done on this baffling problem' and we will look briefly at one aspect of this in the next part of this chapter. Relating time to consciousness Rose (ibid.: 394) says that all higher levels of consciousness are formed by binding between:

1 current input representations, short-term records and current motor efference (something that conducts outwards from the centre) to give retention or protention of the phenomenologists' 'thickness' of experience;

2 various durations of long-term memory . . . to generate conscious awareness of identity and meaning of a stimulus; and

3 long-term autobiographical memory and long-term plans, desires and life goals . . . our memories of the most significant evens so far, and imagined goals of what we want to reach in the future – to give us a sense of who we are and our sense of self.

Consequently, we can see that for as long as we are alive we are compiling our autobiography through experience and learning, and that we are always becoming (see Chapter 17) as we move from experience to experience or even from social status to social status. Phenomenology can be placed within this context since it is a process of 'binding across time to form systematic structures connecting memory, current inflow and plans for the future' (Rose, 2006: 395).

This process is clearly shown in the anthropological studies of van Gennep (1960 [1908]) and V. Turner (1969). More recently, and from a specifically learning perspective, Camilleri (2009) demonstrated this when she followed 10 nursing students through their final year in university and their first 18 months of practice. She showed quite convincingly that it was the experiences in the work place, above all, that provided the basis for the incidental and often pre-conscious learning that led to the students going through the process of playing the role of nurse and being identified as nurses by patients and others to actually identifying with the role, feeling that they were nurses and so eventually they actually became nurses in their own minds. At some stage in their careers they become a nurse – they gain a self-identity as a result of their experiences – in which they identify themselves with the social identity that wearing the uniform generated.

It is not surprising, therefore, that there has grown up in research into human learning the whole field of life history: individuals tracing their life histories and engaging in a process of learning from the experiences of life that they can remember them (see, for instance, West, 1996, 2001, 2007). Noonan (2003: 9) refers to this as 'experience-memory' in order to separate it from the process of memorising: memory of past experiences is quite fundamental to the process of identity building, which is at the heart of our biography.

It is through the process of living and learning that we gain wisdom, as Aristotle (1925: VI.8, 148) noted. Wisdom is the result of experience rather than being a science, like mathematics, that the young can master. Wisdom comes from the practical rather than the theoretical. Ageing also is clearly related to experience as biography and, as we live in an ageing society, it is not surprising that educational gerontology is emerging as a very significant area of study: how older people learn, utilise their learning and also how they feel isolated in a very rapidly changing society since it is hard to keep abreast with everything that is changing. Significantly, however, wisdom is one of the concepts that appears to play a less significant role as our work-orientated society concentrates on technical rationality and competence – knowledge of the present. Wisdom, however, is gained pre-consciously and incidentally in the process of living and learning from experience: it is tacit. Like wisdom, another concept that has not been fully studied in recent years has been the one with which it may be coupled – expertise – and we will turn to this shortly. However, we have to recognise that not all become wise as a result of living because there are many times when we fail to learn from our experiences – we presume upon them and take them for granted. Non-learning from experience is something quite vital to our understanding of learning (Jarvis, 1987), although there may be tacit changes in our understanding of ourselves as a result of this process.

Part 3: Experience as episode/event

In my previous work I did not separate these two terms. Following Donald (2001), I now think that this was a serious mistake, and much of my work has been based on events, which I called episodes, although episodes are actually series of events bound together in conscious awareness of their unity. It is, however, a major flaw in those evolutionary psychologists who consider that the brain is hard-wired as a result of our evolution and that we are programmed by our past to respond to stimuli in specific ways and at specific times. Donald argues that this flaw is exhibited by some of those scholars who believe that they are constructing a science of learning (OECD, 2007b: 11) and consider that our brains are fully wired at birth: scientists can claim that our brains are hard-wired based upon experiments that are no longer than a single event but not for those which span a whole episode, or sequence of events. Laboratory experiments can be carefully designed to record the here and now – they study sensations and very short-term memory – but these are not the limits of consciousness: this has 'a much larger window of experience than short-term memory' (Donald, 2001: 47). We can have an experience of a whole class or even a whole course – experience is an episode in our lives. The capacity of our brains is much larger than that required for the consciousness of a single sensation. We continue to be aware of the situation for a much longer period of time than the immediate and we hold it in our working memory for as long as necessary. No brain can be programmed to respond to a whole episode and this undermines a great deal of the theory of the hard-wired brain. It is what Schutz and Luckmann (1974: 51) called 'a stream of consciousness': experience is a sequence of events that overlap and form a continuous whole and yet, like biography, it is a single episode in our lives.

We sometimes live in the flow of time, an episode in which we seem to have heightened awareness all the time – what Csikszentmihalyi (1990) calls optimal experience – our awareness enables us to learn rapidly and effortlessly without interruption. He (ibid.: 39) describes this as when 'information that keeps coming into awareness is congruent with goals' that leads to psychic energy flowing effortlessly. An interruption to this flow can occur – a disruptive disjuncture – which can refocus our attention on a different event. When I started my own research into learning I was interested in a sense of 'feeling at home' in our own life-world upon which we can presume in an almost unthinking manner – a process which Bergson (1999 [1965]) called *durée*. We take the world for granted and, as it were, act in an 'almost mindless manner' but suddenly something occurs which we can no longer take for granted and we experience a degree of disjuncture: we have a heightened consciousness or awareness and we are forced to question our expectations of the situation. We ask: Why? What for? How do I do it? And so on. These events occur more frequently than optimal experiences; they are common to everyday living whereas flow happens from time to time. A moment in time constitutes the time of an event and it is in this that we experience the situation.

My own model of learning is based on this idea that we learn from events such as this and that episodes are series of events bound together in a continuing awareness, hence in Figure 2.2 I show the start of the next learning cycle. It is important to recognise that awareness spans time and that we learn to live within the flow of time but learning occurs as joined up series of events upon which we concentrate.

Understanding the disjuncture created by the event is important in seeking to grasp the beginning of learning processes: we become aware that we do not know and that we need to know if we are to continue in either doing what we were doing or thinking what we were thinking. We have to re-establish that harmony through learning. Children go through this period early in their lives when they are continually confronted with phenomena that they do not understand: Why this? And why that? All parents are aware of this stage of cognitive development – children need answers so that they can feel at home in their world, parents and significant others provide those answers and we all become part of our culture, or subculture. We all experience this disjuncture when we enter different cultures and subcultures.

As Donald (2001) shows, it is the single event, which is much easier to capture in laboratory experiments, that has formed the basis of certain forms of research and which is even the basis of the conjectures of those scholars who think that most of our learning is hard-wired into our brains. However, an episode is much harder to capture in a laboratory experiment and so the longer time frame actually casts doubt upon the idea that we are hard-wired before birth and places much more focus on learning from continuing conscious experiences through which we construct our biography. Experiences are both single events and elongated episodes and we learn from both.

Part 4: Experience as expertise

An expert is one who 'has extensive skill or knowledge in a particular field' or someone who is 'skilful or knowledgeable' (*Collins English Dictionary*). Perhaps the dictionary should also have offered the possibility that an expert is both skilful and knowledgeable. More recently, Gardner (2007: 82), writing about the creating mind, suggests that:

> For every talented writer or composer who breaks new ground, however, hundreds are content – or resigned – to be 'mere' experts. An expert is an individual who, after a decade or more of training, has reached the pinnacle of practice in her chosen domain. The world depends on experts.

Although the world depends on experts, this is still a restricted definition, but nearly everybody is an expert in the art of living in society. Nevertheless, it would be true to say that for a number of years the word 'expert' has fallen into something like disrepute in some parts of the world as terms such as 'competency' have dominated the vocabulary of political correctness in both work and education. But we should not expect people to stop learning just because they have achieved the state of competence – it is a low expectation of achievement in social living, and this should not be an aim in education. We have all been witnesses to this growth of political correctness in UK that downplays the expert, who is better than others, and yet the sum total of every individual's practice is their experience – their expertise – in this or that area of behaviour. We learn our expertise through experiencing and learning from the experience.

> One becomes an expert not simply by absorbing explicit knowledge of the type found in text-books, but through experience, that is, through repeated trials, 'failing, succeeding, wasting time and effort . . . getting a feel for the problem, learning when to go by the book and when

to break the rules'. Human experts gradually absorb 'a repertory of working rules of thumb, or 'heuristics', that combined with book knowledge, make them expert practitioners. This practical, heuristic knowledge, as attempts to simulate it on the machine have shown, is 'hardest to get at because experts – or anyone else – rarely have the self-awareness to recognize what it is. So it must be mined out of their heads painstakingly, one jewel at a time (all quotations from Feigenbaum and McCorduck, 1984).

(Nyiri, 1988: 20–1)

The whole point here is that we just cannot apply theory to practice: the practice situation is a new learning situation and in it we have to find out if the theory can be utilised in any way, but primarily we have to learn from the situation itself. There is no logical connection between *knowing how* and *being able to*. We have to generate our own practical skill and the ensuing knowledge and ultimately our own practical theories (Jarvis, 1999), which may be a combination of book knowledge and what we have learned from the years in practice, often repeating similar manoeuvres and procedures many times but in each learning and reinforcing our learning. It is those years of experience that constitute the basis of expertise, and expertise is specific to the situation – in many cases it may be a generalisable technique that can be replaced by a machine but in others it is specific to the type of situation in which the actor performs.

As the years go by the experts not only gain knowledge and skills, they might also gain wisdom, but we learn this pre-consciously – and this is one of the fundamental problems in seeking to understand experiential learning. But expertise may not be associated with time in this simple manner because we can repeat behaviours and not learn from them because we do not pay attention to them or to the small differences similar situations have or the slightly different problems each situation poses – only if we treat every experience as an individual learning experience can we gain expertise. Consequently, when we praise someone for their experience we are basically praising them for having continually gained expertise, learned from their experience.

Concluding discussion

From the above discussion, it can be seen that learning is not just a psychological problem, it is a human one, and the study of learning is an existential one. However, we did not start with Descartes' assertion that 'I think, therefore I am'; rather, we reversed it and started with being and the claim that 'I am, therefore I think' or rather, and more accurately, 'I am, therefore I experience', which, in the light of pre-conscious experience, is the more correct claim. Experience, then, is mostly about consciousness and awareness, about being and becoming, about episode and event, about wisdom and expertise: it is also either direct or mediated and it is about the actual process of doing things. We can relate learning to each of them and see how we learn from experience throughout the whole of our lives. There are many other major conceptual problems that surround learning from experience, such as the mind–brain relationship, but in conclusion I want to turn to turn to one major question:

Can I have an experience from which I learn without the end-product of the learning being knowledge?

It is a topic that demands a full chapter rather than one or two conclud-ing paragraphs, but it is included here in order to complete the discussion about experience, and it will be referred to it again later in this book.

In 1999, Jossey-Bass published a book of mine, *The Practitioner Researcher*, and two of my then MSc students (both nuns working in Zam-bia) asked me if I would go out to Zambia and conduct workshops on this study with community doctors and the community, which I did. Towards the end of the week, they asked me what they could do to repay me and I, not knowing the geography of Zambia very well, said 'I would love to see Victoria Falls'. Well on my next to final day, my first free one, they packed me into a small car and drove hundreds of kilometres across Zambia to Victoria Falls – and we stood there as the sun set and watched the won-drous scene of the sun through the haze of the Falls and over the beauty of the Zambezi river. Again, early the following morning, I, amongst only about six people, stood there and watched the sun rise over the river and the Falls. What experiences – words could not describe my feelings – and as we travelled back to the airport, I said to them that no fee could have paid for those experiences.

What I experienced was awe-inspiring – a religious experience (?) – it was a feeling of creature-consciousness that Otto (1959 [1917]) called the numinous. Otto (ibid.: 24) describes this as 'the emotion of a creature, submerged, and overwhelmed by its own nothingness in contrast to that which is supreme above all creatures'. But, significantly, once I describe this non-rational, emotional experience it ceases to be that experience and my description can be transmitted only in words that are non-emotional and rational. Any explication does this to sense experience, and in order to understand it we need to understand something of the nature of experi-ence. In a sense, explaining my feelings is a stage in understanding the situation, but it is a stage removed from the experience itself, and once I try to interpret it I may do so in the language of a community of which I am a member and have generalised a particular. Then, telling you about it creates a secondary experience for you. But the experience had no mean-ing and I only learned in awe about the beauty of the world – cognitive learning was a stage removed from the actual experience. It is this that Ricoeur (1995: 48–55) accurately describes, both capturing the process that I went through and also illustrating the way in which we learn from the senses in general. He makes five points, and these are similar to the process I have described here:

- The 'numinous' element of the sacred is not first of all something to do with language.
- Following Eliade, this is hierophantic, i.e. while we cannot describe the numinous element as such, we can at least describe how it manifests itself – this I have already done.
- The sacred may also reveal itself in significant behaviour – although this is only one modality of the numinous and it may have been my intense concentration, my contemplative nature, and so on that could be described as behavioural.
- The sacred is dramatic.
- Each of these elements point to a logic of meaning – to signify something other than itself.

But the point is that there was no intrinsic meaning to that experience and I learn that not every experience has meaning – the logic of meaning is not necessarily the meaning of the experience, if there is one: the outcome of the learning was awe, wonder – an experience of a lifetime if you like – but then every learning experience is an experience in a lifetime.

There is also another way of responding to this question – the body can learn almost independently of the mind. Pianists, for instance, can practise a very complicated pieces of music so thoroughly that their fingers learn the sequence of notes almost independently of the body: when this has been very thoroughly accomplished then pianists can listen and reflect on the product of their playing and just feel that the fingers played the right notes at the right time, or vice versa.

Before we examine the processes of learning, however, one more concept needs exploration – meaning. We have already met this term in Chapter 3, but it is a concept that underlies our personhood and relates to every aspect of our learning.

Chapter 6

Meaning

We have already been faced with the ideas of both meaning and intention in early childhood. Meaning, however, is a very complex phenomenon and making meaning is certainly crucial to our understanding of both learning and personhood and so we intend to explore some of this complexity in this chapter.

Meaning *per se* has a wide variety of meanings, as *Collins English Dictionary* shows:

- sense of significance;
- the sense underlying or intended by speech;
- the inner, symbolic or true interpretation, value or message;
- valid content, efficacy;
- expressive of some sense, intention, criticism.

When I discussed meaning previously (Jarvis, 1992: 155–76), I covered the following topics:

- existence and knowledge;
- metaphysical meaning;
- socio-cultural meaning;
- meaning as intention;
- meaning and learning;
- meaning and understanding;
- meaning, truth and knowledge;
- meaning, truth and non-learning;
- meaning and legitimation crises.

From these two very similar lists we can see that the concept is not easy to capture. Fundamental to the development of meaning is language which can be both symbolic and narrative – both meaning and language are acquired during socialisation. Nevertheless, there is an underlying assumption that meaning is created as a result of rational thought but Kingwell

(2000: 194) reminds us that there is a 'habitual error of the overweening theorist, of thinking that human meaning can be made entirely transparent by consistent application of human reason'. We are not all reasonable all the time, and neither are our meanings or our intentions. However, we have already touched upon some of these interpretations, and others we will meet in Section II of this book. The aim of this chapter, however, is to provide an overview of the various meanings of the word 'meaning', and, even more, to see how we acquire meaning in order to lay the foundation for the second section of this book. We will, therefore, in the first part of this chapter, look at the metaphysical and socio-cultural interpretations of the term, including its relation to knowledge, truth and belief – a cultural concept. In the second part we will deal with the subjective aspects of intention and significance – a more subjective and personal concept. In the third part, we will look at meaning and learning – a process of acquisition. In this way we will cover the variety of meanings suggested by the above lists.

Part I: Cultural meaning

As a result of our evolution, human beings are born with a propensity to seek meaning. This is something that is a result of our existence: we reflect about ourselves and about the world in which we live, we question existence and seek to devise answers to those questions. It is as if curiosity has been built into us as a result of our evolution, but it is not just a biological phenomenon. Bruner (1990: 34), concerned about the way that psychology was developing, wrote that 'it is culture, not biology, that shapes human life and the human mind, that gives meaning to action by situating its underlying intentional states in an interpretative system'. This has already been argued in the opening chapters of this book, and we have also seen that in early childhood intentional states occur at very young ages. Existentially, Macquarrie (1973: 125) indicates this when he reverses the Cartesian dictum and claims that 'I am, therefore I think'. Once we do this, we question our experiences and seek to give them meaning. Experience itself has no meaning, as we will argue below, but our meanings stem from our relationships with other people in our life-world, from our own interpretations of our experiences, from questions about the cosmos or any combination of these. There are metaphysical and socio-cultural perspectives on this.

Metaphysical

One of the interesting paradoxes about the concept of meaning is that although we are born with this propensity to seek meaning as a result of our evolution we know that there is no intrinsic meaning in the universe. Fromm (1949: 44–5) summarises this paradox thus (italics in original):

Man can react to historical contradictions by annulling them through his own actions: but he cannot annul existential dichotomies, although he can react to them in different ways. He can appease his mind by soothing and harmonizing ideologies. He can try to escape from his inner restlessness by ceaseless activity in pleasure or business. He can try to abrogate his freedom and to turn himself into an instrument of powers outside himself, submerging himself in them. But he remains dissatisfied, anxious and restless. There is only one solution to his problem: to face the truth, to acknowledge his fundamental aloneness and solitude in a universe indifferent to his fate, to recognize that there is no power transcending him which can solve his problem for him. Man must accept responsibility for himself and the fact that only by using his own powers can he give meaning to life. But meaning does not imply certainty. Uncertainty is the very condition to impel man to unfold his powers. If he faces the truth without panic he will recognize that *there is no meaning to life except the meaning that man gives his life by the unfolding of his powers, by living productively;* and that only constant vigilance, activity and effort can keep us from failing in the one task that matters – the full development of our powers within the limitations set by our own existence. Man will never cease to be perplexed, to wonder, to raise new questions.

Although some may not be happy with his conclusions, it is clear that, since there is no intrinsic meaning in matter itself, then there can be no intrinsic meaning nor obvious explanation to the cosmos and that all inter-pretations – whether theist, agnostic, non-theist or atheist – are meanings given by individuals, peoples and cultures in their quest to understand existence. Metaphysical explanations are responses to our human quest to make sense of our existence and to ask if there is an ultimate meaning to it all: they are belief systems, and we will look more closely at this when we examine knowledge and beliefs later in this study. Throughout the ages there have been teachers and preachers who have expounded meanings, and some of these have in different ways become embodied within the cul-tures of different societies and, in this sense, meaning is 'ultimate meaning' for the cultural group which has accepted it. But one of the fundamental paradoxes of meaning – in fact a paradox of human living – is that we think that we have arrived at the ultimate, only to find more questions and more endeavours: meaning can never be ultimate – it is always relative and to be discovered within the socio-cultural world.

Socio-cultural

Some of these teachers and preachers have been very successful within their own or others' cultures and so, in different ways, their interpretations have been accepted and become embedded within cultures as symbolic universes of meaning. These are then learned through the socialisation process and transmitted to children through interaction with significant others. Luckmann (1967: 44) writes of the universes of meaning into which individuals are born:

> Symbolic universes are objectivated meaning systems that relate the experiences of everyday life to a 'transcendental' layer of reality. Other systems of meaning do not point beyond the world of everyday life; that it, they do not contain a 'transcendental reference.

We can see that such systems are slow to change because they are built into national and ethnic cultures and learned in childhood – imprinted, as it were, in newly emerging minds. Children learn to believe them, and it is hard to eradicate these early impressions since they are the institutionalised meanings of society and they are also the meanings that are most significant to the family within which we are born and raised.

However, sociologists have long been preoccupied with the structures of society, and so it would be oversimplistic to talk about meaning as if it were a single entity. Since we also live within our life-worlds, we may find a greater sense of conformity and agreement by those significant others within them than between them. Nevertheless, we are exposed both to the pressures of society as a whole and also to those of our life-worlds: we are going to be exposed to a unique combination of meanings that we learn and which we will in some way combine and reflect. Society's structures have undergone considerable change over the past century or two, and with it a sense of shared meaning has probably become less strong, although there are still shared meanings in such ideas as the imagined community, nationalism, and so on. As early as 1893, however, Durkheim was aware of the significance of the changing social structures on people's lives and even on their consciences or even their consciousness (see Durkheim, 1933 [1893]: ix, in which the translator debates the meaning of the French word *conscience*) are related to their social position. Durkheim traced society through three phases: mechanical, organic and contractual solidarity. Even in his introduction, Durkheim shows his awareness that the way in which people view the world changes with changing social structures. In this sense, meaning is not only social but relative: this relativity could be traced historically across time or socially and hierarchically through a cultural group. Durkheim (ibid.: 43) wrote of education, for instance, that:

> Education is growing more and more specialized. We deem it more and more necessary not to submit children to a uniform culture, as if they were all to lead the same life; but to train them differently in the light of the different functions that they will be called on to fill.

But now in a society having contractual solidarity there is no uniform socio-cultural meaning to life. The changing nature of contemporary society has led to our developing changing meanings to social life and even to life itself. We, in the West, now live in a global consumer society (Jarvis, 2008) in which our children learn that one meaning of life is to be happy and that, in order to achieve this, we have to work in order to acquire goods and finance and spend and consume. It is this consumer culture that I suggest is the basis of an alternative learning society – but for many, this meaning of life is not satisfying. Bellah *et al.* (1985: 290), in their study of individualism and the American way of life, record the fact that 'few have found a life devoted to "personal ambition and consumerism" satisfactory and most are seeking in one way or another to transcend the limitations of a self-centred life'. Hence, the quest for meaning is not socially determined, although the dominant meanings are propounded by those who have the power to perpetuate an interpretation of life that they wish to others to adopt.

Underlying a great deal of advertising are ideologies of life that those who are 'other directed' (Riesman, 1950) may become dependent upon. In contrast, those who are 'tradition directed' may prefer to accept those dominant meaning systems that have been built into the culture over the ages, whereas those who are 'inner directed' may seek to step outside the dominant self-centred ideologies of global capitalism and discover a system of meaning that transcends their social situation. This is an element of the learning process that certainly requires further research.

Clearly, the organisations, groups, social classes, etc., that individuals occupy in society are going to affect, or reinforce, the meanings that they place upon their lives and even the meaning that they give to all other aspects of social life. Meaning is, in this sense, a social construct and even a personal one in the light of our understanding of the nature of society. Meaning is not just a metaphysical quest; it is a social and personal quest to understand the experiences of everyday living. Experiential learning, therefore, must always be seen within the social context within which the learner is living. Although much of the remainder of this chapter assumes psychological overtones, it would be false to view the psychological processes as being divorced from the sociological context within which they occur.

Many of these universes of meaning that assume a significant place in a culture claim that they contain 'the truth'. Indeed, what is the truth? This is a question that has haunted humanity almost since the beginning of time. Can there be an ultimate truth or is Fromm right when he claims that the universe has no meaning? Certainly, there is no obviously ultimate truth, but this does not negate the idea of holding a reasoned belief position about meaning – whether it is religious or not. But this is a matter of belief, faith and commitment to a cultural or a personal position – but not truth. Meaning resides not in phenomena at all but only in those who construct meaning and use it to interpret their experiences of the world.

Individuals, however, carry many of the personally and socio-culturally accepted meanings, as well as their individuality, within their own memories, and they transmit them through their actions and interactions. This is how we are all socialised into the dominant culture of our society and into our own life-worlds – but this is itself a complex process that has received much greater attention in the past few years.

Part 2: Personal and subjective meaning

Children are born into a cultural milieu and they learn the cultural symbols – the language, gestures, artefacts – that carry the institutionalised meaning and which are the symbols of meaning. They are learned, in the first instance, through imitation and trial and error, but this is not really a mindless act, and at about nine months children realise that the significant others with whom they interact are intentional agents, like themselves. Once more we see the significance of relationship. As Tomasello (1999: 89) writes (italics in original):

> As infants begin to follow into and direct the attention of others to outside entities at nine to twelve months of age, it happens on occasion that the other person whose attention the infant is monitoring focuses on the infant herself. The infant then monitors that person's attention to *her* in a way that was not possible previously, . . . She now knows that she is interacting with an intentional agent who perceives her and intends things towards her. When the infant did not understand that others perceive and intend things toward the outside world, there could be no question of how they perceived and intended things toward *me*.

This is the birth of the 'self' – the Me, as George Herbert Mead claimed (see Jarvis, 1987, for a full discussion of Mead's work in relation to learning), the emergence of which happens in the second year – and it can only occur in joint attentional situations. Children begin to learn the socio-cultural meanings that others attach to words, symbols and gestures, and this forms and then transforms the way that they view the world. They do this through imitation and trial and error: they seek to imitate the significant others and they experiment with words and their meanings to discover how they fit into their position in the social structures. They are already beginning to learn to reflect their social position through the significant others with whom they share meaningful situations. They have a shared sense of meaning. As Nelson (2007: 106) points out, this sense of shared meaning means that 'everybody can see me (and perhaps know what I am thinking)'. And so children become capable of reflecting on what others think of their behaviour and even beginning to reflect on their own knowledge.

What can be seen here is that meaning is learned: it is both learned from experience and constructed through the combination of experiences and memories of previous significant events. Nelson (ibid.: 110) suggests that 'these on-going dynamic processes organize memory in terms of meaning structures'. She goes on (ibid.: 111) to suggest that:

> Over time events (the basic unit of experience) may be combined to form generalized, meaningful wholes that are termed schemas or scripts, concept and categories, and they may be broken down into parts that are then made available for organizing into other concepts and categories.

Every event that we experience consciously enters into the memory: it has some degree of significance, although some have much more significance than others. In other words, it is meaningful to us, and in this sense 'memory is meaning' (ibid.: 111) – our memories of events are the building blocks of the meanings that we place on our lives, but our biographies are not unaffected by these meanings. With the development of language, children learn the meaning of words through shared attentional situations and imitating the sounds: these joint situations mean that children will learn words, and the meaning of those words, that reflect their socio-economic position in society, their education, and so on. In this sense, it would be hard to accept the idea propounded by Chomsky that locates language in the brain since there are few, if any, universal meanings to words that do not have an empirical referent. Shared meanings in joint attentional situations enable children and their significant others to communicate, and the same sense of shared meanings exists in linguistic communication throughout life. The process of learning meaning begins with primary experiences in early childhood, but in later life many of the experiences that relate to individual's meaning systems are learned from secondary or mediated experiences, reflecting Durkheim's contractual solidarity.

Having learned word meanings and speech, children have to articulate their meaning, and Bruner (1990: 97) summarises this process thus:

> our capacity to render experience in terms of narrative is not just child's play, but an instrument for making meaning that dominates much of the life of culture – from soliloquies at bed-time to the weighing of testimony in our legal system.

We tell our stories and embody our sense of meaning; indeed, it is in and through the process of articulation that we refine our meaning system as we organise our memories of events to expound our meaning system – or our world-view. Bruner goes on to suggest that the stories we tell and the sense of self that we construct are a result of this process of meaning making. The self, Brunner (ibid.: 138) declares, 'does not arise rootlessly only in response to the present; [it] . . . takes meaning as well from the historical circumstances that give shape to the culture of which they are an expression'. Whether we are anything more than our memories and narratives is another question, but, once we view the development of the 'self' in this way, we can see that the mind is more than just the brain with which we are born.

Part 3: Meaning and learning

In the previous two parts of this chapter we have seen how meaning forms a crucial element in lifelong learning: from the earliest years until late in our lives we seek to understand, to give meaning to, our experiences – the events that occur in our lives. We can see how children from the earliest age have experiences and that from before they are one year old their experiences tend to be meaningful and intentional. New experiences will reinforce or transform these meanings, as will new knowledge, new skills, and so on, and so they continue to grow and develop. Learning, then, is at the heart of growth and development, and a major aspect of that learning is the way that we seek to give experiences meaning and that meaning will change and deepen as our experiences of the world and of the people with whom we interact. This is a process that begins early in life and continues until late in life – but as we do grow and develop so we become aware that some of our meanings do not fit our experiences and so they need to be changed. We learn to reflect on our experiences, and this element of reflection is what Mezirow (2000: 26) regards as the mark of adult learning. Indeed, Mezirow (1991: 7) wrote that 'Adult development is seen as an adult's enhanced capacity to validate prior learning through reflective discourse and to act upon the resulting insights'. However, children from much earlier in life become critical of their meaning systems – for instance, it is well known in sociological studies of religion that adolescence is a time when young people are prepared to reject some of their meaning systems and adopt others. Consequently, I feel that Mezirow makes too great a distinction between adult learning and young people's learning; I prefer to see the distinction between early childhood learning and learning throughout life being drawn more clearly. Indeed, this is always a problem in starting a study of something that is a lifelong process in adulthood, whereas starting with the early years shows how even critical reflectivity develops and reveals that there is not really a sharp distinction to be made between the age groups in the way that some adult educators do – and which in many ways Mezirow acknowledges.

However, for Mezirow (1991: 12), 'Learning may be understood as using a prior interpretation to construe a new or a revised interpretation of the meaning of one's experience in order to guide future action'. A weakness in this definition lies in the fact that he does not explain where the prior interpretation comes from if it was not learned – we get an infinite regress unless we build culture into the equation. Learning involves learning new things as well as reconstructing our own meaning schemes. However, Mezirow regards this process of changing one's perspective as transformative, and it is this that lies at the heart of his understanding of adult learning. His study is extremely comprehensive and is well grounded in research evidence, but the failure to relate it to lifelong learning as a whole is one of the points of criticism, and another is that it is not the meaning system that is necessarily transformed (although it may be), but in human learning it is the experience itself that may be transformed. There are others, such as his concentration on meaning rather than looking at the other elements in the content of learning, such as knowledge or skills. Nevertheless, Mezirow's work has made a considerable impression in the field of adult learning, and he has been a major force in relating learning and meaning.

The idea of transformation underlies two other learning phenomena: 'changing one's mind' and 'conversion'. As we grow and develop we all become aware from time to time that we have made a mistake in our understanding and this might result in our changing our minds, but in religious belief there is also the idea of conversion (Robertson, 1978), which is itself a complex process because it usually involves not only meaning change but emotional changes as well. It is beyond the scope of this study to explore this further here (see Robertson, 1978: 186–222).

But Mezirow's approach to learning and meaning is not the only one: Marton and Saljo (1984: 40) suggested that there are two types of approach to understanding meaning in texts: in the first students seek to memorise the text, seeing themselves, as it were, as empty vessels that have to be filled, whereas, in the second, the learners see themselves as creators of knowledge by examining the text in relation to the world, and so on. The first approach is a 'surface approach' to meaning whereas the second is a 'deep' approach. We will return to this discussion when we examine reading and writing later in the book.

Conclusion

Meaning can also be understood in terms of 'I meant' – or 'I intended' – and as such it relates quite closely to intention and even motivation, subjects upon which we will focus in Chapter 16.

Meaning is, however, the final concept that we look at in the first section of this book: in common with all the other concepts it is basic to learning to be a person in society and, as we have seen, it is itself a learned phenomenon. In Section II of the book we are going to look at what people do or have done to them in the learning processes.

Section II

Processes of learning

Chapter 7

Experiencing

In Chapter 5 we examined the concept of experience and looked at ways in which it relates to human living. But this is not just a concept – we have experiences, and experience, so we argue, is the start of learning, so that in this chapter we examine the idea of experiencing. In a sense the argument of this book is the opposite to Descartes. He argued that because I have experiences I know that I am (*cogito ergo sum*), whereas we argue that because we are we have experiences.

Experience is the way by which the sense organs transmit through our bodies to our minds images of the external world, which we will explore a little more in the following chapter: we are aware of what is external to us and we can have an experience of it. But it is worth making the point from the outset that we actually learn from our experiences of the external world and not from the external world itself – this is a point to which we will return in the next chapter on perception. We all have different forms of experience – in both space and time – and it is we who are affected by our experiences. The fact that we can discuss different forms of experience demonstrates that we can and do actually experience external reality in different ways, and so the following chapters illustrate something of these differences, but they may also relate to the different parts of the brain which process them (Gardner, 1983). All of these mental experiences start from the diverse processes of sense experiencing and perceiving, but, as Gardner points out, we experience different phenomena, such as music and mathematics, with different parts of our brains. In his theory of multiple intelligences, he suggests that we actually have different types of intelligences and that we do not know to what extent there is a general intelligence to which each of these other intelligences correlates. Hence, our experiencing starts with the senses – a biological basis of intelligence – but it does not end there for the biological combines with the cultural to provide a basis for intelligence. Our different experiences occur in time and space and they also affect our biographies. Consequently, this chapter has three parts – in time, in space and in ourselves – and we will show that, for the most part, a great deal of our learning in everyday life is socially and culturally reproductive. At the same time, reproduction does not imply any form of universality, since we live in different strata (e.g. socio-economic class) of society, learn different gender expectations in our social group, and so on. Although there is some universality in humankind, our cultural experiences are our own and are unique.

Part I: In time

There are many ways of examining time, and if we were to write a philosophy of learning we would be bound to look at some of these, but for the purpose of this enquiry we will look briefly at five different aspects/ responses to our experience of time: ageing, *durée*/disjuncture, 'time flies' (being busy), optimum experience, 'time drags' (boredom), and the slow movement and attentive experience.

Ageing

We have started this enquiry with early childhood and have seen how the early years really do affect our future lives, but for many people there has been a belief that as we age we are less able to learn and even that it is almost impossible to learn new things. The old adage 'You can't teach an old dog new tricks' is frequently cited.

Now we know that, as we age, so some of the millions and millions of neurons in the brain are destroyed or become dormant and some of the synaptic connections are severed if they are not used – 'use it or lose it' as the saying goes. But, as we have seen here, learning is not entirely biological but is also experiential, and we continue to have experiences for as long as we stay involved in the world. Naturally, some of our potential experiences are curtailed if we do not have the physical abilities or acuities to take advantage of the possibilities, but this does not mean that we cannot learn within our physical limitations.

Indeed, the story of Gail Sheehy's (1995) *New Passages* is that through every age in life we can continue to learn and to live life to the full for as long as we remain engaged in the world of relationships and activities, although our dominant emotions do change with the ageing process (Erikson, 1965: 239–66). Manheimer (1999), for instance, records how he taught philosophy classes to the very old and so it is – until we decide to disengage we can continue to learn. Havighurst (1970) suggested that the last two stages of life are deciding when to disengage and disengagement itself: indeed, it is only in death that we are entirely alone. Until that time, we can continue to learn and to play an active role in the world (see Jarvis, 2001).

From before birth to death we can keep on having experiences from which we learn and add new memories, interpretation and meanings to our lives. We will return to this at the end of the book – but the story of learning to be a person in society is the story of being and becoming a person through all the ages of life.

Duration/disjuncture

Time, says Bergson (see Lacey, 1989: 26–32), is like a melody: we are not aware of the individual notes. Or we live in harmony with our life-world and the world is unproblematic. Lacey (ibid.: 29) describes Bergson's conception of duration thus: 'duration implies consciousness', its 'essence is to flow without ceasing, and consequently not to exist except for a consciousness and a memory'. However, the very ceaseless flow makes the experience almost unconscious – that is, that we are not conscious of the passing of time, only of the world upon which we can presume and act. There is a taken-for-grantedness about this form of harmony but less awareness than there is in Csikszentmihalyi's optimal experience (see below), when we are fully aware of our situation. But when discord occurs in either duration or optimal situations, we can become aware that we are not in harmony – we are faced with a situation that we cannot take for granted and we have to stop and think and learn. It is this that I have called disjuncture and which we discussed earlier in this book. We have a conscious experience when we are aware that we do not know, although the degree of consciousness varies, as we showed in Figure 2.3. Now we are conscious of the situation and may not be conscious of time at all – except that it is the present 'now'. This is the awareness of a specific moment in time when we become conscious of our situation and we experience it.

Disjuncture does not automatically result in applying ourselves to a learning experience: it may be because we have been doing things rapidly because we have been too busy and so, when a disjunctural situation arises, it is just an additional burden – one that we do not want at that time and so we actually do not consider the situation and reject the opportunity to learn. There are others, such as when the potential learning will potentially affect our attitudes, disrupt our meaning about life, and so on, in ways that we do not wish – then we also reject the opportunity to learn. These I (Jarvis, 1987) have called non-learning. However, as we will see later in this chapter, although we may reject the content of the potential learning experience, we may well be affected as selves, and this may result in the occurrence of some unintentional and perhaps pre-conscious learning.

Optimal experience

In a very similar manner, Csikszentmihalyi (1990: 39) writes of optimal experience: 'When the information that keeps coming into the awareness is congruent with goals'. He suggests that when this happens 'psychic energy flows effortlessly' (ibid.). This is the same sense of harmony that we mention in the above paragraph, but there is a greater sense of awareness than with duration – it is something that enables us to deal with the information almost unthinkingly because previous experiences have equipped us to respond to the new stimulus in a rapid way because we have trained ourselves to be aware of the situation. In this way, time appears to fly because every moment is filled with expectation. Csikszentmihalyi argues that people find greater satisfaction in this form of activity, and that this leads to happiness or contentment: in a real sense the experience has meaning because we have prepared ourselves (learned) in readiness for each new experience – we become absorbed in the activity that we are undertaking. Like the previous situation, when the unexpected occurs, we have a disjunctural experience, but we may be more ready and able to respond to it since we have prepared ourselves for the expected experience.

Although Csikszentmihalyi does not suggest this, his work is also a reflection of society's demands for efficiency and speed: fast food, etc. Everything has to be done with optimum efficiency and, although this might lead to satisfaction, it is not the type of happiness that we get when we are having optimal experiences. In this world, we are just too busy to appreciate our experiences to the full and so we may learn less from them.

Boredom – time drags

Quite the opposite is the sense of boredom – this can be because we have nothing to do or because what we do is apparently meaningless to us – meaningless because we go through the motions of doing things but without being committed to the meaning that the social group gives to the actions, or because we actually have nothing meaningful to do. Everything seems to drag and, because we are so wrapped up in this meaningless experience, we may be unable or unready to have a new experience. In this sense, we actually miss the opportunity and, since time does not repeat itself, that specific opportunity has gone for ever, even though similar ones might arise at other times and we might be more able to respond to them.

Slowness and attentive experience

The world in which we live is a rapidly moving world, and the experiences we have may be partial or directed in one specific direction so that our perception is incomplete – or at least we get less from the experience than we might have done had we tackled it differently. Almost as a protest to the demands of rapidity and efficiency of contemporary society a movement seeking slowness has emerged. In fact, the slow movement has become a social movement in contemporary society (Honoré, 2004: 33–46):

it aims at getting people to slow down and to appreciate their experiences more deeply. This movement has precisely the same type of concerns as Crawford (2005) captured in her discussion of attentiveness in her feminist interpretation of attentive love. However, I do not want to emphasise the gender base that she claims for attentive love (agape – see also Jarvis, 2008) since it is a characteristic that men can adopt as well; instead I will argue that disinterested love is the one sole good. Crawford (2005: 115) argues that the current conditions of Western culture militate against attentiveness. Slowing down, being attentive to persons and experiences, changes one's perceptions of the world – it creates a more spiritual, caring, human approach. Slowness is using time to the best possible advantage so that we can plumb the depths of meaning in order to understand more fully the experiences that we have.

Part 2: Space

Like time, there are a number of facets of space, four of which will be explored briefly here: social position/group membership, environment, primary experience (interaction with people in our life-world in holistic experiences) and secondary experience (mediated content, including being taught).

Social position/group membership

As we live in a familiar life-world so our experiences will be restricted, in a sense, because our life-world itself provides parameters within which most of our life is lived. Thus, Schutz and Luckmann (1974: 36–45) discuss fully the spatial arrangements of the life-world, distinguishing between the world within actual reach and that within potential reach. However, the significance of their discussion lies in the way in which they show how individual life-worlds overlap and yet remain individual: there is a sense in which we can presume on our life-world because it is familiar. In this sense, a great deal of our social living is socially and culturally repetitive and re-productive – we are interacting with others who share a great deal of our life-world. However, there is a potentiality to reach beyond the immediate, since a great deal of that is also familiar to us.

Consequently, we can see that there is a considerable propensity for us to live socially and culturally reproductive lives – to be conformists – this is in relation to all forms of subcultural activity including knowledge and the emotions. The potential for change comes when we can no longer take the world for granted: when there is a disjunctural situation. Then learning something new might, but does not necessarily, occur.

Environment

In the Delors Report (1996), four pillars of learning are mentioned: learning to know, to be, to do and to live together. From the outset I have always argued for a fifth pillar – learning to care for the environment. Because of the threats of global warming, we have become much more conscious of the significance of caring for the planet, and O'Sullivan (1999) argues that global capitalism is destructive to both the earth and humanity and that we need to develop a new vision of creation and all within it. In this a major factor is the earth, which needs to be cared for in a way that humankind has not done. In the past decade the concerns of global warming are being brought home to us, and the more that we experience this, the more we learn about what is occurring. In my own experience, I recall that in the early 1990s I visited an area in Alaska not far from Anchorage and stood beside icebergs in July, but only a decade later I revisited the same area in May and there were no icebergs – they had all melted. The experience of the changed planet made me more aware than ever of the need to be concerned about the earth – we experience the external world and its conditions and we learn from our experiences of the environment. I had a primary experience of the changing environment.

Primary experience

Primary experience corresponds to the world within our reach:

> The world in my actual reach contains, apart from this sector's orientation to proximity and distance, which is centred on me, and arrangement according to the modalities of meaning. Through this the Objects of this sector are given to me. This arrangement in visual range, in auditory range, indeed in the field of reach, is certainly overlaid by the identity (which is taken for granted in the natural attitude) of things as seen, heard, etc.
>
> (Schutz and Luckmann, 1974: 37)

Here then we see the taken-for-granted of daily living but, as we have just seen, primary experience need not be taken for granted and habitual – it can be disjunctural. However, Schutz and Luckmann (1974) also discuss the world of potential reach; that is, when we move our location, there are worlds beyond our primary experience that can become primary but, although we may be familiar with these worlds, there is a greater likelihood of disjunctural experiences when we are in a new situation. They regard the zone in which we are likely to have primary experiences as the zone of operation and they recognise that there is a world beyond this that we experience differently.

Secondary experience

These might also be called mediated experiences since they are experiences we have of different times and places although we are not actually present in the situation: they can be provided through discussions in personal interaction, or by media, wireless and electronic communication. Whereas some secondary experiences are interactive, the majority of them are more impersonal: people are exposed to hours of television and wireless broadcasting everyday and to the advertising on the web and so on (see Jarvis, 2008). We are recipients of information and, as the amount grows, there is a tendency to scan it rapidly, as discussed above, and to spend less time considering the content of the communication. Nevertheless, much of this communication has effects on our lives and, as I have argued (Jarvis, 2008), the creation of desire occurs through advertising, as the advertisers endeavour to generate in everybody, but especially young children, the desire to purchase, to have, to own, to consume, and so on. Nevertheless, advertising, in its educative form, can actually form a more legitimate purpose, which is to inform, although it is usually used with an 'educational' purpose. As recipients of secondary experiences, we learn a lot, but we can also be manipulated or indoctrinated to perform the actions that those who transmit the information wish because we do not spend time analysing the information that we receive. But not all secondary experiences are of this nature.

Learning by being taught

All teaching, except where a practical element is introduced, is a combination of secondary experiences in the content of what is taught and the primary experience of being present in the classroom with the teacher and other students, or even of the students operating their computers or other electronic devices. However, the more rational the presentation, the less likelihood that it will result in indoctrination. Where opportunity exists to test out what is propounded, to debate and discuss the information, and so on, so that we change our views and grow and develop, indoctrination cannot occur. Although there need not be a socially reproductive element in teaching Bourdieu (1973) argues that education is both socially and culturally reproductive, and it can be argued that one of the functions of children's education and of vocational training is to learn the best of what is already known. Many teachers use teaching methods that encourage learners to think critically about what they are experiencing, but many do not, and in this current examination-orientated educational climate there is a greater tendency to teach to the examination than there is to encourage lateral and critical thought. Good teachers, however, leave space for independent thought.

But here we are faced with all the problems that the sociology of education has revealed about children with different social class, cultural and socio-linguistic backgrounds being more able to grasp the meaning of what they are taught than others – indeed, this is true for our understanding of learning. Children use their previous experiences in their life-worlds – social class, gender, and so on – to understand the knowledge and to make meaning of their secondary experiences. Hence, these experiences also tend to lead to reproduction, both socially and culturally. The more closed the social structures, the greater the likelihood that we reproduce the social and cultural background since it is explicit in our previous learning. We learn to be the people we are because we utilise our previous experiences to understand our present ones: it is only through good and sympathetic teaching that children and adult learners can learn to transcend their socio-cultural background. However, as society becomes more open and change more rapid, there are more opportunities to have experiences that force us to challenge our previous experiences and to change the direction of our development.

Part 3: Experiencing ourselves

We have already discussed how children develop their sense of self, and I have referred to this situation as an I–Me situation. In every learning or non-learning situation, we do not only experience the content of the experience or even that plus the situation in which the experience occurs – we also take the meaning of these experiences into ourselves and are affected by them. In this sense, we are building our biography, but much of this construction goes on either coincidentally or pre-consciously.

As James (1963 [1892]: 166) wrote in what McAdams (2001: 590) calls the most famous chapter ever written on the nature of the self:

> Whatever I may be thinking of, I am always at the same time more or less aware of *myself*, of my *personal existence*. At the same time it is *I* who am aware; so that the total self of me, being as it were duplex, partly known and partly knower, partly object and partly subject, must have two aspects discriminated in it, of which for shortness we may call one *Me* and the other one the *I*.

In the course of our daily living, we actually learn and remember a great deal. It is this memory that becomes a source for some of our future knowing because we learn from our own lives (Dominice, 2000). We will return to this later when we also refer to some of the contemporary research of how we learn from our own lives – but there is a sense in which many of us are inner-directed and learn from our previous experiences. Indeed, we seek to impose our plans, desires, and so on, on the rhythm of our existence: for instance, we decide how we are going to live on a specific day and what we are going to do on it, and this structures our life and may alter the normal rhythm of our daily living. These decisions are made as a result of our social situation and our previous learning. But not only do we impose our intentions on the rhythm of the day in order to determine our experiences, our experiences also feed back on us and alter our biographies to some lesser or greater degree. Our experiences are embedded within our own biographies and many of them are very private and subjective. Whereas we are aware of some of them, we may be less aware of others – we may be aware of liking or approving of something we experience in our life-world but less aware of others. Our emotions, beliefs, attitudes and values are affected by these experiences although we may not be fully aware of what is happening until such time as we are asked to discuss our attitudes, beliefs, etc. As Schutz and Luckmann (1974: 58) argue, 'When we as adults turn to past segments of our life, we can discover very "decisive" experiences that subsequently determined our lives'. Many of those that could be called 'life-changing' are conscious and occur as a result of a disjunctural experience: they fit into our flow of time. However, they need not all be pre-planned. We discover the significance of pre-conscious and unintended ones only when they surface in our future conscious actions. In this way we acquire and learn some of our beliefs, values and attitudes – these often occur unintentionally and even pre-consciously, and these affect our future actions.

Our biographies are the sum total of our memories of our experiences which occur in our life-world. Many of these learning experiences are socially and culturally repetitive and reproductive, but there are others that can cause considerable changes. At the same time, we each develop a unique biography which includes attitudes, values and beliefs that we may have learned incidentally and even pre-consciously during the process of living.

Conclusion

Most of our experiences in our life-worlds occur in familiar situations, but secondary experiences can take us beyond these into a wider world; they can take us from a familiar to unfamiliar culture; they can create learning situations that need not be reproductive. At the same time in a more open society, and one that changes rapidly, we may have an increasing number of experiences that are innovative and, at the same time, we can reflect on those experiences and not respond to them in the way that others have done.

Chapter 8

Perceiving

Perception is a much studied subject – both philosophers and psychologists have focused upon it. In a psychological dictionary (Reber and Reber, 2001), for instance, it is defined as:

- the processes that give coherence and unity to sensory input;
- the actual experiencing of a chain of (organic) processes initiated by some external or internal stimulus;
- a synthesis or fusion of the elements of sensation (structuralism);
- a hypothetical internal events that results directly from the stimulation of sensory preceptors and is affected by drive, level and habit (behaviourism);
- an awareness of truth;
- a label in the field of psychology that studies any of the above.

A philosophical dictionary (Speake, 1984) offers the following discussion: the study of perception asks the question 'Can an external object be a source of knowledge or, as perceptions are often wrong, should we not recognise that objects in the external world stimulate us into having sense data and so we are never directly aware of external events?' Thus, we have two other theories of perception, the causal and the representative, and these are much debated by philosophers (see, for instance, Crane, 1992).

Naturally enough, each discipline has its own starting place, or places, and it is not our intention here to explore their differences so much as to try to throw light on how our perceiving affects our learning in different ways, which in turn affects our development as persons in society. Although the philosophical questions are interesting in themselves, the philosophical discussion *per se* is only just touched upon in this chapter – apart from the crucial and central point that this book assumes that we learn from sense data rather than directly from the external world. Thereafter, the questions that we will look at are from psychological and sociological perspectives. Crane (1992: 1), however, illustrates the questions that concern us when we consider perception as the basis of experiences from which we learn:

Any full understanding of the mind must give a central place to perception, since it is through perception that the world meets our minds. But the nature of perceptual states is perplexing: do they give us access to the world that is in any sense 'direct'? Or is perception mediated by the awareness of some mental or nonmental intermediary? Are perceptions essential conscious? Do they essentially involve sensation? Do they represent the world – do they have *content* – in the way that beliefs and judgments do, and if so, can they be reduced to beliefs? In any case how do they get their content? And how do perceptions and their content relate to the structure of the rest of the mind, especially to belief, desire and action. But even before we get this far Merleau-Ponty (1962) reminds us that we have to start with sensation and understand that perception is about the way that we have sense experiences as a result of our being open to the external world. Consequently, the first part of this chapter will examine briefly the relation between perception and the body. Thereafter, we will look at different factors that affect our perception: Reber and Reber (2001) suggest a list and we will include within the context of our discussion, although we will not follow it directly and we will add to it in order to construct an understanding of this complex process.

Part 1: Perception and the body

As we have already pointed out, we take our world for granted and our behaviour is habitual because we have already learned it from previous experiences, until such time as we are forced to think about it because of a disjunctural experience or because we want to impose our own intentions upon it. At times such as this we become more conscious of our world – we are more aware of it – and are able to experience sensations about it. Our initial contact with the external world is always through the sensations that we experience through our body: we feel/touch, hear, see, smell or taste that which is external to us through bodily experience. If our sight or hearing is deficient, then we will have a less than perfect experience of the external event that we are experiencing and so what is transmitted through the nervous system is a less than perfect reflection of the eternal event – this is crucial when we think of children in school who are slightly deaf or who have deficient vision and whose experience of the external world, and even of the data with which their senses are presented, is deficient. This is significant to teaching as teachers need to be aware of how children perceive their world, so that the philosophical debate has tremendous practical significance (see Crane, 1992). What we experience through our bodies is some form of representation of the external object.

It is through our bodies that we have sensations which are 'units of experience' (Merleau-Ponty, 1962: 3–12). But sense data have no meaning in themselves:

> to see is to have colours or lights, to hear is to have sounds, to sense (*sentir*) is to have qualities. To know what sense-experience is, then, is it not enough to have to have seen a red, or to have heard an A? But red and green are not sensations, they are the sensed (*sensibles*), and quality is not an element of consciousness but a property of the object.
>
> (ibid.: 4)

But to say that we experience a red carpet is to make a double error – the quality lies in our experience and the fact that it is red and a carpet lies in our previous learning about both the phenomenon that we experience and the name that we give it. In the first instance we can see that the sensation experienced by the body is transmitted through the nervous system to the social brain from the point at which it enters the mind. But if the light changes, then the red may appear to be of a different shade of red, or if the room darkens we may see not a carpet but something on the floor. If the external conditions change then our senses change and the sensations our body experiences may change, and this leads to different sense data arriving in the brain. It is this that leads Merleau-Ponty (ibid.: 215) to suggest that, consequently, 'I ought to say that *one* perceives in me, and not I perceive'. But upon reception of the sense data we may take the conditions into account and construct a representation of the red carpet on the floor that makes sense to us and that we might have seen had the light been better. We are, therefore, combining previous learning with the sense data that we receive and, in so doing, the world that we 'perceive' is actually different from the direct sensations that we receive (see Merleau-Ponty, 1962: 207–42 for a discussion on sense experience).

Goleman (1995: 19) shows how visual sensation – visual perception in the one sense most frequently used by scholars in discussing sensation – passes from the retina to the thalamus, where it is translated into the language of the brain. From the thalamus the great majority of neurons go on to the visual cortex, but just a few take a different route to the amygdala – the seat of the emotions – and so the amygdala actually receives some of the input from our senses nanoseconds before the cortex receives it. Consequently, sometimes our immediate response to a situation is emotional – before we have time to think about it. We can all think of situations that have taken us by surprise, leading us to register fear, anger, happiness, etc., in the immediate moment of the experience and then, when we have thought about it, giving the experience a different connotation because the cortex is now processing the sensory input. This basic emotion comes from the mammalian brain rather than the cortex (social brain), and it reflects part of our evolutionary process, when primitive human beings needed to react immediately to dangerous situations, etc. The brain has many information processing mechanisms which are hard-wired into our system as a result of our evolution (Gardner, 1983: 55) although, as we have seen, the cortex is the final stage in the brain's evolution to date, but it is also affected by the sensory stimuli that enable us to reflect upon what we are experiencing. But the stimuli have their effect upon the brain.

The more we are exposed to external stimuli, the more input enters our social brain (cortex) and the more active our brains are likely to be. Gardner (ibid.: 42) records an experiment with rats. Rats fed the same diet were exposed or not exposed to many visual stimuli. After 80 days, the rats were killed and their brains examined and it was found that the cerebral cortexes of the rats that experienced the enriched environment were 4 per cent larger than those of rats which had experienced a normal environment. The greater our exposure to the external world, the more likely it is that the external stimuli that this generates will ensure that our brains are activated and grow: a phenomenon that will probably increase our intelligence.

At a basic level, the stimuli that we receive are merely sensations that are transmitted through a pathway in the body to the brain, the effectiveness of this transmission depending on the state of the body at the time of perception. However, as a result of our being in the world and learning about it from our birth, many of these sensations appear to us not just as sensation but as reality itself, since we automatically relate the sensation to the larger picture drawn from our experience and previous learning: we see, for example, the carpet as a carpet because that is what we have previously learned it to be. Because we do this, we learn to take many of our sensations for granted – we see what we expect to see or hear what we expect to hear, and so on.

Part 2: Factors that affect our perception

It is clear, even from the brief discussion above, that perception is a very complex process and all that we can do in this section is to try to understand some of the factors that affect the way that we perceive the world. Reber and Reber (2001) list different factors that affect our perceptions: attention, constancy, motivation, organisation, set (cognitive and/or emotional stance), learning, distortion/hallucination and illusion. They also discuss subliminal perception – which comes very close to our discussion of pre-conscious learning. We want to add three other factors: early childhood development, level of expectation and our place in the social world. Clearly, these 12 different factors overlap in some ways and we will not discuss them individually but, rather, we will start our examination by looking at our early childhood development since it underlies all the others.

Early childhood development

It is clear from the above that our initial learning is from the senses and has a biological dimension. Whilst in the uterus the fetus is already learning through the senses, and this process continues throughout the whole of life although it is more complex after we have left the womb and as we grow and develop. In all experiencing and learning, the process begins with the bodily processes of sight, smell, sound, taste and touch. In itself each sense experience is meaningless and so we need to respond to it, use it or give it meaning, a use-value and name, and this we begin to do soon after birth. Tomasello (1999: 124) points out that from very early in life (a few weeks old) children begin to remember learning experiences and 'they begin to form perceptual categories of objects and events from fairly early in development as well'. From this early age, children begin to learn perceptions and remember learning experiences.

> The ability of organisms to operate not only with perceptions of the environment but also with sensory–motor representations of the environment – especially object categories and image schemas of dynamic events – is one of the most remarkable phenomena of the natural world. More importantly it gives organisms the ability to profit from personal experience via memory and categorization and so be less dependent on Nature's ability to foresee the future via specific, and often inflexible, biological adaptations.
>
> (ibid.: 125)

The ability to imitate and then to give subjective meaning is important, but as we grow that subjective meaning has to relate to an external meaning that lies outside of ourselves; this is to be found in culture, which is also carried by other people and which we all learn through interaction. Over time and with repeated experiences, children learn that the same experience that they have memorised can be given a generalised response, which they take for granted and which is usually embedded in culture and transmitted through interaction with significant others. My criticism of Kolb's (1984) idea of generalisation in his learning cycle is that he does not convey the idea that we can generalise, or habitualise, only after we have successfully performed an action on a number of occasions. Once we take our world for granted we begin to perceive it through these lenses of habit.

Learning

In the first instance we have to ask the question: 'Is perception innate or is it learned in some way?' Tomasello perhaps (1993: 53) provides an answer when he suggests that we have all inherited the capacity to live culturally, and that our only evolutionary tendency is that we have learned to live together and develop our own cultural inheritance.

When babies have experiences, or sensations, that they do not understand these are, in the first instance, memorised, the brain storing these sensations as early memories. However, from the very earliest of days a baby has to distinguish between its memories and new sensations – both sensations of different phenomena and, even more difficult, sensations of the same phenomenon. Hence, a baby has to distinguish between a new experience and the memory of the past sensations of the same phenomenon, and this lies at the initial stages of conscious awareness. Learning, then, is about memory, and memory is the reconstruction of earlier experiences. In this sense we learn to be conscious, but our experiences are meaningless in themselves until we can contextualise them – we have to learn to become conscious through a process of constructing and reconstructing our experiences, to develop our own perception of the world. We can be conscious only of something!

However, as they mature very young children begin to use and to give meaning to those initial sensations of sight, smell, sound, taste and touch, and their learning moves from the senses to the cognitions, and the knowledge that they learn from the sensations is conveyed in language. So later learning occurs primarily in the cognitive domain and the sense experiences are relegated to a secondary position. These early individual experiences are natural – Vygotsky (1978) calls them the 'natural line' (Tomasello, 1999: 51). Children learn from these very early experiences without the aid of culture. Thereafter, learning becomes a cultural phenomenon. At this point we are both perceiving and learning perception. Children learn to respond to, or give a meaning to, their sensations that is acceptable to their social group, or to their immediate significant others, so that once they have attached a meaning or a use-value to a sensation it will be the one internalised and then presumed upon for future similar situations and sensations. They will perceive social reality in accord with these learning experiences and reflect the culture of their life-world. In this sense, perception is itself a learning process that is going to lead to cultural reproduction and during which we learn to take our sensations and our life-world for granted.

When children have an experience with which they are unfamiliar (box 2 in Figure 8.1), it creates a dilemma for them that they may solve either for themselves – self-directed learning (Vygotsky's natural route) – or by imitating others (box 3). If they do not resolve the dilemma, then they revert to box 2 and try again. Once they have a solution, they try it out and, if it does not work, they revert to the earlier stages in the process, so that the arrows between boxes 2 and 3 and between boxes 3 and 4 are not unidirectional, illustrating that there is a process of trial-and-error learning going on at both stages. Having worked out an answer to the problem, i.e. to give a subjective response to the sensation, perhaps as a result of self-directed learning (box 3), the child is able to practise it in a social situation. If the subjective response is acceptable, in as much as the people with whom the child interacts and practises the answer do not contradict the response in some way, then the child can assume that the response is

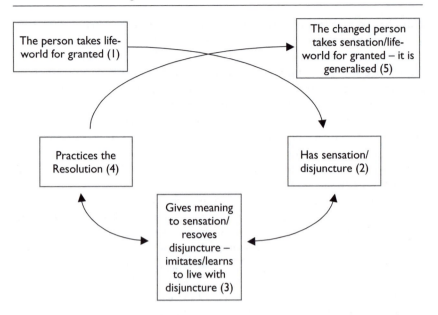

Figure 8.1 The transformation of the senses.

socially correct, even though it may not be technically correct. If it is not technically correct – that is close to the 'truth' or even the 'truth' as other social groups perceive it – then the child may be faced with a new learning situation later in life. With continued practice, so the child is able to universalise the response and take it for granted (box 5), until the next time that a disjunctural situation occurs. Kolb (1984) actually includes generalisation in his learning cycle, but my research suggests that generalisation occurs not immediately following a new learning experience but only after the resolution to disjuncture has been tried out on several occasions. In a sense, once we have developed these habitual responses to sensations, we have learned to perceive the world in a taken-for-granted manner.

But we rarely experience single senses, or have an experience of a single phenomenon. Vygotsky (1978: 33) has shown that from a very early stage in development language, perception and speech require sequential processing so that each element is dealt with separately. But he claims 'that a special feature of human perception – which arises at a very early age – is the *perception of real objects*' (ibid.) so that we see the world not just as colour and shape but also as sense and meaning. Vygotsky concludes from this that 'all human perception consists of categorized rather than isolated perceptions' (ibid.), which relates to Reber and Reber's point about the way that we organise our perceptions. Consequently, young children have to choose individual elements from within the wider whole and they then have to isolate elements. Vygotsky shows that children do not choose the stimulus in the first instance but they carry out the physical movements that the choice requires and resolve the issue of choice through physical movement, rather than making a single decision based upon their perception of the situation and then acting accordingly: only later with the use of language and signs do children actually choose the stimulus because the signs have allowed them to structure the choice process differently. Vygotsky (ibid.: 35) writes that 'Movement detaches itself from direct perception and comes under the control of sign functions included in the choice response'. It is language and sign that enables perception to develop and, through this and attention, the memory develops. Vygotsky suggests that this also enables children to break up fragments of the past and relate them to the present, which helps to develop a sense of time – but they then become aware that they exist within time.

Consequently, we can see that our experiences of anything, e.g. any single sensation, are always embedded in a wider context. Marton and Booth (1997: 100) discuss this type of awareness within the framework of appresentation, which is:

> the fact that although phenomena are, as a rule, only partially exposed to us, we do not experience the parts as themselves, we experience the wholes of which the parts are parts. We do not experience silhouettes but phenomena (material or conceptual) in all their complexity of space and time.

However, the level of our attention can vary: we may perceive a situation clearly when we are fully conscious, but if we are tired, or if we are focusing upon another aspect of the whole, we may only be dimly aware of the external object, or even hardly conscious of it at all. This situation generates the pre-conscious learning that we have already discussed in all these cases; the level of our consciousness affects our perception of the external. This is slightly different from the fact that we can and do receive images though subliminal stimuli that affect our orientation towards an external object and, consequently, make us perceive it differently in the future, a phenomenon widely utilised in advertising.

As a result of all our previous learned experiences, our perceptions become much more complex, but we can see that our perceptions are never of the direct external object but are always learned from our earliest days, and they will change slowly as our understanding of the object of our experience changes. This will come through learning, which will begin when some aspects of the external object do not appear 'right' and this creates a disjuncture that leads to further learning.

However, our attitudes may be formed as a result of previous learning experiences, and so our own orientation towards the external object – our perceptions – will be affected by our attitudes. In Figure 8.1 the final box shows that, when we take things for granted, we habitualise our orientation towards certain external objects and that this affects our future perceptions of them. We may perceive things negatively simply because we disagree with them, or because they anger us, or we may view things from an upper or lower social class viewpoint simply because we were born and grew up in this type of social environment and our perceptions are always affected by our previous experiences and our previous learning, and so on.

Hallucination and illusion

Sometimes it may not be the object which has changed, but us: our state changes under the influence of drugs, tiredness, hunger and thirst, and so on. In these instances our bodies are unable to process the stimuli in the normal manner, and as a result we get a distorted perception: we believe things are easier than they are – that things are different colours and shapes – mirages, and so on. In these instances our perceptions are controlled by our bodies and once again we become aware that we do not experience the external object directly. But, as Descartes pointed out, it is still we who have the hallucinations – it is not our bodies.

In a similar manner, if we are very hungry or thirsty, we can see food and drink in situations where people who are not hungry do not see it. We 'see' what we are looking for or what our bodies need, even though the external object does not necessarily have any direct reference to food and drink. In this sense, once again, our perception is affected by the state of our bodies – it is a response to a bodily need.

As we noted earlier, we rarely perceive single sensations but whole situations, and on occasions the whole situation produces an illusion that can result in immediate perception misleading us unless we are very aware of it and focus upon the specific. Perhaps the most common illusion is the Muller–Lyer diagram (Figure 8.2).

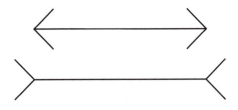

Figure 8.2 The Muller–Lyer illusion.

The two horizontal lines are precisely the same length but the upper one appears shorter as a result of the direction of the arrowheads and the lower one appears longer for the same reason. The illusion is created by the way in which we perceive the external objects as a whole. A similar type of illusion can be created by the power of the group within which we act: in this sense we can be field dependent or field independent. In another experiment, Asch (1952) demonstrated how group pressure can affect perception since each member of the group is aware of the pressure exerted by all the other members. A majority of a group offered a false judgement unbeknown to another member. Often, not only did the unknowing subjects conform to the group's judgement so as not to appear different, but some individuals actually came to perceive the situation in the same way as they thought that the social group perceived it. Thus, the power of the group can distort the perception of the external object.

Conclusion

Perception, then, is the result of our being in the world and internalising our image of it. We cannot be conscious unless we are aware of something, and that is what we have internalised from the external world. The only trouble is that, although we may internalise the external world, it still remains external to us, and so what we have internalised is an appearance of the external world. This was what concerned Descartes in the first instance, or, as Feser (2005: 5) succinctly puts it about this appearance of the world in us: 'In perception we know that appearance immediately and intimately; what we know of reality is another and problematic matter'. What we can know directly is that we exist even though the problem of the external world still remains. However, this has a major implication for all of our learning: we never actually learn from the real external world itself – we always learn from our perception of it which we have internalised and, as we have seen already, that perception may approach the empirical reality but might be quite a long way removed from it. This clearly has implications for teaching, but that is another subject and one that takes us far beyond the ambit of this study. We might, however, want to pose the question: 'How can we be sure that what we perceive approaches reality?' How can we be sure that what we learn is actually about the real world in which we live? This question can be answered in a number of ways, for example by discovering that what we think we have learned is actually practical in our experience in the real world, or by reaching agreement with others who are undergoing their own individual perceptual processes about the world about what is out there. At the same time, it is easy to understand that it is possible to disagree with others about our perception of events, simply because there are so many different states that affect our perception of any event and different people are in different state when they perceive something. We know this to be true from common everyday occurrences, especially in giving police evidence or evidence in a court of law, when one person's evidence about an event may differ from that of others who also witnessed the event.

What is clear is that this complex process of perceiving, which is both sense based and cognitive, underlies all our learning and it is also the base upon which the following chapters are constructed.

Chapter 9

Thinking

After the sense experience, whether primary or secondary, we think about it. This statement comes close to Dewey's (1991 [1910]: 8–9) definition of thinking as 'that operation in which present facts suggest other facts (or truths) in such a way as to induce belief in the latter upon the ground or warrant of the former'. Perhaps Dewey's use of the term 'fact' is a problematic claim and 'present perceived facts' might be more accurate in today's climate. But even this broad definition, which focuses on a sequence in the thought process, omits the possibility that remembering is a thought process since it does not have the same sequence of constructing new ideas from present ones. Thinking, then, is the operation of the mind, but the mind itself develops as we develop as persons.

Thinking, then, is rather an ill-defined process, although Gilhooley (1996: 1) extends Dewey's basic idea and suggests that it is 'a set of processes whereby people assemble, use and revise internal symbolic models'. Underlying most of our ideas about thinking is the idea of rationality, although we will meet at least three types of thought below: creative, inspired – which may be creative – and undirected thinking. In each of these cases the rules of rationality do not always apply.

Rational thought takes two forms: one which looks back and seeks to explain and one which looks forward, i.e. planning. Both, however, demand that our arguments are carefully and logically constructed often from a priori knowledge, although some theorists seek to characterise it in terms of irrationality (Moser *et al.*, 1998: 123). Heidegger (1968) regards this logical thinking as thinking *per se*, although thought can be illogical. For him, it follows the rules of logic, starting from a premise and building an argument upon it. It has come to reflect modern society – with it, beliefs and superstitions were to be eradicated and all thought should follow the rules of logic. As we have already pointed out, it is one way through which knowledge itself can be legitimised. Despite its high reputation, however, we certainly do not all abide by the rules of logic, as my own research (Jarvis, 1980) into superstition has demonstrated. Freud's research is, of course, the most significant when we consider the prevalence, or otherwise, of logical thought. He has shown how our unconscious mind influences a great deal of our thought and behaviour. Indeed, we certainly need to understand the unconscious a great deal better in our endeavours to understand human thought and learning. Handy (1990) also pointed us to the fact that this is an 'age of unreason'.

Nevertheless, we are frequently confronted with the ideas of instrumental rationality – we have already discussed this with reference to external history – when we try to master time in order to achieve our ends by the most efficient means. Indeed, this approach to rationality is quite common, although there is another mainstream school of thought, stemming from Aristotle and Kant, which claims that rationality should be thought orientated to the well-being of humankind. In this sense, it reflects certain basic moral beliefs based upon rational argument.

Fundamentally, we live in an age in which rationality is prized although it is something that is not frequently practised. However, as Moser *et al.* (1998: 127) write: 'If theories of rationality are anything, they are about making epistemically responsible inferences in the light of available evidence'. Consequently, we can see that not only can we examine rational thought for its logical processes, but we can also evaluate it in terms of 'sound' judgement, and so on.

Fundamentally, however, there are two ways of looking at rational thought, as either non-reflective or reflective, although we recognise that there can always be a combination of the two. The first two parts of this chapter will, therefore, examine non-reflective and reflective thought; in the next parts we will look cognitive development and then styles of thinking; in the fifth part we will look at ways of reasoning; in the final part we will look at the term 'ways of knowing' rather than thinking or learning. Ways of knowing tries to overcome the limitations of normal thought about both the terms 'learning' and 'thinking' and yet it relates closely to both.

Part 1: Non-reflective thought

We are not born with the ability to think; thought, like most other aspects of the human being, develops as the person develops. In the first instance, memories are stored within networks of neurons in the tertiary cortex of the brain. In addition, we know that the higher animals, such as the apes, have a cognitive capacity that we can call memory. Tomasello (1999: 124) points out that infants can remember some learning experiences from the very first weeks of life, but memory develops as we develop as people and in the first instance it is a very private affair. Nelson (2007: 111) suggests that experienced events are memorised since everything that enters the memory is meaningful to the individual. Memory is meaning – it is where meaning is conserved.

As children develop and their awareness of the world broadens, so they become aware of the fact that there are more possible realities than the one that they have experienced thus far, and so in the pre-school years memory takes two forms – episodic and semantic. This distinction is rather like the distinction between primary experience and secondary experience since episodic memory is autobiographical and semantic memory is the awareness and recall of other people's experiences and general knowledge (Nelson, 2007: 184). Autobiographical memory requires a sense of the self, which is developed through the combination of episodic memories, and a sense of time, and it emerges as children gain language ability and the ability to share experiences. Consequently, Nelson (ibid.: 193) argues that 'the distinctively autobiographical memory emerges from a collaborative construction created by the child and social partners (adults and peers) through verbal representations of past and future experience'. However, Nelson (ibid. 200–1) makes the significant point that not all autobiographical memory develops in the same way for different persons; for instance, East Asian people have later and more general and impersonal early memories than do Europeans and Americans. Fundamentally, then, autobiographical memory is the repository of personal meaning constructed from the combination of experiential episodes that happen to the person and, as we have seen in our understanding of experience in Chapter 5 – it consists of episodes and events. However, it is not long before young people begin to reflect on their memories and question them since they begin to enter conversation with others about themselves and about meanings of events, and so on.

Non-reflective memory also occurs when we internalise, and perhaps do, precisely what we are told in an unthinking manner and this can occur throughout life. It also occurs when we merely observe an incident or a scene and do not really think about it. In precisely the same way, we may internalise these experiences without being consciously aware of them, and only when we have a later experience do we recall the scene that we have previously internalised without giving it conscious thought: it is this that I have discussed in the process of pre-conscious learning. Additionally, non-reflective learning occurs in what Marton and Saljo (1984) refer to as surface learning, when students try to memorise the texts that they are reading rather than looking for their underlying meaning. Fundamentally, non-reflective learning does not introduce change into society: it is reproductive.

However, non-reflective thinking is probably a much rarer phenomenon than generally supposed because we rarely just internalise information without giving it some thought, e.g. strict obedience to commands without thinking about them may be rare as recipients may well think about them but say nothing – thought and action do not always have to be congruent.

Part 2: Reflective thought

It is interesting that one of the meanings of the concept of 'reflection' is reproduction in a mirror, in which the image is a reflection of the original, whereas reflective thought carries a completely opposite connotation – it should not rehearse the information that has been presented to the thinker.

Dewey (1933) limits his discussion of thought to reflective thought, deliberately excluding any possible non-reflective elements: he (ibid.: 6) defines it as 'Active, persistent and careful consideration of any belief or supposed form of knowledge in the light of the grounds that support it, and the further conclusions to which it tends'. Two pages later he offers another definition, 'that operation in which present facts suggest other facts (or truths) in such a way as to induce belief in the latter upon the ground or warrant of the former'. He (ibid.: 72) goes on to suggest that there is a five-step sequence to reflective thought: a felt difficulty; location and definition of the problem; suggestion of possible solution; reasoning based on the possible solution; further observation and reflection leading to its acceptance or rejection. This sequence is clearly appropriate for reflective thinking and problem solving, but he des not discuss non-reflective thought.

Since the time Dewey discussed this, there has been a tremendous amount of research on reflective thought, and it is not my intention here to examine all of the literature on the topic. For instance, it is possible to analyse reflection on meaning (Moon, 1999), on actions (Schön, 1983; Newman, 2006), on facts and beliefs, values, and so on. It is also possible to look at critical thought (Brookfield, 1987) and the debates that occurred around that time as to whether all thought should be critical, or at least reflective in the way that Dewey defined it. Reflection, consequently, takes on a number of different forms and it should be analytical, creative and evaluative. We will try to capture its essence under these three subheadings of analysis, creativity and evaluation.

Analytical

Dewey (1933) was concerned that reflective thought should be reasoned or logical, whereas Brookfield (1987) regarded critical thought as analytical thought. Indeed, analytical and critical have precisely the same meaning, but critical can also carry the other meaning of disagreement. Brookfield (ibid.: 26–8) suggests a five-step sequence of thinking which is very similar to Dewey's: a trigger event, appraisal, exploration, developing alternative perspectives and integration. Fundamentally, both sequences describe a logical chain of thought that does not take as given the initial stimulus. This initial stimulus is the experience of disjuncture which leads to our becoming consciously aware of the situation, i.e. experiencing it, which in its turn leads to thought and learning which is then integrated into our own biographical memory.

Analysis is the process of breaking down ideas/propositions into their component parts and determining the validity of each, and also examining the connections between the parts to ensure that there is a logical development between them. Where this does not occur, then it is necessary to seek alternative propositions/solutions and test them out in precisely the same manner, which is a learning process.

Creative

The act of creation usually occurs through the synthesis of two or more diverse thoughts, elements or situations to create a new whole: it is the exact opposite of the analytical process. In this sense, it is typified by the idea that 'two minds are better than one'. In this instance, the trigger event is often an insight or a hunch that brings together two ideas so that a better understanding may develop. As early as 1926 Wallis suggested that there are four stages to creative thought: preparation, incubation, illumination/verification and verification – it is certainly a reflective process.

Another way of looking at creative thought is by regarding successful creative thinking as inspired. When individuals answer questions in a creative manner, they may be regarded as inspired and the knowledge they present may be regarded as inspired knowledge. Now, inspired knowledge is very different from the claims of revealed knowledge – something that some but not all religious believers maintain. For instance, it is possible to regard the Bible as inspired without believing in its being revealed knowledge. Inspired knowledge is creative and based upon human creativity and learning.

Reflective thinking can also be creative in as much as there can be forward planning and, significantly, intention to act in a specific manner, so that we can see that reflective thought is also related to meaning.

Evaluative

Evaluative thought is a matter of judging the relevance or significance of meaning of knowledge, beliefs, attitudes, values, and so on. It is a process of determining how the propositions were reached and looking at their relationship to 'truth' or even to meaningful existence and reality itself. There are both subjective and objective elements in this process. Evaluative thought also examines actions, which I will discuss below.

It is objective in as far as it assesses the methodological sequence by which the knowledge was gained: if the methods do not stand the test of scientific scrutiny then the conclusions are invalid, but if the methods do stand the test there is a likelihood that the conclusions have some validity.

However, this is by no means always the case. For example, scientists can undertake perfectly valid pieces of research and achieve factual answers that are correct, but, since facts have no meanings, the meaning and relevance that scientists place upon their research must always be assessed since their research is always subjective and can be completely ideological.

The subjective elements in evaluation are to be found in examining the relevance or significance of the knowledge either for the individual or for society as a whole, and this requires a thorough analysis of the reasons given for the significance or relevance, and so on. Once more it relates to subjective meaning; new learning stems from such an evaluation.

In precisely the same way, actions can be evaluated to see whether the action is correct, effective or efficient. Clearly, this is the type of distinction Schön (1983) makes when he looks at reflection in action and reflection on action. In the former, reflection is a form of problem solving, trying to find the best action in the given situation, whereas reflection on action is looking back and assessing its effectiveness and efficiency, and so on. If the evaluation is less than positive it generates another learning process.

On the other hand, Newman's (2006) analysis, which leads to defiance, stems from an assessment of the situation, or an action in which power is exercised to force individuals to conform to a situation that those in power wish. When the evaluation is that such a situation is wrong, immoral, etc., then Newman claims that individuals should be taught to defy those forms of authority – in this sense it is both evaluative and critical.

Reflective thought, therefore, is diverse and the ways that we undertake it reflect, in some way, the types of person we are and the forms of learning that we undertake: but then so do our styles of thinking.

Part 3: Cognitive development

It was Piaget (1929) who pioneered research into this in the West: he suggested that children go through a five-stage cognitive developmental process and that the level of development will affect children's understanding of their own experience. He suggested that this process is related to biological age, although his sample was much too small for him to demonstrate this clearly and we feel that this form of development, like many others, is experiential. His findings may be summarised as shown in Table 9.1, which I initially prepared for my own Masters degree work.

As we have seen from the research into early childhood learning (Tomasello, 1999; Nelson, 2007), there have been many developments since Piaget's pioneering work, and his sensorimotor stage has been much more thoroughly researched. His sample size was also rather too small, although in order to study small children in depth it is necessary to focus on individual children rather than large samples. Obviously, we do not pass from one stage to another and leave the former one behind at a specific biological age

Table 9.1 Piaget's stages of cognitive development

Stage 1	Sensorimotor	0–2 years	Infant learns to differentiate between self and objects in the external world
Stage 2	Pre-operational thought	2–4 years	Child is egocentric but classifies objects by single salient features
Stage 3	Intuitive	4–7 years	Child thinks in classificatory way but may be unaware of classifications
Stage 4	Concrete thought	7–11 years	Child able to use logical operations such as reversibility, classification and serialisation
Stage 5	Formal operations	11–15 years	Trial steps towards abstract conceptualisation occurs

so that there are indistinct boundaries – and our level of thinking also varies from situation to situation so that the stages are further blurred. In any case, our conceptual development cannot be reduced to biological development although there might be some linkage between the two. However, as Tomasello argued, a specific change occurs at the age of around nine months. In addition, we do not know all the aspects of the relationship between conceptual development and culture or ethnicity, although we are aware that there are cultural differences and, as Nisbett (2005: 157) points out, 'Western languages force a pre-occupation with focal objects as opposed to context' whereas Asian languages start by establishing the context. Indeed, the experiences that children have within their life-world, rather than their biological age, probably constitute the major factor in conceptual development, as our understanding of learning suggests. Additionally, we do not know whether cognitive developmental learning is the same in other cultures in which world-views are extremely different.

Finally, our conceptual development does not stop when we reach the abstract level, and Riegel (1973) highlighted the fact that adults think in, what he called, dialectical operations terms, which is the ability to tolerate problems and contradictions (Allman, 1984: 76).

This process of cognitive development is probably not automatic: some people may not move beyond certain stages and some may remain in those stages because they reflect the social milieu, group or organisation of which they are members. However, if we have not achieved a certain stage necessary to understand the meaning of the information given, it may also lead to profound misunderstanding of the meaning of the communication unless careful instruction is provided, and, as we will see later in this study when we look at hermeneutics, the art of understanding the meaning of the communicator is often very sophisticated.

Part 4: Styles of thinking

Sternberg (1997) set out to show how thinking styles both help individuals to fit into their environment and also reflect their social position: thinking styles are preferred ways of thinking (Sternberg, 1997: 19). This is about how we prefer to use the abilities we have rather than about the abilities themselves. We do not have just one preferred style but a profile, and he produces a comprehensive framework that revolves around three major dimensions of mental self-government (Table 9.2) (ibid.: 22–6).

In this typology we can see how different patterns of thought enable people to play their roles in society but, even more than this, we can see how these types tell us something about the person who adopts them. However, Biggs (2001: 79) is not clear why Sternberg chose the metaphor of mental self-government, and he suggests that had he chosen another one he might have developed a different complex of styles. Nevertheless, this question illustrates the fact that we are not dealing with a universalistic typology – only a theoretical framework within which the notion of thinking styles fits. There is nothing in our evolution that would suggest that this is in any way biological: it is social and, as we have seen so far, we are socialised into different cultures and we learn to think differently. Once again we see the divide between the Greek/Judeo-Christian West and the

Table 9.2 Sternberg's styles of thinking

Functions	Legislative	People who decide to do things for themselves
	Executive	Rule followers who prefer pre-structured problems
	Judicial	People who like to evaluate rules and problems
Forms	Monarchic	Single-minded people
	Hierarchic	People who have a hierarchy of goals and set priorities
	Oligarchic	People who have competing goals of equal importance
	Anarchic	People who take a random approach to problems
Levels	Global	People who prefer to deal with large issues
	Local	People who like concrete problems
Scope	Internal	People who like to work alone and are concerned with internal affairs
	External	People who like working with others and are extroverts
Leanings	Liberal	People who like to go beyond existing rules
	Conservative	People who like to adhere to existing rules and behaviours

Confucian heritage East. But another distinction can be found, and that is between Protestant West and Catholic West – the Catholic West is less individualistic than the Protestant West, reflecting precisely the same distinction that Max Weber (1930) made in his famous *Protestant Ethic* thesis. The Protestant West is much more individualistic and liberal whereas in Catholic and Confucian heritage countries the group and collective orientations are much more favoured. Nesbitt (2005: 51), for instance, suggests that Eastern and Western values play an important part in our thinking: he notes that in Chinese there is no word for individualism – the nearest word is the one meaning selfishness – and the Japanese rarely use 'I' in conversation. In precisely the same way, we find that there are gender differences in thinking styles. Ageing is another variable and, although it is possible to distinguish between those thinking styles encouraged in the young and the way that expectations change as children age, there is no research, as far as I can discover, that looks at the development of thinking styles over the lifespan, although one would expect to find differences especially after individuals retire from their work. Sternberg also suggests that parenting styles and school and work situation also affect thinking styles.

Understanding the way that people prefer to think can perhaps tell us quite a lot about the persons who describe their thinking styles, but whether the style is a dominant causal factor in the development of personality or whether personality is a causal factor in preferences to thinking style is another matter. However, Sternberg's thesis is that all people exercise mental self-government, and that the forms of government in the world are not coincidental but are 'mirrors of our minds' (Sternberg, 1997: 19), and in this sense we learn which forms of thinking are acceptable in our place in society and we may well choose to practise them. However, had he looked at the cultural values of another country, Sternberg's analysis might have been very different, for 'self-government' would have different connotations.

Part 5: Ways of reasoning

There are two basic ways of reasoning: deductive and inductive. Deduction is the process of inferring a particular instance from a general law; conversely, induction is the process of inferring a general law from a particular instance and is also about the production of facts to demonstrate the validity of a general statement.

Deduction is the process that is carried out in decision making, when a number of facts, which are assumed to be true, have to be considered and a conclusion reached about them which must, therefore, be true – provided the thought processes have been logical. However, we have already highlighted how dominant discourses occupy the educational vocabulary and so we have to be prepared to question the initial facts as well as the assumptions underlying the process of reasoning. Our subconscious thoughts and emotions, and even our conscious ones, might well affect the process and, consequently, the logical progression of an argument has always to be carefully constructed and checked.

Induction, however, is the converse of this and is, in a sense, a process of generating hypotheses and, perhaps, theorising from them. Theorising is similar in some ways to rational thought, although it may include hunches and intuitions, but it is not necessarily irrational thought. In another sense it is similar to generalisation (box 5 in Figure 8.1), when individuals learn by experience that the outcomes of their actions appear to be patterned and repeatable – it is about the creation of habitual thought processes and occurs only in the process of time. Generalisation does not occur with every learning incident, but when things appear to repeat themselves then we seek to theorise about them. Moser *et al.* (1998: 183) suggest that (italics in original)

> human knowers are primarily *theorizers* rather than simple fact gatherers. One can find evidence for this in the earliest recorded human history. We theorize about each other, in order to try to understand what makes us tick, to explain why people behave the way that they do.

They go on to say that we also theorise about our environment in order to try to control it. In a sense, then, this also reflects the idea that every person is a scientist (Kelly, 1955) since it starts from a disjunctural experience but it seeks to postulate answers to the question 'Why?' in a more general sense. It contains a mixture of some of the previous forms of thinking and yet, in the end, it becomes a distinct form in itself.

Even our ways of reasoning in the West may differ from that in the East: Nisbett (2005: 171) makes the point that 'East Asians, then, are more likely to set logic aside in favor of typicality and plausibility of conclusions. They are also more likely to set logic aside in favor of desirability of conclusion'. Hence, the way we reason may also be guided by culture and we reflect our cultures in these thinking processes.

Part 6: Ways of knowing

In Dominice's (2000: 87) work on educational biography we can see the truth in his claim that preparing 'the biographical narrative is itself an experience that discloses a way of knowing' since it helps us clarify our own meaning perspectives and the significance of learning events in our lives. However, it is Josso (1991), a colleague of Dominice, who provides a theoretical framework for ways of knowing. She does so in a book with an English translation *Approaching Oneself,* which captures something of the theme of aspects of this book. She suggests that there are three different ways of knowing for adults: existential, pragmatic and comprehensive. In each of these categories, there are six subdivisions: psychological, sociological, economic, psycho-sociological, political and cultural (in Dominice, 2000: 87). The existential way relates to psychosomatic learning; the pragmatic to instrumental or relational learning; the comprehensive to reflective learning. However, I am unhappy about the term 'psychosomatic' since it does not really fit the examples given in the book and it appears to relate to personal interpretation of events that happen to the individual and, in this sense, it comes close to meaning. Thus, we can say that the three ways of knowing are about the person's meaning, instrumental or relational and reflective. We do think about what happens to us, to what we can do, and we do reflect upon all the events that befall us, and we do so from a wide variety of perspectives: it is these that contribute towards our personhood.

Gardner (2007) uses the term 'mind' rather than thinking or knowing, but his description of mind comes close to Josso's although it is not based on empirical work – rather Gardner predicts the types of mind that we will need to cope with life in the future. He suggests that there are five ways of knowing and thinking: disciplined, synthesising, creating, respectful and ethical.

- The disciplined mind is one that views the external world from the perspective of a specific academic discipline, although it also includes the ideas of high motivation to master rigorous thought within this framework.
- The synthesising mind is one that seeks to draw together diverse perspectives on the world to achieve a coherent whole – we can synthesise narratives, concepts, and so on. In this sense, Gardner is appealing for a multidisciplined perspective as we are living in a very complex world.
- The creative mind is one which draws together different perspectives or synthesises or combines ideas from several people. In a sense, synthesising and creativity are very close, and I have already combined them earlier in this chapter.
- The respectful mind is one which has respect for other persons and their viewpoints: it is about toleration of all forms of difference and, although Gardner acknowledges intolerance, he does not really enter the debate about the value of intolerance or even criticality, even though he mentions both. The term conjures up the type of person who has respect for authority and who is always politically correct – but Gardner seems to be outlining an approach to respect that actually underlies social living.
- The ethical mind is one, Gardner claims, which focuses on good work, although he recognises that ethics is rather broader than this. However, he does not really explore values to any extent in this piece of work.

Of course, Gardner has not exhausted the ways of knowing or the types of mind that we need for the future, for this is rather a subjective book in which he seeks to extend his thinking beyond the perspectives upon which most of his writing have been based, and this is a descriptive study rather than one in which he rigorously argues his case. However, Gardner considers that these ways of knowing and acting can be taught and learned, and perhaps this is one of the most important claims in this book – we can learn to be the people we are.

Another study which examines ways of knowing which is important to this book is Belenky *et al.*'s (1986) study of women's ways of knowing but this is much more than just a study of learning – it is about knowing and so we will examine it in the following chapter.

Conclusion

Thinking is closely related to our being: it is the processes of conscious daily living. In exploring this complex phenomenon we can see how some of the ways in which we think underlie our actions and consequently the type of person we are. Some of this learning is conscious, but other elements of it are pre-conscious, some intended and other unintended, some formal but many informal. Our thinking does to a considerable extent reflect our position in society but we are not mirrors of our social position – we are individuals in relationship and we do have the opportunity to develop our thinking in and beyond our own social context.

Chapter 10

Knowing

Knowing is not quite the same as learning – it is more the situation of having learned – and as a result it is about understanding or being able to give meaning to a situation, often a personal situation. In this sense it is akin to perception. *Collins English Dictionary* gives three meanings to knowing: suggesting secret information; wise, shrewd or clever; deliberate or intentional. Yet none of these meanings quite captures the idea of one's own personal (secret/subjective) understanding of a situation that the term 'knowing' also seems to suggest. It is a matter of having personal 'knowledge', but the word 'knowledge' here needs qualifying: this constitutes the first part of this chapter. The second examines that idea that personal meaning is articulated and is, in this sense, narrative knowing; the third part is specifically devoted to women's ways of knowing; fourth, we will discuss knowing as a way of knowing ourselves; finally, knowing is related to our theory of learning.

Part 1: Knowing and personal knowledge

In Polanyi's (1962) study of personal knowledge, he makes it clear that there is almost a contradiction between an active comprehension (personal) of things known and the more universal and objective conception of knowledge. He (1962: viii) is clear that:

> into every act of knowing there enters a passionate contribution of the person knowing what is being known, and that this coefficient is no mere imperfection but a vital component of his knowledge. And around this central fact I have tried to construct a system of correlative beliefs which I can sincerely hold, and to which I can see no acceptable alternatives. But ultimately, it is my allegiance that upholds these convictions.

Herein lies the problem with the subjectivity of 'knowing' (a verb): it can be both a matter of knowledge or belief and commitment and it can even relate to 'doing' or 'experiencing'. The ancient Hebrew word *yada'*, for instance, means 'knowing intellectually', 'experiencing' and even 'being acquainted with'. *Yada'* is used in the mythical story of 'Adam and Eve' to describe Adam having intercourse with Eve – 'knowing' her (see Von Rad 1961: 100). In this sense, it captures the complexity of 'knowing', 'personal experiential learning' and 'doing'. Knowing is more than cognition and is a very complex phenomenon.

The fact that we know something does not mean that it is true in terms of objective knowledge but we believe it as true because we are committed to it and because we can see no acceptable alternatives for us even though there may be some for other people. Objective knowledge (a noun) is legitimised provided it fulfils one of three basic criteria: it is based upon rational and logical argument constructed from indisputable premises; it is grounded in empirical fact; and its application works in practice (pragmatism). Each of these three criteria requires considerably more discussion than we can give in this brief chapter but we will discuss each in turn.

Logical argument based on indisputable premises

There are two components to this proposition – that the premise is indisputable and that the argument is rational or logical. Even if we can agree on indisputable premises, and there are fewer of them that we might suppose, we then have to construct a logical or a rational argument based upon such premises. The distinction is made here between rational and logical because it is possible to feel that we have constructed a logical argument when we have built into it some of our own prejudices that might be slightly irrational and since, as we have argued here and elsewhere, human beings are not computers and thus our own arguments may sometimes be less than entirely rational. Fundamentally, this means that knowledge based on argument requires considerable examination before it is acceptable as fact, but then we are still confronted by another problem – fact has no intrinsic meaning – and this is one of the problems with the second approach to knowledge.

Empirical facts

We can make the assumption that knowledge discovered through hard scientific and empirical research is fact. Hence, we frequently ask questions about the methods used to obtain the facts and claim that if the methods employed are wrong then the conclusions reached might be false. Examination of the method, therefore, becomes important if the facts are to be verified. But the problem still remains that the meaning given to the fact is not intrinsic to it, although there is a tendency to assume that it is.

Pragmatism

It is this form of knowledge that Lyotard (1984) called performative and which he saw as being significant in the late modern world. If it works, then it must contain true knowledge, even though its application might be questionable. In other words, 'the end justifies the means' might well be regarded as a maxim of contemporary society which has downgraded the morality of action so that it is no more than subsidiary to outcome. However, there are problems with this form of knowledge since, although we can assume that because something has worked in the past it will work again the future, this can be true only if we are dealing with machines that function in an unchangeable manner: we cannot assume that people will always act in precisely the same manner. Hence, technological pragmatism may be possible (but even then the machine may break down) whereas pragmatism in the social and human world is less certain and we must always talk in terms of possibilities and probabilities.

Habermas (1972) adopted a slightly different version of knowledge from this. His three forms were empirical–analytic sciences, historical–hermeneutic sciences and disinterested contemplation. The first two are very similar to the three that we have discussed and the third points us in the direction of the issue of meaning – it might be through disinterested contemplation that researchers can give meaning to their research findings, but the application of meaning may be a little less objective than Habermas would suppose, so that the issue of uncertainty is built into any assertion of meaning based upon empirical facts or, in other words, a belief component is built into personal knowing.

But 'knowing' also emerges as a result of personal experience, and in this sense the main philosophical arguments do not capture its meaning – 'I know because I have experienced it'. However, we then enter a Cartesian-type argument of how we know that our experience is valid, and so on – or we accept the validity of our experience.

It is, therefore, easy to understand that there can be a little confusion in assertions of personal knowing. We see this perhaps most clearly in statements by religious and political fundamentalists, who claim to know what they believe, and so they do, but their knowledge contains a non-empirical knowledge (belief) component that they may not acknowledge. Both the theist and the atheist may make their assertions based upon scientific facts, but both assertions contain that belief component that gives meaning to facts which exist without meaning (but not meaningless facts). In this sense, we have logically to be agnostic in the face of scientific fact even though we might logically and rationally hold beliefs about them. (This argument is one echoed by a recent study by Vernon, 2007.) It is at this point that we can see that a great deal of personal knowing may be based upon careful scientific thought but, since no empirical fact has meaning, we always build a meaning, or subjective component, into our personal knowing, and this subjective component may just possibly be wrong, so that although no other alternative may be seen, it cannot rule out that possibility.

At the same time, there are other claims to personal knowing that are based upon less factual evidence – sometime religious fundamentalists will claim this to be revealed knowledge. Revealed knowledge is always a faith position, and its levels of logicality and rationality are always open to discussion. Most people who believe in revealed knowledge also believe that that knowledge is not relative but always true and valid, so that it opens itself up to problems when the content of that knowledge is seen to be out of date and open to challenge by modern knowledge. Revealed knowledge is not a scientific position about learning – rather it may reflect either culture or power, or both, although, as we saw in the previous chapter, inspired thinking may be perfectly valid. Revealed knowledge makes presuppositions that are questionable, at the very least.

Knowing, as a verb, is about human being – it is part of us, part of our own biography – whereas knowledge, as noun, is something we possess – it is about having. This is a fundamental distinction in as much as knowing is related to both our biography and our social situation, whereas knowledge can be conceptualised as what is learned (acquired) as a result of being recipients of information. Personal knowing, then, is a matter of giving or constructing meaning in the face of a level of factual understanding about the world in which we live. By contrast, knowledge is a narrower concept and only an element, albeit a major one, in the process of knowing.

Part 2: Narrative knowing

One of the things that make us human beings is being able to ascribe meaning and communicate meaning to each other. Meanings that are accepted by a people become embedded within their culture and transmitted from generation to generation until such time as the meaning is perceived to be out of date or just plain wrong. Consequently, meaning making is basic to our humanity and embedded in pre-history. Psychologists have demonstrated how as very young children we develop the capacity to make meaning. Nelson (2007: 110), for instance, holds that 'making sense processes derive meaning from experience, relating elements of current experience to self-interest and goals and to past experience conserved in memory. These on-going dynamic processes organize memory in terms of meaning structures'. But meaning systems pre-date individuals and are embedded in cultures, so that as we are socialised into our culture we are also socialised into the relevant meaning systems and ascribe meaning to events and experiences in our lives that reflect that socialisation process. The very survival of society depends upon its successful transmission of culture from one generation to another, and in this way culture is traditional and we all learn the traditions of our society. As we learn language, so we acquire the ability to articulate those meanings but, like everything else in our socialisation process, we do not just soak up what we learn and reflect it unthinkingly thereafter but we try to make sense of each of our experiences and we begin to combine separate events and relate meanings to sequences or categories of episodes and events.

As Bruner (1990: 49), referring to disjunctural situations, writes:

> when you encounter an exception to the ordinary, and ask somebody what is happening, the person you ask will virtually always tell a story that contains *reasons* (or some other specification of an intentional state). The story, moreover, will almost invariably be an account of a possible world in which the encountered exception is somehow made to make sense or have 'meaning'.

The story seeks to embed the meaning within the culture in some way or other – it is as if we reflect knowledge in narrative or story. However, as Ricoeur (1984) makes very clear, each of these narratives is embedded not only within culture, but also within a time frame, and so the stories are relative to historical situations. Narratives are essential cognitive constructions that we have accepted and then articulate in order to explain ourselves, our intentions or our meanings. As Polkinghorne (1988: 15) writes, 'Human experience is enveloped in a personal and cultural realm of non-material meanings and thoughts', and these interpretations of reality and experience change with every new experience but will always be related to the surrounding culture. Our response to these stories and meanings is also related both to our previous experiences and to our positions within the social structures. As a result, some people are likely to reflect the story in their lives more clearly than others.

But we are also story-tellers when we try to account for our lives as we age: when asked to talk about ourselves, we usually tell a sequence of short stories about the different stages in our lives to provide a meaning for the whole rather than to philosophise about the meaning of life and our place within it. Autobiographies are often a series of stories strung together in a sequence that seeks to convey an overall sense of meaning about the life lived. As Polkinghorne (ibid.: 119) suggests:

> People use self-stories to interpret and account for their lives. The basic dimension of human existence is temporality, and narrative transforms the mere passing away of time into a meaningful unity, the self. The study of a person's own experience of her or his life-span requires attending to the operations of the narrative form and to how this life story is related to the stories of others.

We find the knowledge and beliefs, the meaning systems that people have embedded in their stories – often the knowledge and beliefs are not explicit but in some way buried within the narrative, which it is told in relation to the social situation of the story-teller and in this sense it is often left to the listener(s) to interpret the story. Indeed, the narrative often contains meaning that the story-teller might find difficult to tell in any other form since it is a form of tacit knowledge. Indeed, 'to affirm anything implies, then, to this extent an appraisal of our own art of knowing, and the establishment of truth becomes decisively dependent on a set of personal criteria of our own which cannot be formally defined' (Polanyi, 1962: 71). In this sense, we know – even though we might discover at a later date that our knowledge was deficient or relative to our time and place.

Part 3: Women's way of knowing

One study, above all, reflects the relativity of our personal knowledge, and that is Belenky *et al.*'s (1986) study of women's ways of knowing. Although this book records analyses of interviews with 135 women, the ways of knowing discussed could just as easily relate to men – and this is something that the authors recognise. They suggested that there are five ways of knowing although two of them are subdivided:

1 silence;
2 received knowledge – listening to the voices of others;
3 subjective knowledge
     – the inner voice
     – the quest for self;
4 procedural knowledge
     – the voice of reason
     – separate and connected knowing;
5 constructed knowledge – integrating voices.

Each will now be briefly discussed in turn.

Silence

In this study, those who are silent are among the most socially and economically deprived people and have no confidence in themselves. They conform without question, feel powerless and think that even knowledge about themselves is to be found in other people rather than in themselves. Belenky *et al.* describe them as 'deaf and dumb'.

Received knowledge

This type of learning is exhibited by those who listen to the voices of others but have no confidence to articulate their own thoughts. They assume that the others know and that there is only one answer to most problems. In the same way, those who are the receivers of knowledge listen to the voice of authority, including teachers and well-known personalities, and this is one of the reasons why many advertisers use well-known personalities to promote their brands. Since others know, they even know about us and so we, the receivers of knowledge, look to them to tell us about ourselves.

Subjective knowledge – the inner voice

The women in this survey moved from passivity to active knowing at different ages in their lives as a result of listening to their own 'inner voice'. This move resulted in a greater sense of independence, and Belenky *et al.* (ibid.: 56) suggest that it is a change in their personal lives that enabled them to have this freedom. Similarly, Aslanian and Brickell (1980), who surveyed 744 adult learners by telephone, found that 83 per cent specified a life transition as the reason why they started learning, or became engaged in education again. The socialisation process enables us to learn to play our role in society but we need to feel free of the social structures if we are to grow and develop beyond the level into which we are socialised. It is when we are removed from the support mechanisms into which we have been socialised that we learn that we are a valuable resource for our own knowing and so we begin to listen to our own thoughts.

Subjective knowledge – the quest for self

As we develop, we leave our past behind but we still find it difficult to reflect upon our thoughts since this is a transition stage: while we are both still listening to others and trying to listen to ourselves, we are going through a preparatory phase for critical and reflective thought.

Procedural knowledge – the voice of reason

This emerges out of the clash between the external voice of authority and the inner voice of subjectivism. It is in this phase that we learn that it is not our opinion but the procedures that we use to gain that knowledge that are being assessed. Here we have to be given licence to disagree openly with those in authority and learn the procedures for gaining and justifying our own knowledge – 'form predominates over content' (Belenky *et al.*, 1986: 95) – and there is a development of objectivity.

Procedural knowledge – separate and connected knowing

At the heart of separate knowing, suggest Belenky *et al.* (ibid.: 104), is critical thinking since we have to be critical of our own ideas. There is a sense of objectivity so that we try to dissociate ourselves from the subjectivism of other earlier positions and examine the propositions without reference to the people – this is an impersonal world. Connected knowing, by contrast, is based on the idea that knowing comes from personal experience and knowers have to be able to empathise with each other since knowers try to appreciate each other's experience. They (ibid.: 121) suggest that connected knowing is also procedural but the procedures have not yet been elaborately codified, although interaction rituals are thoroughly researched and Clark (1997) has subsequently undertaken a lot of research into sympathy, especially in interaction situations, which may illustrate some of the interaction dynamics that underlie connected knowing.

The things that make these two forms of knowing similar are that there are procedures and that there is an attempt to ensure that both forms of knowledge are objective.

Constructed knowledge

This is the form of knowledge when knowers seek to integrate both their own subjective intuitions and knowledge with that which comes from outside of themselves: it is the construction of our own personal knowledge. Belenky *et al.* (1986: 137) note that all knowledge is constructed and the knower is part of the construction.

Belenky *et al.*'s study is not only a study of women, it is a very thorough study of the different ways of knowing and how women grow through these stages as they change their social position and gain more confidence in themselves. At the same time it reflects something of the relativity of knowing and demonstrates that personal knowing is not the same as objective knowledge – there is a sense that although personal knowing is about meaning it is also related very closely to beliefs – beliefs about our own lives and about the world in which we live.

Part 4: Knowing ourselves

This is a section that might have been placed in the section on reflection but it is deliberately separated here because there is a form of reflection when we reflect upon ourselves and upon our actions: it is a way of knowing about ourselves. It is the inner conversation that we have with ourselves – the I–Me relationship. We all think in language and occasionally talk to ourselves, either aloud or silently – but this conversation is a way of articulating our intentions and in some ways asserting ourselves. It is our self-consciousness. The 'I' is the actor, the agent, but we are also conscious of our place in society and so an internal conversation ensues. The 'Me' is, as Archer (2000: 264–5) suggests, the social person – we have to know our place in society – and this internal discussion is a way of knowing ourselves and our place in society.

This way of knowing, as we reflect upon our lives, has been developed by Dominice (2000) – as we learn from our lives, the information from which we learn is already within us and as we reflect, or meditate, we learn from what we have done or what we feel that we ought to have done in a given situation. This sense of self-awareness is being aware of how we act in society and with people – it is both being aware of it at the time when we are role playing and being aware of it when we review the way that we have performed. This is a mode of awareness that requires our social brain and Goleman (1995: 47) regards it as a neutral mode which maintains its equilibrium even in times of turbulent emotions – it is the socially learned 'Me' when the 'I' reacts to the situation: the I–Me debate is a way of knowing ourselves and the process of reflecting upon it is a learning process.

Part 5: Learning and knowing

Knowing is a biographical phenomenon and, in a sense, reflects the culture of our life-world; even more specifically it reflects our biography within the context of our place in our life-world – or at least the place that we assume. For as long as our interaction with others follows the pattern of previous interactions our knowing is undisturbed – we can presume upon the situation and our knowing is unaffected except that our self-image is reinforced. However, when we have a disjunctural experience, our sense of knowing about the world is disturbed and we have to reassess the situation. This requires new learning, which may be cognitive, affective or action learning, and the outcome of this is biographical change. The disjunctural situations may have arisen through interaction with another in formal or informal situations, through teaching or example, by intention or incidentally, but however it occurs it results in learning.

As we pointed out earlier, knowing is a verb and so it captures something of the temporal nature of personal knowledge – its transience is the very opposite to the idea of unchanging knowledge and knowledge as truth. As we learn, so our way of knowing about the world and our place in it changes. In the Belenky study, above, the women were able to develop and as their social position changed so did their way of knowing and as their way of knowing changed so did their attitude to the world, and so on. In a sense, they became changed – or more experienced – persons.

Conclusion

As we are beginning to see, in the whole person it is hard to distinguish knowing from thinking, perception, meaning, and so on. This reflects the integrated nature of the person in society and the next chapter reinforces this assertion, since the paradoxical question might be posed here – is knowing a sense of believing about ourselves and our place in the world or is believing one way of knowing about ourselves and our place in the world?

Chapter 11

Believing

The word 'believe' carries connotations of having an attitude towards religion, but it is a much more complex word than this: *Collins English Dictionary* provides us with a list of differing meanings:

- to accept a statement as true or real;
- to be convinced of the existence of;
- to have religious faith;
- to think, suppose or assume;
- to think that someone is able to do, e.g. I think she can do it.

From the above definitions, it is clear that believing is similar to knowing and we can understand why this is since a great deal of personal knowledge cannot easily be legitimised and, even if it could be, it is subjective rather than objective. Subjectivity might be equated with a belief as opposed to knowledge. However, in everyday thinking, believing is to do with religious faith or uncertainty, and the fact that both of these connotations are built into the same word carries its own message. Although we can see all of these meanings here, the main focus of this chapter will revolve around belief, whether it is political, religious or ideological, and this is because belief is very closely associated with the concepts of 'meaning' and truth. In this chapter, therefore, we will first of all discuss believing in relation to meaning and truth; then we will look at the nature of religion, religious belief and theological interpretation; third, we will examine faith development; and, finally, we will look at learning and spirituality – including both the spiritual elements of learning itself and spiritual (emotional) experience.

Part I: Believing, meaning and truth

Clearly, we learn to believe in the potentiality of someone, or something (the fifth meaning given above), as a result of previous experiences with/ of that person or phenomenon. Carrying those previous meanings of what we have learned about that person or phenomenon in our mind, we can express the belief that that person or phenomenon is capable of doing a certain thing or achieving a specified condition. We might say, 'I know she can do it', and this expresses an even greater element of certainty. In this case our beliefs are clearly based upon our previous experiences of a phenomenon or person and what we have either intentionally or more often unintentionally learned about them

Such statements are usually circumspect, and the only truth in them is that this is the belief that we hold – not that the belief itself is true. Nevertheless, there are times when people express what others would see as beliefs in terms of personal truths or even objective truths. This is true of religious and political fundamentalism and even anti-religious fundamentalism. Religious fundamentalism is often based on the belief of revealed knowledge, that is that a thing is true because 'God has said so', and we see this belief expressed in beliefs about the inerrant accuracy of the Bible or the religious claims, maybe, of the Church of Rome. Anti-religious fundamentalism is based on similar claims about both the accuracy and the meaning of scientific research. Perhaps a classical contemporary example is the claim that there is no God because the facts of biological and genetic evolution do not need a God to enact the process of natural selection. Clearly, there is a great deal of evidence for biological and a growing amount for genetic evolution, but facts have no meaning in themselves and so there is a great jump in logic to claim that because evolution is true we have proven that there is no God – all we have actually proven is that biological and genetic evolution occurs and that the previous believed function of God in this process is not a precisely accurate belief. In this sense, we learn our beliefs from experience in precisely the same way as any other learning, and we place meaning on facts. Thus, some people, for example thinkers such as Dawkins (2006) and Dennett (2006), place an anti-religious meaning (belief) on the facts of evolution. The claim of truth for their position is suspect because the leap from the fact to the meaning is based not on evidence, only on beliefs. Without wanting to enter this debate here, since it is beyond the parameters of this book, one would do well to point out that others who hold similar views to Dawkins about science draw completely opposite conclusions from the data (see McGrath, 2007). Belief is not truth, as this simple example makes clear; although the facts themselves might be indisputable, the meaning placed upon them is disputable. The meaning might be inferred from the facts, but it is not intrinsic to them – meanings are, therefore, belief statements, with the degree of certainty varying from high to low.

Thus, we give meaning to experiences and also to events and phenomena, and this meaning is based upon our beliefs, even if the evidence for attributing the meaning seems very strong. In this way, we can claim that the meaning we give phenomena and experiences is true only in as far as the evidence that we have implies that this is the case. There is a human potentiality to attribute meaning to facts, and this is also one of the under-lying foundations for religion itself. However, we are now confronted with two very similar dangers: that we equate the meaning that we give to the situation with the event itself – and this is common in everyday learning – and the meaning is actually treated as the reality since in the ideas of some post-modern thinkers the reality is contained within the language. For instance, when we hear a sound that we do not know, we are conscious of the sound, in other words we are having a primary experience, but it is only when we know the meaning of a sound that we give the sound meaning – a secondary experience. In the same way, when we have a pri-mary experience of a taste of a food that we do not know we are perhaps more conscious of the taste. However, when we have learned the meaning that our society gives to the sound we tend to take the sound for granted and use the meaning in everyday speech, and when we try to explain the meaning to someone else we provide them with a secondary experience. Similarly with taste – once we know the name of the food, the sense experi-ence becomes secondary to the cognitive use of the word – we have named the experience – and we can talk about it without reference to the primary experience any more. Then the second danger is that the meaning that we give the experience is actually treated as the reality itself rather than a mediation of that reality – what Foucault (1979) called discursive fact; that is, we treat a subjective description of an event as if it were the event itself rather than an interpretation of a primary experience which is then presented to us, our secondary experience, as if it is a fact. Hence we can begin to see the need for critical thinking in order to deconstruct language and try to understand the event itself.

The question may then be posed as to whether there is an objective truth or whether everything is a matter of belief. Perhaps one answer to this lies in the fact that when we discussed knowledge we examined ways of legitimising it; we argued that empirical and historical facts are true but meaningless and pragmatic fact is true but only in specified conditions when it 'works'. We also discussed the logical/rational position, but in this case we have to start with a premise that we accept, otherwise the out-come of the argument is not valid. Meaning is always a matter of belief, and fanatics claim that their meaning is true whereas a faith position is essentially agnostic although accepting of the cultural meaning is respect of personal belief.

Part 2: Towards an understanding of religious and theological interpretation

From the previous discussion, I want to emphasise five things here:

1 We all experience disjuncture; that is, we all ask questions such as 'Why?' 'How?'

2 We all have primary experiences about existence, our being, the world, the cosmos, and so on – these are universal primary experiences.
3 We all seek answers to those questions, which is a form of learning from secondary experience if we accept the cultural propositions of our society – these answers are ones previously devised and incorporated into a social narrative.
4 We actually transform experience through our learning – Foucault (1979) terms it discursive fact.
5 We all seek to transmit social narratives to others.

It is necessary to recognise that all academic disciplines and, indeed, all learning begin from these points. Learning truly is an existential phenomenon. Having established these points, it is now necessary to distinguish between religious experience and theological understanding, and it is necessary to point out that there are a wide variety of definitions on both ideas and so the ones that are produced here are no more than working definitions that enable us to understand the learning process a little more clearly.

At one end of the spectrum, Otto (1959 [1917]) sought to analyse religious experience. For him, the heart of the religion is the experience of the *numen* – a mental state which is irreducible to any other (ibid.: 21) – which he regarded as *mysterium tremendum*. Included in the experience are a sense of creature dependency in the face of the aweful and overpoweringness of the wholly other, which is both full of energy and completely encapsulating. In a similar manner, William James (1960 [1901–02]: 53–4) wrestled with this problem:

> The sense of the world's presence, appealing as it does to our peculiar individual temperament, make us either strenuous or careless, devout or blasphemous, gloomy or exultant, about life at large; and our reaction, involuntary and inarticulate and often half-conscious as it is, is the completest of all our answers to the question, 'What is the character of this universe in which we dwell?'

He goes on to argue that the quality of the experience is what makes it religious and he (ibid.: 64) concludes this element of his argument by stating:

> There is a state of mind, known to religious men and no others, in which the will to assert ourselves and hold our own has been displaced by a willingness to close our mouths and be as nothing in the floods and waterspouts of God. In this state of mind, what we most dreaded has become the habitation of our safety, and the hour of our mortal death has turned into our spiritual birthday.

This is a more theistic response; it contains within it something of a cognitive, theological interpretation but it still points back to the primary experience. However, James is more precise about religious experience when he writes (ibid.: 50) that religion is:

> The feelings, acts, and experiences of individual men in their solitude, as far as they apprehend themselves to stand in relation to whatever they may consider the divine.

Elsewhere, James (Capps and Capps, 2005: 144–61) points us to the other aspect of experience – radical empiricism. We live in a world in which we have to make sense of the sensations that we experience and our making sense of them is a scientific enterprise. We also learn facts from empirical investigations into phenomena, and these can also be transmitted and learned. In contrast Berger (1969: 26) suggests that religion is 'the human enterprise by which a sacred cosmos is established'. It is a making sense of the world and giving explanation to it. Consequently, we can say that at the heart of religion itself is the sense of disjuncture caused by experiences both of being and/or of the cosmos, which raise these questions for which there is no obvious answer but for which we we try to provide the answers: this is both universal and subjective. We cannot learn subjective experience: we can only experience it. Indeed, it is part of the human condition. However, we try to make sense of these experiences and give them meaning – often the meaning that we give them is taken from a narrative that has been propounded in the historical past and has become embedded in societies' cultures. These religious stories are the narratives of established religions, although few of them exist in a single form – there are usually many variations on the theme – orthodoxies and heresies, and so on. Naturally, not all explanations of these experiences either get accepted or become embedded into any society's culture: many teachers are not charismatic, do not gain a following or expound their views at times when the people are unable to accept or receive them. However, as these teachings get incorporated into society's culture, the socially ascribed meaning becomes a discursive fact and those teachers whose explanations are accepted are generally legitimised with special status or even 'divine' acclamation: this is true in many cultures of the world and for most of the world's great religions.

But these interpretations, built into different cultures, tend to emphasise the difference between them rather than the similarity of the experiences upon which these interpretations are built. At a study day held during the time this book was being written (10 September 2008 – in Swindon, UK) five speakers from different religions (Buddhist, Christian, Hindu, Jewish and Muslim) each spoke about their beliefs to an audience of over 50 people. At the end there was both a sense of surprise and agreement that there was so little difference between them. The organiser for that day, the author of this book, was subsequently asked if he would organise another day when extremists were invited to speak so that the differences that divide the world could be understood.

We are now in a position to return to our understanding of learning. Learning is an existential phenomenon, but there are two different ways in which we experience the world – through primary and secondary experience. From the primary experience, we may be able to gain a sense of meaning or we may be just lost in the wonder of creation itself – we may call these experiences religious or they may go by some other name, such as spiritual. However, once we seek to give meaning to them we begin to move from primary to secondary experience, and when we try to teach others about the explanations that we have accepted we are providing them with secondary experiences. Significantly, in religious conversion, primary experiences are created or recreated and their explanation is often fitted into the narrative of the secondary experience. At this point, it is possible to discuss the idea of teaching theology, or belief systems, religious education, and so on.

But it is necessary to point out that we cannot teach anybody religious experience – they have to experience that for themselves and learn from it; perhaps, however, traditional religious systems of meaning can actually help us interpret our experience from within the framework of our own religious narrative and we can also provide individuals with many opportunities to learn theology, religious history, philosophy and morality, and so on. For instance, Ricoeur (1995: 56), in his discussion of proclamation, points out that the whole of the Hebraic faith of the Old Testament is based around discourses, not experiences of the numinous. This is also the logic of any form of communication since it is just not possible to communicate the numinous experience, and so we are confined to language and, therefore, to the meaning that can provide secondary experience. The meanings need to gain acceptance in the community, and either they will be those ascribed by the elite of the community of practice to their own numinous experiences or they will reflect the meanings assumed and accepted by the community leaders. The logic of this is that gradually prevailing interpretations achieve an accepted status – an orthodoxy, if you like – which reflects one's membership of the community of practice. Significantly, the orthodoxy is based upon secondary experience and, therefore, is learned from secondary experience rather than primary ones; it is learned through socialisation – both primary and secondary socialisation – and children tend to reflect their communities of origin's belief systems although later in life they can grow beyond them.

Consequently, new members of any faith community need not have had the numinous experience so long as they accept the meaning system that they are taught by the community, and this system can change in dialogue with other systems of meaning without reference to any primary experience. Interestingly enough, this is precisely what Mezirow (1991: 12–13) regards as learning. He writes (ibid.: 12) that

> Learning may be understood as the process of using a prior interpretation to construe a new or a revised interpretation of the meaning of one's experience in order to guide a future action.

Consequently, we can see how transformative learning theory has emerged and how it deals with other than the linguistic and cognitive level of learning. Although Mezirow might not use his theory in the way that we are applying it here, its use here also fits within the overall theory of experiential and existential leaning that we have developed.

But there is another scenario that we might paint at this time. Imagine two people standing together, one a Christian and the other a Muslim. Both view a magnificently beautiful scene and have a profound religious experience but one interprets it from a Christian perspective and the other from a Muslim one. Each interpretation makes sense to the person who has the experience, and both individually make sense when related to the members of their faith community, but they may appear totally different experiences because they are described differently on account of the different cognitive starting points of the two people. Indeed, this might now be taken one stage further since we can only describe how the numinous manifests itself rather than the experience itself; we do not know whether we experienced the same thing. Even if we assume it was, we are still faced with the problem of bridging the gap between different life-worlds, and only through intensive dialogue between the two people who have these experiences are we in a position to reach agreement, which is precisely how Habermas (1987) understands communicative action. At this point different faiths can join together, and this lies at the heart of inter-faith dialogue.

But do those people who claim no religious adherence have similar experiences? Newman (2006: 218), a scholar who now claims no religious adherence, wrote these words:

> Things happened when I walked out on that hillside in the far south of France. I was struck, confronted, taken over, by the context. Background suddenly became all-enveloping foreground. I was in the middle of a huge globe made up of sharp clear blue sky, the mountains, the hills, the vines, the brown earth and the stone walls, and the roadway, I felt the heat. My feet were firmly planted on the roadway, but I felt a 'pull' down into the floor of the valley and up the hillside to the mountains and the sky. There was no sound, but it was if there were a noise giving a texture and a volume and density to the entire space. I stood still for a time but it was, as the hackneyed phrase has it, time itself stood still.

Newman recognises that he was disorientated by an experience that he could not explain – he was left in a disjunctural situation with his experience, but still he had it. Perhaps it was a rumour – in Berger's words – that he did not hear, or perhaps it leaves itself open to another interpretation, as Newman (2008) himself suggests. The point is that the experience takes us beyond the bounds of normal rationality and we might be agnostic as to its having any meaning, and we might even contemplate it – as Newman did – but we might give it a meaning or accept one that others give and have faith in it.

Part 3: Faith development

Having faith, in one sense, is a trust that what has previously happened in our lives will continue to happen, so that as children we can trust, or have faith, that our significant others will continue to love us and care for us. Faith is not always a religious phenomenon but it is an existential one. But an extension of this is in making a step between recognising that the meaning we give, or we learn about anything, is not merely a belief or a trust statement, but either a hope or a belief that it is a statement of truth. In this sense, theist and atheist are in the same boat in that they both express a faith position, whereas the only logically rational position is an agnostic one: a position that recognises that there is insufficient evidence to claim that a meaning is true. Certain scientists may claim that their evidence for atheism is extremely strong, but the position they espouse is still a faith position – even though they may proclaim it as the truth. We learn meaning or even theological systems of meaning, and we might invest emotional energy in that meaning system and it is this that leads to faith and commitment.

Religions have systems of meaning and they exist in every culture, so that children are socialised into the meaning system or systems of their society or life-world: they learn that they are true. But there have often been doubters as to the truth of these statements, and such doubters may seek new explanations, which they then expound, in the process sometimes becoming the teachers of new systems of meaning. This is especially true in times of rapid social change, either when people are mobile or because the structures of society have changed and new knowledge has been introduced. But people still seek to understand and give meaning to their existence. Faith is, according to Fowler (1981: 14), 'the most human category in the human quest for relation to transcendence. Faith, it appears, is generic, a universal feature of human living'. In a later book, Fowler (1996) argued that faith actually sustains people through these times of rapid individual, interpersonal and systemic change.

In this sense, we can see that faith, like learning itself, is an existential phenomenon and will therefore depend upon our learning and will change as we grow and develop, so that we can see that it is possible to understand it in relation to cognitive development: this is precisely what Fowler (1981) endeavoured to do. Taking as a base the work of Piaget (see Chapter 9), Kohlberg (see Chapter 14), Erikson (1965) and Levinson *et al.* (1978), Fowler studied people's faith and constructed a developmental system starting with infancy and having six stages thereafter.

Recognising the significance of infancy, Fowler sees this initial stage as 'undifferentiated faith' since during these early days of life babies exist only because of the love and concern of significant others and so they learn love, trust, hope, and so on, in these relationships and in the people. We briefly looked at this stage during the opening chapters of this book and saw just how significant it is in human development.

Thereafter, Fowler suggests six stages. The first is intuitive–projective faith, which emerges with language and symbolic representation and is a response to the 'why?' questions that children raise during this period, which is a very imaginative time. This stages covers the years from three to seven; it is a phase of imitation, which reflects Tomasello's understanding, and which we discussed earlier, and is permanently influenced by other people's behaviour. Stage 2 is the mythic–literal stage in which children take on the stories of their culture or life-world: it is a literal phase but it is also one of morality in as much as fairness in relationships comes to the fore. This is the school child's faith, and it predominates until contradictory stories of meaning cause the young child to reflect on them and to begin to make decisions about them

Stage 3 is that of conventional–synthetic faith, which emerges in early adolescence although many adults will remain at this stage in their faith development. This stage is reached when our individual life-world transcends school or the immediate family as the various sectors of social living have to fit into the meaning system of the young person. Fowler (1981: 172–3) describes this stage thus:

> It structures the ultimate environment in interpersonal terms. Its images of unifying value and power derive from the extension of qualities experienced in personal relationships. It is a 'conformist' stage in the sense that it is acutely attuned to the expectations and judgments of significant others and as yet does not have a sure enough grasp on its own identity or autonomous judgment to construct and maintain an independent perspective. While beliefs and values are deeply felt, they are tacitly held – the person 'dwells' in them and in the meaning world they mediate. But there has not been occasion to step outside them to reflect on or examine them explicitly or systematically.

Once we can step outside of this world then there may be clashes in the orthodoxies that we have accepted and even clashes with those significant others, or even authority figures, who have been regarded as the sources of our meaning system. This clash may well reflect the adolescents' drive for independence, and this gives rise to an individual thoughtful stage which Fowler called 'individuative–reflective'. This is stage 4: now our identity has been freed from the constraints of the group and the self is differentiated from others. This is clearly a cultural phase, which may be very different in Westerners from in people from Confucian heritage countries, where the family and the social group are much more significant than they are in the West; in the West, according to Fowler, this is a dymythologising stage. However, Fowler's work was conducted about 30 years ago, and so the technological/scientific culture of contemporary culture may well have shifted this change in faith development to an earlier age. It is a much more complex understanding of meaning, and often one that is also quite secular but it is, nevertheless, still a faith position.

Fowler suggests that the next stage, conjunctive faith, rarely begins for those who move from the fourth stage until middle age: it seeks to combine different interpretations of meaning – even different meaning systems. Now the knower has to be 'capable of dialogue' (ibid.: 185) and self-certainty has to decline. It is, as it were, 'the mid-life crisis', when we begin to look back and, at the same time, face an unknown future aware that there may be no truth. But this phase may never occur in those who are certain of their beliefs, whether they are theist or atheist. In this phase there is a paradoxical relationship between the relativity of belief systems and the desire to hold on to an unchanging system of meaning or the truth.

Finally, there is a universalising faith which occurs but rarely:

> The persons described by it have generated faith compositions in which their felt sense of an ultimate environment is inclusive of all being. They have become incarnators and actualizers of the spirit of an inclusive and fulfilled world community.

They are people who have stepped outside the normal faith development process; they provide their own answers to the ultimate questions, they develop their own systems of meaning and sometimes they seek converts to their systems. It is these who are persecuted by those whom they try to change because they are seeking to introduce something new and which has, apparently, stood the test of time.

Fowler's approach, albeit Judeo-Christian in its theoretical framework, does seek to point beyond the traditionally Western Christian, although it is not really capable of being extended to other cultures without considerably more research. Nevertheless, it does point us to the fact that our faith is learned, often non-reflectively and often unintentionally, through experience. His approach fits clearly into our understanding experiential learning and it points us to the need for more comparative research into how we learn and become committed to religious stories and how we remain committed to them even after we have apparently developed beyond them.

Part 4: Spiritual dimensions of human learning

In this part we will show that learning itself points to a spiritual dimension in human existence, a dimension that presupposes no theological interpretations at all. We will explore the idea of learning itself; disjuncture and experience; aspects of reflection; meaning; self-identity.

Human learning

It is impossible to conceptualise a human being who has never learned since learning epitomises our humanity and, in a similar manner, it is as impossible to think of a time when the living human being stops learning – apart from the vegetative state. Learning is intrinsic to our humanity – it is world-forming (Heidegger cited in Agamben, 2004: 51) – but, as Luckmann (1967) suggests, when we transcend our biological nature then a religious experience occurs. In this sense all our leaning is religious. But if we continue to grow and develop as a result of our learning, then humanity is an unfinished project, and this raises another, unanswerable, question: what is the end of our learning? What, then, is the end of our humanity? Why are we here? Are we here just to keep on learning? No answer to these questions, secular or sacred, is completely satisfactory, and so, if we ask them, we are confronted with an unanswerable: a void that reflects the human condition itself. This 'nothingness' points us beyond the scientific and empirical to perhaps a spiritual space, but once it has done this we can learn little more about the unfathomable mystery of human existence itself.

Disjuncture and experience

As we have argued in earlier parts of this book, our lives comprise a series of experiences made up in such a way that our biography appears as continuous experience added to by each unique event of learning which we call an experience. But each of these begins with the same type of question that we posed earlier: Why has this occurred? How do I do this? What does this mean? And so on. It can be cognitive, emotional or a combination of the two: this is disjuncture. Whereas we learn to live with our ultimate disjunctural questions, we are frequently confronted with less ultimate ones that stimulate our learning or which leave us in a state of having learned once again that we do not know all the answers to our questions. Consequently, we can see that it is disjuncture itself that drives learning – it is emptiness and void that underlie our need to learn, for our learning is the continuous attempt to establish harmony between our experience and our understanding of the world. In this sense, it reflects our need to discover answers that enable us to live in harmony both with our environment and with ourselves. But we sometimes feel the need to reach out beyond our taken-for-granted, beyond our everyday, since there are still more things to learn and to do – for a paradox of our responding to our disjunctural experiences is that we are immediately confronted with new disjunctures – for life is a journey to we know not where.

Experience, as we have already noted, is a problematic concept since our primary ones are sense experiences and secondary ones are cognitive. Each of the five senses (sight, smell, sound, taste and touch) can be the start of a learning experience. Children seek to give meaning to their sense experiences, and we might wonder why they do this since no fact or arte-fact has intrinsic meaning, but, as we have pointed out already, the very process of human learning is an element of the human condition in which we endeavour to give meaning to the apparently meaninglessness. Children give names to the artefacts with which they play – the names are usually approved of by our culture, but it is these sense experiences that can take us beyond the cognitive to the emotional: What a gorgeous sound! How beautiful is this scene! What a tranquil moment! And so on. In these situations the experience is disjunctural because the beauty, tranquillity, etc., take us outside of our taken-for-granted world and we are confronted with the extraordinary – something that has no meaning or explanation in itself but is something so extraordinary that we want to hang on to it for as long as we can – a magic moment – yet, paradoxically, we know that we can give no empirical meaning to it. It was, as we noted above, James's (1960 [1901–02]) starting point for religious experience.

Reflection

It is here that attentive experiencing becomes contemplation – a form of reflective learning that I have discussed in all my models of learning from the very first (Jarvis, 1987). But that reflection need not be the cold rational learning of modernity; it might well be wonder at the mystery of the experience (Otto, 1959 [1917]), the admiration, even the worshipful attitude, of the believer. Reflective learning can take learners outside themselves provided that they have the time to think about their experience – a point that Crawford makes very strongly. We learn through reflection, but our answers might merely reveal that the world in which we are learning is itself a mystery that is slowly being uncovered by science but that beauty, awe, wonder are emotions that can take us beyond the scientific to make us aware of the non-material dimensions of human existence.

Meaning

Learning is a process of meaning making, but writers such as Mezirow (1991) regard it as a process of transforming meaning whereas I regard learning as a process of transforming experience and giving it meaning as well as transforming meaning into new meaning. The search for meaning is a paradoxical experience (Jarvis, 1992); from the moment we discover a meaning it leads to new questions, and so on. As soon as we begin the endeavour we realise that there is no intrinsic meaning to existence itself and that we have to give it meaning – something that has been recognised from time immemorial. In the creation myth, recorded just a few hundred years before the beginning of the Christian era, Adam gave names to the animals of the world. Every meaning that we produce gives rise to further questions about Being itself for, like learning, the human condition is always a journey that appears to have no end. Meaning is transient and a matter of belief since there is no empirical answer to the question of meaning itself.

Self-identity

The outcome of every learning experience is that it is incorporated into our identities: through our learning we are creating our biographies. We are continually becoming – an existential being; but what are we becoming and why we are becoming remain the problematics of existence itself. Our identity is neither an empirical nor a scientific phenomenon – it is not intrinsic to our body but is constructed as a result of our being and acting and from our learning. Indeed, we become selves but Chalmers (1996), amongst other philosophers, concludes that we do not merely have psychological selves residing in the brain but that there is a metaphysical self that occurs beyond it. Significantly, once we enter the debate about the brain and the mind, some of the more 'scientific' theories of learning, such as behaviourism and information processing, appear unsustainable philosophically. To be able to claim an identity is to make a spiritual statement for 'I' have become myself as a result of my learning.

Amongst the four aims of lifelong learning in the European Commission (2001) policy document is that of fulfilling our human potential: this one is rarely discussed in depth since the word 'potential' is itself a problem. Potential seems to suggest that there is an innate set of abilities that can be drawn out from us as we learn but it is a restrictive concept. But the nature of our humanity is potentiality itself (Agamben, 1990: 42). If we can keep on learning we can transcend totality, in Levinas's (1991) sense, and he argues that in relationship with others, which is the beginning of religion, we can learn to reach towards infinity:

> To approach the other in conversation is to welcome his expression, in which at each instance he overflows the idea a thought would carry away with it. It is therefore to *receive* from the Other beyond the capacity of the I, which means exactly: to have the idea of infinity. But this also means: to be taught. The relation with the Other, or Conversation, is a non-allergic relation; but in as much as it is welcomed this conversation is teaching (enseignment). Teaching is not reducible

to maieutics; it comes from the exterior and brings me more than I contain. In its non-violent transitivity the very epiphany of the face is produced.

(ibid.: 51; italics in original)

So, then, in a learning relationship we can transcend ourselves and reach towards infinity. There are, therefore, in the learning processes dimensions that reflect spirituality as being intrinsic to the human being.

Conclusion

Through this process of believing we can see that learning is often un-intended and even pre-conscious, but it is clear that belief is rarely entirely cognitive: it is also emotional since it often demands commitment. As Fowler points out, some of those who achieve the highest stages of faith development are persecuted by their peers, especially if they try to teach others to accept their own interpretations of reality and the meaning system that they develop and to which they become committed. However, commitment is not merely an intellectual phenomenon – it is also an emotional one.

Chapter 12

Feeling – emotions

In recent years, as we have gradually recognised that the rationality of modernity is not actually the controlling force of human action, the study of emotions has become much more prevalent and we have begun to see it creeping into learning theory. Yet we have always known about the significance of the emotions since we have been aware of the 'cold fish', e.g. an intellectual who does not enjoy human company, and the homely woman who just delights in people – the one socially inept and the other socially adept. But it would be unwise to juxtapose cognitive intellect with social behaviour. At the same time the psychologist and the sociologist may view emotion differently. In this chapter we will examine the concept of emotions, seek to understand their base in the human being, recognise their place in human experience, explore their place in learning theory, and see both how we can learn them and also how we can learn to control them.

Collins English Dictionary defines emotions as 'any strong feeling' but the same dictionary provides many definitions of feeling – sense of touch; the ability to experience sensations; a state of mind; physical or mental impressions, such as a sense of warmth, fondness, sympathy; to feel deeply about a person; a sentiment; a mood or an emotional disturbance; intuitive understanding, sensibility; and so on. All common words and common experiences, and so it is surprising that for so long studies of the emotions were to a considerable extent the preserve of novelists and therapists. Among the few scholars from other disciplines who recognised the significance of emotions in human behaviour even fewer actually provide us with a definition that captures the essence of this sense of feeling which we regard as emotional.

Part 1: The concept of emotion

As the wide variety of definitions noted above indicate, the concept of emotion is a very complex one – almost impossible to define. From the outset there is a major conceptual problem – a feeling is a conscious state but it could well be argued that many of our emotions occur in unconscious states and still affect our behaviour and so we should not regard the two terms as synonymous.

Philosophically, emotion is probably best known in the theory of emotivism developed in ethics, in which statements such as 'she is a good student' are regarded not as statements of fact – being neither true nor false – but as merely conveying a positive feeling. We all know that we have used language in this way, but we may wish to convey more than our emotions, we wish to convey some construction of reality about the student. We will not enter this debate any further here, but it does demonstrate how emotion was viewed by schools of philosophers in the twentieth century. In psychology, for many years, there were debates between those who considered emotion to be physiological and those who regarded it as cognitive awareness. Indeed, even in the late 1970s, Hilgard *et al.* (1979: 329) asserted that the 'nature of the relationship between motivation and emotion, as well as the definition of emotion itself, is an unresolved issue in psychology'. A few years later, McAdams (2000: 636–7) recognised the central significance of emotion to life itself, and he cites Tompkins (1981: 322) when he suggested that 'the primary function of the affect is urgency . . . to make one care by feeling'. Following Tompkins, he also recognised the difference between primary and secondary emotions and also the positive and negative valences of the emotions. The primary emotions are biological whereas the secondary have a more cultural basis. But the whole idea of the human being as a sophisticated machine with a computer-like mind has hindered the development of the study of the emotions. Goleman (1995), however, captures a much more solid understanding of the emotions within the person, and we will return to some of his discussion below.

In contrast, sociologists have spent much more time examining the social functions of the emotions since they have long recognised that emotions are the social glue by which society is held together and that many emotional states are the outcome of social situations – but this highlights one of the problems that some sociologists have experienced since they tend to overemphasise the cultural dynamic. But emotions are also divisive and split society, and they even lead to individualism. For instance, many years ago, in 1903, Simmel realised the significance of the money economy on lifestyle and even on thinking itself: he claimed that as a result people have become more calculative (Simmel, 1971: 82–93) and act with their head rather than their heart and so the money economy society was producing a more individualistic and rational society – even human rationality might be a product of the emotions. By contrast, other sociologists, such as Durkheim (1915), were looking for those elements that helped society to gel – such as emotion in religion and ritual. Even in sociology it is recognised that the terms that relate to emotions and feelings are used very loosely, and this may be because of the complexity of the human experience.

One very close relationship that needs to be highlighted from the outset is that between emotion and motivation – motivation drives behaviour in a way that rationality cannot. Collins (1990; quoted in Turner and Stets, 2005) uses the term 'emotional energy' to reflect this drive to act, in the way that Goleman (1995) used emotional intelligence to describe people's expertise in social behaviour, which has led to his subsequent study on what he calls 'social intelligence (Goleman, 2006).

However, there is a danger in seeking to define a phenomenon by its functions, which is that anything that performs those functions may be regarded as part of that phenomenon and yet, at the present time, it is still problematic to try to delineate emotions from other similar phenomena.

Part 2: Emotions within the human being

From the above discussion we can see that emotions have been divided into primary and secondary ones and the primary ones are those that have been built into ourselves as a result of our evolutionary past – that is, they are hard-wired. This means that the emotions may be generated before conscious awareness because the seat of the emotions in the mammalian brain is the amygdala. Although most sense experiences are transferred to the brain via the thalamus, some neurons take a shortcut to the amygdala, which as a result receives sense information milliseconds before the social brain does; thus, our immediate reactions are emotional, occurring before they are rational. Goleman (1995: 16) regards this as an emotional sentinel that is able to highjack the brain but, moreover, this direct route to the brain can speed up reactions by minute fractions of a second that may have been significant for survival in our prehistoric past. Consequently, we may show some physical response to experiences just a moment before our cognition kicks in, and this is where sensitivity can occur in human interaction since we can read the non-verbal behaviours in the persons with whom we interact, and these influence the subsequent behaviour. However, as we grow and develop we learn to control our emotions, and we will return to this below. There is, however, some debate about which emotions reflect our evolutionary past and which are more cultural: that is, which are primary and which are secondary. As Turner and Stets (2005) show, there is little agreement between scholars about what constitute the secondary emotions, although there is greater agreement about some of the primary emotions, such as happiness, fear, anger, sadness and disgust (ibid.: 14–15). Turner and Stets (ibid.: 274) make the point that

> Expanded neurological capacities in emotional centers of the brain should be reflected in a wider range of emotional responses. This enhanced emotionality is still built from the few primary emotions of all mammals, but the combination of a larger neo-cortex coupled with

larger limbic systems may help explain how humans are able to generate the complex and subtle emotions they use to forge social bonds and
to sanction each other.

What becomes clear immediately from this discussion is that primary
emotions are universal and hard-wired into our human being and so we do
not learn these, but what we might well learn is how to control them since
our behaviour is both social and cultural – this is also in part the preserve
of therapy, but we also learn this during our socialisation process from a
very early age. Our temperaments reflect both our ethnic culture and our
socialisation process, and we will return to this later in the chapter.

Emotions, then, are a significant feature in our early evolution, occurring
before the emergence of human rationality, but which are these emotions?
There is considerable debate about which are the primary, hard-wired,
emotions but Turner and Stets (ibid.: 13) suggest that there are at least four
primary emotional continua: satisfaction–happiness, aversion–fear, assertion–anger and disappointment–sadness. Each of these continua reflects
levels of intensity of the relevant emotional state. Turner and Stets refer to
the work of Plutchik (1962, 1980, 2002), who draws the analogy between
primary and secondary colours and primary and secondary emotions: secondary colours are made by mixing the primary colours and so, perhaps,
might not secondary emotions occur in the same manner? But even then
there is some debate as to whether secondary emotions are hard-wired or
whether they are cultural constructs (see Kemper, 1987) but the universality of some secondary emotions may point in the direction of hard-wiring
although cultural differences either deny it or suggest that socialisation
enables them to be controlled, e.g. we can learn to manage our emotions.

Turner and Stets (2005) note that sociologists have studied emotions
from within a dramaturgical framework (Goffman, 1959, *inter alia*); ritualism (Collins, 1987, *inter alia*); symbolic interaction (Freud, 1900; Mead,
1938); exchange theory (Homans, 1961); social structures (Kemper, 1990);
and evolutionary theory (J. Turner, 2000). Clearly, this is not the place to
review all of these approaches, but we can see immediately that many of
these perspectives impinge on learning theory – we learn our emotions or
learn to control them in all the things that we do, and even think, and in
all the interactions that we have. We can see that how we think and behave
reflects our emotional learning, and so it is not surprising that Goleman
(2006) moves on from emotional to social intelligence. From the framework provided by Turner and Stets it would be possible to write a whole
book on learning and the emotions, but this is not the place to do it. Suffice
to note here the centrality of behaviour and the extent to which we learn
emotions or learn to control them, although we will extend this discussion
just a little when we look at emotions and experience.

Part 3: Emotions and experience

At the heart of our understanding of learning is experience: it is the whole person who has the experience and not a part of that person. But, as we have seen, we can have both conscious and pre-conscious experiences and the latter occur before the conscious ones. The pre-conscious ones are those sense experiences – a sight, a sound, a feeling, an emotion, and so on – which are transmitted to the amygdala more directly, and so our first impulse is to respond to the emotive experience rather than the rational explanation that follows soon after. At the same time it is difficult to conceive of an experience that does not have an emotional dimension, so that we can see immediately that the emotional dimension may help determine the experience itself; that is, we feel positive or negative about the experience we are having. Since the emotion actually precedes our rational understanding it is not surprising that Goleman (1995: 17) refers to it as 'the emotional sentinel'. Those experiences that are emotionally charged are more likely to be recalled at a later date than others that are more ordinary and everyday. Hence our biographical memory is likely to be biased in favour of those emotionally changed experiences.

Being aware of our emotional state can help us understand the experiences that we have and also how to transform them in learning episodes – self-awareness is then at the heart of many of our learning experiences, and as such it is transformed with our learning. However, some of our emotional responses may reflect past experiences that we have built into our memories rather than present ones: we may recall traumatic experiences, and these emotions may be triggered by other experiences before the social mind begins to operate, so that our immediate reaction to the present may be out of date and faulty, reflecting those unpleasant experiences in the past. It is when we have these experiences that we need therapy in order to learn how to cope with these more extreme cases in our biographical past and the emotions generated by them.

In sociological studies of the emotions we can see how ritual – of all social forms – can heighten our emotional awareness and affect the type of experience that we have. Ritual heightens the emotions of the group and lowers the barriers between individuals, and the emotion generated affects our experience greatly. In the same way, all forms of social interaction also generate emotions in both actors, unless one or both of them does not have the ability to generate emotions because of a brain state. The ability to control the emotions in social behaviour is learned as part of our socialisation process and controlled by our sensitivity to other people in social interaction. At the centre of learning is both emotion and thought, and the former precedes the latter although, as we can see here, the action dimension is also quite important to the experience itself.

Part 4: Emotions and learning

If we revert to our initial understanding of learning, it is the whole person who has the experience, and we have shown quite clearly that the emotions are at the forefront of personal experience. Understanding how the emotions affect our experience is an important step in understanding our learning. Indeed, disjuncture itself is often a very emotional state since it occurs at times when we can no longer take our life-world for granted: it can lead to anger, frustration, a sense of anticipation and adventure, and so on. The emotional state is likely to occur milliseconds before the cognitive processes and may influence the way that we respond to our experience.

However, we have argued throughout our study of human learning that experience is generated by a sense of disjuncture: when there is a gap between what we expect and what experience in a given situation. We have pointed out that this leads us to ask questions, such as Why? How? and so on. But there is also an emotional response to disjuncture: it may lead to a positive response, since our experience is better than we thought it would be, or negative because it is worse. Learning can be exciting or frightening – we may approach learning differently as a result of our age, our previous experiences, and so on. Nevertheless, this emotional response both affects our understanding of the situation and is built into our learning from the experience. Consequently, all satisfying and stressful experiences might begin with emotional disjuncture. In a very similar manner, but on a macro-scale, Davies (1969; cited in Turner and Stets, 2005: 313) suggested that political and social revolutions are more likely to occur at times when the gap between expectations and the experienced condition increases – in a sense, there is macro-social disjuncture – and people are disappointed with the present or anticipate a better future.

Experiences from which we learn most are nearly always emotionally charged, and these experiences are not necessarily always beneficial, although many are. For instance, advertisements are nearly always full of emotion because they want to persuade people to do something: desire is one of the most frequent emotions portrayed in advertisements – especially in those aimed at children (see Jarvis, 2008): children are targeted because they can be taught to desire to consume and they can pressurise their parents to purchase commodities for them. This is also true of advertisements to adults: adults can be persuaded to do something – to purchase – because they want to be like the others who have already done so, and so on. We can learn emotions from the media because what is offered appeals to our sense of need, ego, identity, and so on.

This brings into question the manner by which we can control our emotions: from the time of our childhood we learn to interact with other people and in the process learn to control our emotions, and much of this occurs incidentally, or even pre-consciously, as a result of social living. In a sense this is one of the tacit skills that we learn in everyday life. But there are also times when we have to do this consciously, and then we need to be self-aware, both of our mood and of our thoughts about our mood (Goleman, 1995: 47). Part of our reflection upon our experience should be an analysis of our emotions as we were having the experience, but an awareness of the thought processes generated by the mood and the ability to reflect in this manner is something that we also have to learn. We have to recognise that feelings are also 'indispensable for rational decisions since they point us in the proper direction, where dry logic can then be of best use' (ibid.: 28).

Learning from our moods teaches us more about ourselves – this meta-cognitive process is a significant part of the way that we learn to be ourselves, since as we learn these things about ourselves, so they are then incorporated into our subsequent behaviour and biography. The aim of our learning, then, is the whole person – one who is emotional and cognitively aware – but the whole person is also a practical person, and we will return to this in the next chapter on 'doing'.

Part 5: Learning to control our emotions

From our early socialisation we learn how to interact with others, what Tomasello (1999) sees as learning to have joint attention in early childhood (and it is in this interaction we also learn how others view our emotional response to situations): it is often a fairly painful learning process as young children learn that they are not the centre of the universe but that other people and their perceptions of our behaviour also matter. Consequently, socialisation, and the tacit knowledge we learn in this process, is a major control mechanism for all of us. In this sense, our behaviour and the way that we express our emotions is learned from within a cultural framework and we reflect the subcultures of our life-worlds, but we also know that positive thinking within this framework breeds success, popularity, and so on – as many popular writers and gurus have reminded us over the years.

However, we are not conformists all the time, and sometimes we deviate from what is expected from us: if we deviate badly and our behaviour becomes either socially or personally destructive, then we need therapy, as Goleman, Rogers and others remind us. In this sense, therapy is a learning experience in which the emotions are as important as, or more important than, the cognition. But we also need to deviate sometimes, just as we need the deviants, who feel strongly about injustice and have visions of better worlds – prophets, leaders and teachers (see Jarvis, 2008) – people who are prepared to stand alone for their convictions: when one emotion, commitment, is stronger than another, which is the will to conform. It is here, in the clash of emotions, that we see other emotions emerge, such as confidence, conviction, and so on.

What we are faced with here is crucial to our understanding of learning. It is interesting that Pinker (1999) called for a new way of thinking about learning, as we saw in an earlier chapter of this book; significantly, Goleman (1998: 244) also calls for a new model of learning. His model, however, is not really a new model, since it can be and has been built into the model offered in this book – but the important thing is that he calls for a model that emphasises the emotional aspects of human life:

> Learning in school is, in essence, adding information and understanding to the memory banks of the neocortex. The neocortex learns by fitting new data and insights into existing frameworks of association and understanding, extending and enriching the corresponding neural circuitry.
>
> But learning an emotional competence involves that and more – it requires that we also engage our emotional circuitry, where our social and emotional habits are stored. Changing such habits – learning to approach people positively instead of avoiding them, to listen better, or to give feedback skilfully – is a more challenging task than simply adding new facts to old. Emotional learning demands a more profound change at the neurobiological level: both weakening the existing habit and replacing it with a better one.
>
> (ibid.: 244)

Goleman goes on to outline the emotional competences that, in his opinion, need to be built into future learning. These are central to human living, and we need to spend more time on these competences than we do on the competences of the work place. In a sense, this is one of the central pillars of learning in the Delors Report (1996), a hope that through lifelong learning we can learn to live together, but Goleman (1998: 245) goes further and suggests that we waste millions of dollars on training programmes that have no lasting impact. This is because we have a deficient understanding of human learning and, although Pinker is correct in calling for a new way of thinking about learning, we are not sure that we would agree entirely with the way that he wishes to develop it. We would argue, however, that correcting this deficiency in our understanding is socially extremely important at the present time in history.

Conclusion

We respond to, and learn from, our experiences, as we are all aware, in cognitive, emotive and practical ways – but there is little connection between cognition and the act of doing. However, there is a much greater connection between emotion and doing, as has already been suggested in reference to advertising: we will purchase because we desire, and therein lies the heart of motivation, to which we will turn in the final chapter in this second section of the book.

People who cannot live with disjuncture are motivated to heal it and to bridge the gap: it is this that is a key to learning, as we have argued in many books and papers, but those who cannot live with emotional disjuncture are those who are motivated to act. It may be a desire to create, to achieve, to help others, a desire to help make a better world, and so on. Goleman (1998: 104–25) gives many examples of ways in which these desires operate, and he emphasises achievement need, commitment, and optimism and initiative – and at the time we put them into action we may not know how to do what is demanded, etc. but we know that if we are to achieve our desires we have to do something about them and we learn in the doing since we will probably not know when we set out!

Chapter 13

Doing

Traditionally, philosophers have talked about *knowing how* and *knowing that* to refer to the practical side of human living, but neither of these terms conveys the actual sense of doing. After all, I can know that if I do a certain thing, it will result in something else occurring, or I could describe how 'x' is performed but it is still not doing 'x'. For instance, I tell people how to play a game of cards but they will not be able to play cards until they have actually held the cards and played the game. The point is that there is no conceptual relationship between *knowing how* or *knowing that* and *being able to*. It is this concern that is the focus of this chapter. At the same time, doing is not just a process of externalising, trying to affect the external world in some way through work or through creative activity; it is experiencing what others do: doing is interaction with the external world and learning through the interaction – learning by doing and learning by having been done by.

Many definitions of learning, including my own, have included skills in order to convey this dimension of living and learning, but in common parlance 'skills' has been restricted to expertise at work, which I feel is too narrow, and so this dimension is here called 'doing', and it seeks to convey a sense of agency of which skills are but a limited aspect. Consequently, the first part of this chapter concentrates on the practicalities of everyday life, the second on learning to be an expert and the third on skills learning; in the fourth we look at tacit knowledge and, finally, we examine creative doing.

Part 1: Practical living

Throughout this study, I have tried to show that consciousness, language and practical living all develop together and that each affects the other and it would be wrong to say that any one was the prime cause. We develop as human beings as the different dimensions of our life emerge and we certainly do not see language as the prevalent cause of human development although it is a very significant one because it helps us conceptualise and externalise. In Chapter 4, however, we pointed to the fact that action is a fundamental aspect of human living, although it is unwise to separate it from thinking and knowing. We have done so here for heuristic purposes only, and in the same way we have discussed thinking before we examine doing, although we recognised in those earlier chapters that we cannot separate thinking from doing. In fact, doing is a major cause of learning and Archer (2000: 27), for instance, makes the point that 'we learn because of its utility to practical living': we learn as a result of our interests and the relevance of what we learn to our doing. This is not just a feature of adult learning, as Knowles (1980) suggested – it is a feature of human living itself. Interest and relevance are generated by doing (practice), and as we focus upon specific concerns we become aware of them and maybe also that we cannot presume upon them – a disjunctural situation emerges from which we may begin to learn.

Learning in everyday life assumes that the degree of harmony between us and our world has been interrupted and that we need to recreate it through what we are doing so that we can rediscover that sense of belonging to the community or cultural group that makes us feel at home in the world. Consequently, we have to adapt our behaviour to the prevailing situation. We all make different responses at different times and Table 13.1 depicts some of the ways in which we adapt to disjuncture, showing our responses to both the expectations and the means of achieving them, which are helped by our group/society. This table provides us with a useful basis of discussion, but it is not sufficiently complex to capture all the elements of human behaviour.

Conformity is at the heart of social living, and in some ways we have to recognise that it is very necessary for society to exist – this is habitual, taken for granted: there is a sense in which stable society is founded on the expectation that once we have learned the procedures of social living we will conform to them and no longer continue to learn. Bureaucratic organisation is founded on the same assumptions: it is the basis of certain forms of rationality. One thing concepts such as *the learning society* and the *learning*

Table 13.1 Modes of individual adaptation

Mode of adaptation	Culture goals	Institutional means
I: Conformity	+	+
II: Innovation	+	–
III: Ritualism	–	+
IV: Retreatism	–	–
V: Rebellion	+–	+–

Source: Merton (1968: 194)
Key: +, accept; –, reject; +–, innovate.

organisation have done is to focus on change; although neither society nor organisations learn, change makes us aware that other people have learned and adapted their behaviour and that, as a result, they do not always fit into the established procedures: leadership, for instance, demands a degree of individualism and different behavioural forms.

But, then, none of us always conforms in a simple process of merely accepting either the goals or the means – or both – and, in fact, conformity is not always an intellectual acceptance of the situation. Our conformity may also reflect the fact that we have learned something different but that we decide for one reason or another not to reveal that we know other goals or that we have other means of achieving those goals or have other knowledge. It may be that we conform because we fear the consequences of non-conformity – another learning process – or because we are committed to the organisation/society, etc. and our sense of commitment overrides our learning. This is one of the ways that conformity coincides with what Merton (1968) calls ritualism – we are seen to conform even though intellectually or emotionally we either do not accept or do not care about the cultural goals – or we are alienated and do not have the power or the skills to change the situation. We can see immediately from this discussion that one of the fundamental weaknesses of all forms of behaviourism is the assumption that we will respond to the stimulus in an unthinking manner. We are neither unthinking animals nor morons but, as thinking individuals, our behaviour is much more complex than it often appears on the surface, and that it is not simply a result of our learning. At the same time, we have to recognise that in some learning situations, such as therapy, conformity to expectations might be both the goal and the means to that goal since it is basically about stimulus and response.

Nevertheless, we adapt to disjunctive situations by either changing or rejecting the goals or the means of the society or the organisation into which we have been socialised. Much of our socialisation has been through stimulus–response learning. As very young children we learn to be aware of the outside world and even to focus our attention on it, so we learn to respond to external stimuli in approved ways and are often rewarded for it. Nevertheless, as we see from Table 13.1, as we grow older, we do not necessarily conform, and in our initial behavioural adaptation we try out two other basic forms of learning: imitation and trial-and-error learning.

Imitation can be said to have occurred 'only when the imitator has not been exposed to an appropriate stimulus for the behaviour except the sight of the "model's" actions' (Borger and Seaborne, 1966: 102): it is according to Tomasello (1999: 5) one of the three most basic types of learning, the other two being instructed learning and collaborative learning. However, imitation is practised as an adaptive form of behaviour when our role model is not a conformist, so that we do not conform to the norm. Imitation, or modelling, occurs at all stages of our lives and for a wide variety of reasons, as Ormrod (1995) shows. But in the first instance, children imitate their significant others' behaviour and as Nelson (2007: 93) says, 'In the latter part of the first year, infants delight in imitating the novel actions of other persons and observing others imitating them'. More significantly, Bauer *et al.* (2000) (cited in Nelson, 2007: 94) introduced the idea of delayed imitation, i.e. that having been exposed to an action sequence infants remember it and can then use it at a later period to reproduce the observed behaviour. In this way, young children are building into their biographies memories that will then form the basis of a future behaviour and so they are able to copy the other's behaviour.

Considerable research in social learning has demonstrated the significance of imitation and modelling. Bandura (1973, 1977a,b), for instance, has demonstrated how young children copy aggressive and loving behaviour in their role models. Bandura was also concerned with the idea of self-efficacy – that is that we are likely to choose to act in certain ways because we believe that we can carry our those actions successfully and achieve our desired ends.

Perhaps the most common form of adaptive behaviour is trial-and-error (discovery) learning, whereby we respond to a situation and seek out a practical or pragmatic response. We all experience this when we are in new situations and we have to discover how to behave in them – this is something every traveller knows well: indeed, travelling has been recognised as one of the most common ways of learning by doing. If our theory-in-use is tacit, then our actions are not actually determined by theory at all but by the situation and the extent to which the action is successful. This is the heart of everyday living and learning. Heller (1984: 166) suggests that pragmatism 'denotes the direct unity of theory and practice' but she probably overemphasises the place of theory in such experimental behaviour. Indeed, Nyiri (1988: 20–1) makes a similar point:

> One becomes an expert not simply by absorbing explicit knowledge found in textbooks, but through experience, that is, through repeated trials, 'failing, succeeding, wasting time and effort, . . . getting a feel for a problem, learning to go by the book and when to break the rules'. Human experts usually absorb 'a repertory of working rules of thumb, or "heuristics", that, combined with book knowledge, make them expert practitioners'. This practical heuristic knowledge, as attempts to simulate in one the machine have shown is 'hardest to get at because experts – or anyone else – rarely have the self-awareness to recognize what it is. So it must be mined from their heads painstakingly, one jewel at a time'.
>
> (Feigenbaum and McCorduck, 1984: 67, 67, 84)

The tacitness of practical knowledge in everyday life is apparent here, but, in the hermeneutic cycle discussed in a future chapter, explanation and interpretation are seen as stages beyond understanding. However, neither explanation nor interpretation is about practical knowledge – they are more theoretical – whereas understanding has the practical dimension of *'being able'*, which is the basis of expertise. In the pragmatic domain, learning to become an expert entails not sophisticated theory but precise and exact practice, and this is learned experimentally. However, the process from novice to expert is not inevitable and, as Merton (1968: 202–7) showed, our behaviour may become merely ritualistic and so we need not progress towards expertise.

Part 2: Learning to be an expert

The process of learning to do – learning to become an expert – has been popularised in nursing education by Benner (1984), although it was Aristotle who first focused on this practical knowledge, which he called practical wisdom, something that could be learned only with the passing of years. Indeed, he said that subjects such as mathematics were for young people; practical wisdom is a much more mature concept. Through these complex learning experiences, novices might move gradually towards the status of expert, a process which was first discussed by Dreyfus and Dreyfus (1980). They posited that a learner goes through five stages in becoming an expert: novice, advanced beginner, competent, proficient and expert (cited from Benner, 1984: 13; see also Tuomi, 1999: 285–340). In precisely the same way, more experienced workers might continue to learn and continue to develop new knowledge through the process of practice. But there is no short timescale on this process – Benner (1984: 25), for instance, suggested that competency in nursing (the field of her own research) might come after two or three years of practice and proficiency between three and five years (ibid.: 31). One of my own doctoral students (Camilleri, 2009) has argued that competence can occur earlier than Benner suggests since student nurses can spend considerable time in practice whilst they are undertaking their initial professional education. This suggests that expertise might also occur more rapidly, although the feeling that we are experts might take longer than the acknowledgement by others that we are experts. However, we have also highlighted non-learning situations, so that for some people 25 years of practice is one year of learning since they have been ritualistic in their practice, whereas for others it is 25 years of learning: this is the distinction between innovative and ritualistic action. This may be so, or it may be that perception of competence occurs sooner, but when do wisdom and expertise appear? All of these points call for further research.

Additionally, practice itself is not static but rapidly changing, so that practitioners are not simply using knowledge gained in the classroom or in any form of initial vocational education. Indeed, they may reach the stage that they have to innovate within their own practice or, in other words, they have to create new knowledge and new ways of doing things and their expertise means that they also need to be creative – they become experts. Significantly, Joas (1996) sees human action as creative: practitioners also have to gain that wisdom – the ability to 'maintain a creative and flexible tension between irreconcilables and allow conscience, impulse, reality, and attachment all to have places at the center stage' of practice, since these tend to develop with expertise. Immediately we see that practice is no longer just a matter of knowledge and skill; it is about the practitioner being confident and creative, having the right impulses, commitment, and so on. But more than this, in practice, practitioners work with others – patients, clients, colleagues, and so on. It is a social activity and, although expertise is very important, Maister (cited in Daloz et al., 1996: 25) wrote that 'Your clients don't care how much you know until they know how much you care'. In other words, practice is a moral undertaking; it is about trust and respect for others. Practice is ultimately about the nature of the practitioners them- selves. Practice is about the person – as practitioner. This points us to a broader understanding of vocational education since it is about developing the person as well as teaching knowledge and skills – which includes the wider spectrum of knowledge that Scheler (1980 [1926]) discussed – and it is this which is at the heart of whole-person learning.

Part 3: Skills learning

The learning of practical skills is, nevertheless, a very important part of social living and the maxim 'practice makes perfect' may well sum up the process that we have just described, but some skills and procedures are very complicated and in many cases we learn through imitation. In this case, however, we try to imitate what we have had demonstrated to us in formal teaching and learning situations. The expert shows us how to do it, but even then we learn how to do it only at such a time as when we have successfully mastered the practice. But complicated procedures cannot be learned holistically. As long ago as 1972, Belbin and Belbin (1972: 44–5) suggested that these complicated procedures should be broken down into discrete stages and each stage taught and learned separately. They go on to make the point that people of all ages and abilities can learn most skills given the opportunity to work at their own pace, but one of the problems with contemporary society is that we live and work by the clock – time matters – and if individuals cannot master a procedure in a specified time they are removed from that level of work and expected to undertake less complicated tasks.

With the growth of technology, we have opportunity to learn these more complicated skills through simulation and in practice laboratories – these are utilised in both initial and continuing vocational preparation. Skills learning is about learning procedures that are already known and practised by others: it is a matter of conforming to established, rational practices and fits into theories of production. But according to Merton (see Table 13.1), we are introduced to innovation or creativity – something that we cannot be taught or which does not fall into labour theory. Even so, Schön (1983) showed that some work situations need to be innovative in his theory of reflective practice since technical rationality is insufficient. Schön (1983: 68–9) writes:

> When someone reflects-in-action, he becomes a researcher in the practice context. He is not dependent on the categories of established theory and technique, but constructs a new theory of the unique case. His inquiry is not limited to a deliberation about means which depends upon prior agreement about ends. He does not keep means and ends separate, but defines them interactively as he frames a problematic situation. He does not separate thinking from doing, ratiocinating his way to a decision which he must later convert to action. Because his experimenting is a kind of action, implementation is built into is inquiry. Thus reflection-in-action can proceed, even in situations of uncertainty or uniqueness, because it is not bound by the dichotomies of Technical Rationality.

In my own doctoral research (Jarvis, 1977) I discovered that professionals – defined as experts in practice – experienced lower job satisfaction in bureaucratic organisations than those who were organisationally orientated, who might be regarded as experts according to another definition of expert. Being creative is perhaps a sign of some forms of professionalism, and it is certainly another way of looking at doing.

Part 4: Tacit knowledge

In our everyday life we often experience phenomena or events to which we give little or no consideration at the time. We internalise the experiences pre-consciously or pre-cognitively, and the knowledge that we internalise becomes tacit. Unlike explicit knowledge, tacit knowledge cannot be critical (Polanyi, 1962: 264) since it cannot be articulated: tacit knowledge is, according to Polanyi, 'a-critical'. Tacitness is an aspect of everyday learning. We have internalised a great deal of knowledge about which we are consciously unaware: Polanyi's (1967) well-known example of knowing a face, being able to recognise it in a crowd but unable to describe it accurately, depicts this phenomenon. The point about recognising the face in a crowd is that we have a primary experience and we are able to crystallise our tacit knowing in a practical manner. Polanyi (1962: 53) gives another example that catches the idea of tacit knowledge very clearly and he shows how it relates to an acceptance of the social and cultural means to achieve the desired ends:

> By watching the master and emulating his efforts in the presence of his example, the apprentice unconsciously picks up the rules of the art, including those which are not explicitly known to the master himself. These hidden rules can be assimilated only by a person who surrenders himself to that extent uncritically to the imitation of another. A society which wants to preserve a fund of personal knowledge must submit to tradition.

For Polanyi, the acquisition of this form of personal knowledge – tacit – is a-critical learning of a pre-conscious nature that becomes explicit only in conscious situations. In the same way, wherever there is personal interaction, individuals both learn and, to use Goffman's well-known expression, 'give off' more than the explicit communication in which they are involved. It is not surprising therefore, that people working in organisations regularly assimilate knowledge that is not known: this is a significant factor in the light of the theory–practice dichotomy – theory is always known knowledge but practical knowledge contains tacit knowledge. Baumard (1999: 76), for instance, provides an extensive list of knowledge that we cannot see but which we have learned, and in most cases in his study he actually mentions those who have researched it:

- learning without being aware of what is learned (Thorndike and Rock, 1934);
- complex information processed unconsciously (Reber, 1967);
- implicit unconscious rules within patterns of perception (Gibson, 1969, 1979);
- weak signals being perceived without our being aware of them (Gordon and Holoyak, 1983);
- we perceive more than we think we perceive and this is unknown to us (Uleman and Bargh, 1989);
- filters hamper our perception (Starbuck and Milliken, 1988);
- contingency and inherence of our perception (Mace, 1974);
- we use tacit knowledge in explanation (Nisbett and Ross, 1980);
- we use placebo-information (Langer, 1978).

In addition, Baumard discusses Polanyi, Dewey (1922) and Ryle (1945) in looking at practical knowledge; he makes the point that organisations actually both are aware of and use tacit knowledge. But from our perspective we can see that a great deal of research has been conducted that points us to the prevalence and persistence of tacit knowing and its significance in our learning.

Tacit knowledge is learned and not something that is hard-wired into our brains, but Tremlin (2006) suggests that 'tacit knowledge' is hard-wired into the brain so that even very young children understand rules governing material objects. For him, tacit knowledge is not some form of incidental learning but evolutionary knowledge and, as we have pointed out elsewhere in this book, although I do not dispute evolution I question the reductionist idea that knowledge can be hard-wired into the brain since the brain structure is the mechanism though which sensations can be processed and perhaps transformed in the learning process. At the same time, it is perfectly understandable and acceptable that some of the emotions, and so on, that are hard-wired into the system can be regarded as having tacit outcomes in our behaviour.

What is clear from the main psychological work on tacit knowing is that we acquire a great deal of knowledge, unintentionally and often pre-consciously, in the course of our daily living, and it becomes explicit knowledge only when what we have acquired is brought to the conscious mind as a result of an event or a specific experience.

Part 5: Creative doing

When we think about being creative, we need to break the means–end syndrome of technical rationality. In fact, we must recognise that learning 'correct' skills and procedures might inhibit creativity. Creativity is not necessarily about *knowing how* or *knowing that* but it might be: for instance, good creative artists may have learned all the skills of the artist before they become creative. Creativity is not necessarily about means, but it is about ends. Learning the skills might actually be a means to an end but it is not an end in itself. Moreover, creative doing is not something that can be hard-wired into the brain: it is cultural and even beyond traditional formulations of culture. Joas (1996) uses five metaphors that are most frequently employed about creativity: expression, production, revolution, life, and intelligence and reconstruction. All of these terms capture something of the nature of creativity and all refer to aspects of our doing, but they are not only about doing but about being.

We cannot learn to be creative but we can learn to throw off some of the inhibitions that hinder our creativity: we do have to innovate, and this is in accord with Merton's schema discussed above. There are social conditions in which creativity is more likely to occur: and that is when the social structures which inhibit, i.e. those we learn in our socialisation, are lowered so that the social norms of behaviour are weakened. In this instance we enter liminality (V. Turner, 1969), a point that I (Jarvis, 2008) discussed quite fully elsewhere and so I do not need to rehearse it here. But the point about liminality is that it does have specified goals and in my study I did note that the generation of *communitas*, when people relate to people without the inhibitions of social structures, is the end product and, in a similar manner, Joas (1996) discusses the idea of creative democracy.

But we might also look at Merton's category 'rebellion' here and ask if substituting means and ends is also creative. It is difficult to see how actions that are designed to substitute new goals and new norms might not be classified as creative, but this also carries with it a sense of the destructive, and this cannot be conceived of as being creative although, politically, it might be conceived of as a necessary stage in changing society as a whole – the extent to which this can actually be successful is a much more debate-able point since we tend to recreate structures with which we are already familiar.

Conclusion

In this chapter we have began to explore the notion of doing and learning and we can see that a great deal of what we learn is self-directed, although this does not mean that we learn without a teacher, only that we learn by undertaking tasks for themselves, and in the process of doing we actually learn. Much doing is self-directed, but not all of it. But the next chapter expands on some of these ideas as we look at speaking and listening, reading and writing – which may be seen to be at the heart of formal education.

Chapter 14

Interacting

In a wide variety of ways we all interact with our world and with our life-world: we interact with people. We both initiate interaction and are recipients of it. We have claimed throughout this study that we are not born as individuals but that we are born in relationship:

> the child discovers himself as an individual by contrasting himself, and indeed wilfully opposing himself to the family *to which he belongs;* and this *discovery* of his individuality is at the same time the *realization* of his individuality. We are part of that from which we distinguish ourselves and to which, as agents, we oppose ourselves.
>
> (MacMurray, 1979 [1961]: 91)

During this process we do not just copy others' behaviour or experiment with our own – we also interact with others, as Tomasello (1999) makes clear, and we also engage in conversation with others: it is through conversation that we learn to understand better other people's behaviour. In everyday life, conversation is a major way of learning: at the extremes, it can be a one-way exposition, such as in didactic teaching, or a two-way equal exchange of views, as in the ideal speech act of Habermas. But we also engage in interaction through writing – we write letters and receive them, we read books and newspapers, and so on – in all of this we engage in learning processes. Our interaction, then, is a process both of externalising and also of internalising: in the former we speak and write and in the latter we listen to others speak and we read what they have written. Consequently, this chapter has two parts: externalising and internalising.

In our interaction we both take for granted and we suffer disjunctural experiences: for instance, we may not understand the meaning of a sound/word, we may not understand the meaning of a discourse, or we may not be able to think of the right word to say. In our speaking and writing, we intend meaning, and so we will need to look briefly at the idea of intention in the first part, in which we will examine narrative knowledge; but in our listening and reading we try to decipher the meaning that the other intends and this is hermeneutics – the rules, or processes, of interpretation – which we will explore in the second part.

However, it will also be recalled that although we can be programmed for short and specific events, Donald (2001: 51) made the point that a conversation is evidence that we cannot be hard-wired for behaviour that extends over time – it is much too complicated. Indeed, all human interaction is extremely complex and its sophistication has only emerged with the growth and development of both language and culture.

Part 1: Externalising

There are similarities in speaking and writing: both require authors (agents) and the agents must intend meaning. We cannot depersonalise interactive discourse in the way that social constructivism and even linguistics seeks to – it is meaningful intention; when we say 'we mean' when we might, in some cases, also have said 'we intend'. We begin to act in an intention manner very early in our lives through gestures:

> The use of gestures to express pragmatic needs or wants is quite common among older infants and young toddlers. Such gestures often derive from natural action schemes, such as holding up the arms to indicate a desire to be picked up. Such a gesture externalizes simultaneously a felt need and a meaning that inheres in the movement. At the same time, it is a move toward intentional communication using conventional signs – that is, those signs whose meanings are shared by two or more people, at least the signer and the interpreter. Late in the first year and into the second, infants also appear to use personal gestures to express knowledge, for example in lifting a cup to the lips in a 'drinking' gesture or in stirring a container with a spoon.
>
> (Nelson, 2007: 96)

From this early age we can see the idea of intention that indicates the existence of agency – a sense of an acting self that can externalise from learned experiences that have already been internalised. But gesture, like speech, is momentary and fleeting. Consequently, in daily interaction we need to be perceptively aware of body language (gestures – intended and unintended) in order to catch some of the intention behind the communication, and this is something that we also learn often quite unconsciously. This meaning is specific to the situation within which the action occurs. However, speech or discourse and language are different phenomena and we are more concerned here with the former: as Ricoeur (1981: 198) points out, there are four distinct differences between these.

- Discourse is temporary and in the present; language is a system outside of time and virtual.
- Discourse is personal; the language system is impersonal.
- Discourse is about something; the language system just refers to other signs.
- Discourse is a means of exchanging messages; language is only the condition for communication.

Speech occurs as a communicative event and, if we do not succeed in communicating our message, we can reinforce it with emphases, gesticulations and dialogue. But we can also convey meaning through writing, and although writing has a 'life of its own' that makes it profoundly different from speech, the processes of understanding both are similar and may be regarded as hermeneutical. However, modern technology has now provided an intermediate possibility – the filmed/video-taped interaction, which conveys a sense of the lived present even though that lived present is actually a past event but it is not interactive; in this sense it is closer to writing – it is text.

Both speech and writing seek to convey meaning using previously learned words so that there is an inherent phenomenology within this since the meaning of the words that have been learned is that which has been derived from our perception and experience of the external world. In a sense, in both speech and writing we engage in narrative: Bruner (1990: 77) maintains that there are four criteria for narrative: agency, sequential order, sensitivity to human order and, finally, a narrator's perspective. In other words, the narrative is a personal story created by the story-teller. But we now need to examine how narratives arise and how they fit into our understanding of learning.

Polkinghorne (1988: 119) suggests that:

> People use self-stories to interpret and account for their lives. The basic dimension of human existence is temporality, and narrative transforms the mere passing of time into a meaningful unity, the self. The study of a person's own experience of her or his life-span requires attending to the operations of the narrative firm and to how this life story is related to the stories of others.

When we tell our story we may describe a happening or a series of events in our lives or, as many older people write, it may be an autobiography or even reminiscence. To achieve a sense of psychological satisfaction or justification, we draw together some of those events and episodes that have imprinted themselves firmly in our memories – even though they may not be precise recollections of events and what we remember may actually be only an interpretation – and from these we construct our story. This is not a social construction but a personal one, although it may be influenced by social conventions, and so forth. What we construct is something of a continuous whole – something approaching the music score – but its sequence may bear little relation to the actual historical sequence in which the events and episodes occurred. We may emphasise some parts because of the emotional response, etc., that they demanded from us but underplay others which other people may regard as much more important. Significantly, story-tellers are relatively free agents and they rarely, if ever, fit their stories into prescribed or innately prescribed structures – we are not hard-wired to do this.

In telling our story we are imposing, or constructing, meaning – or reflective meaning – on these past experiences. It may be that the very act of constructing the story becomes a learning experience for the agents. We actually construct a meaning or explanation, since we are bringing to our consciousness tacit knowledge that has been stored away as a result of previous experiences and we are enabled to learn from it. Indeed, Husserl (see Ricoeur, 1981: 50) actually argued that 'mental life is characterised by intentionality'.

In our constructing meaning in this manner we are engaged in an I–Me dialogue, but when we tell our story to others it becomes an I–Thou experience. We learn about ourselves and about our experiences both from the reflective I–Me dialogue and also in our communication (I–Thou), because we now tell and hear the story – we are experiencing it through different media and the story might itself be disjunctive and begin a reflective learning process about ourselves and our lives, as well as about the knowledge we are seeking to convey in the story. Additionally, we can see the reactions of the recipients of our story and so we may adapt it to be more relevant to what we perceive the situation to be; indeed, it may be told for the recipients' benefit. Assessing the recipients' reaction to our story becomes a learning experience for us, the story-tellers, since we learn about ourselves both by what we say and by our perceptions of the recipients' reactions. Consequently, we can see that the story asks us to understand what is said – the epistemology – but also to understand the story-teller's ontology.

Speech, then, provides a basis for learning in two different ways: first we have to compose our message – in other words reflect upon things – and by so doing we actually learn more about what we wish to talk about. In the most formal sense, many a teacher has told me that they learn more about their subjects by teaching it because teaching requires them to re-interpret their own understanding of the topic in a way that enables it to be understood by those to whom they wish to communicate it. By actually engaging in speech, we learn – but the process is one in which we move from understanding to interpretation and explanation and back again. These are different stages in the hermeneutic cycle – these are different stages of learning and, in a sense, reaching for different levels of meaning.

But by being the recipient of the message, we also learn, and if the message is unclear we can engage in dialogue (unless we are in a formal teaching/ lecture situation) and ask questions until we can agree on the meaning of the message. Otherwise, we go through the same first stages in the hermeneutic cycle – understanding, explaining and interpreting – but, as we will see later, there is another element to this learning, and that is criticality. We will examine this later. It is at this point, however, that we see most clearly the nature of inter-subjectivity. Learning through the speech act is always inter-subjective and interpersonal – in fact we can anticipate our brief discussion on hermeneutics below by saying, with Gadamer, that there is a fusion of horizons in which interpersonal communication occurs. Gadamer (1976: 32) says '[i]n language, and only in it, can we meet what we ever "encounter" in the world, because we are in it'. Language is not a mirror of reality; it is working out what we have already learned, but it is more:

> Hermeneutics bridges the distance between minds and reveals the foreignness of the other mind. But revealing what is unfamiliar does not merely mean reconstructing historically the 'world' in which the work had its original meaning and function. It also means apprehending what is said to us, which is always more than the declared and comprehended meaning.
>
> (ibid.: 100–1)

Learning, then, is apprehending more than the empirical reality of the phenomenon about which we learn – it is more than a simple empirical phenomenon. In a similar manner to speaking, we also learn from writing. We write letters and essays and students are often asked to write essays. Sometimes teachers see the act of writing as merely recording what has already been learned – a sense of understanding – but this is to misunderstand the process of writing for, like story-telling, we are constructing our narrative. We noted above that speech occurs in a fleeting moment, the passing of time, whereas writing is more like didactic speech that assumes a degree of fixation in time. In writing, we move from understanding to both interpretation and explanation. Ricoeur (1981: 147) makes the point that:

> what comes to writing is discourse as intention-to-say and that writing is the direct inscription of this intention, even if historically and psychologically, writing began with the graphic transcription of the signs of speech. This emancipation of writing, which places the latter at the site of speech, is the birth of the text.

We may not always recognise it, but while we are writing we are actually learning by doing – we are not only deepening our understanding but interpreting and explaining it. Once again, however, we might not be consciously learning when we are constructing our discourse – it may be pre-conscious and certainly it is often unintended.

Part 2: Internalising

In the same way as we externalise by speaking and writing, so we internalise by listening and reading. Listening can itself be subdivided into listening to sounds, enjoining conversation and being taught didactically, although not always formally. Sounds are sensations, and we learn about the origins of sounds or their meaning from previous experience. For instance, we learn about sounds from previous associations – a song of a bird, for instance, will enable a bird watcher to know the type of bird making the sound. When we listen to the bird song we hear and recognise (understand), although we might also understand that the bird is communicating fear or warning to other birds through the sounds that it makes. A sound (word) will carry meaning, but often the meaning has to be contextualised before we can interpret it, so that we can see a learning cycle of experience and meaning – but this meaning can also actually mean understanding, or at least it can lead to understanding – so that we actually learn sounds in three stages – hearing (experiencing the sensation), giving meaning to the sensation and then understanding it. But it is not really as straightforward as this since we might understand the word and then give meaning to the sentence, and so on. In addition, there are four aspects that we need to consider in this process of learning from hearing: first, we learn something about the speaker; second, we need to know that we have understood the meaning that the speaker intended the words to convey; and, third, we might accept the meaning that we have understood even though it is not the meaning that the speaker wished to convey – this form of interpretation actually occurs more frequently in reading than in listening, as we will see below. Finally, we then need to ask ourselves whether we actually agree with the sentiments being conveyed and so the notion of criticality becomes central to the process. Failure to be critical may reflect the power of the speaker or the weakness or gullibility of the listeners. But criticality is not value free and so we cannot just assume that criticism is more objective than the original statement – in this sense we are now in the realm of interests and prejudices, since criticality reflects something of our own humanity and our previous learning experiences. There is a tendency for listeners to regard their own position as objective and their criticisms of statements they hear to be based on their own 'objective' knowledge/understanding that is actually a subjective statement, or a claim to their own freedom and emancipation from traditional interpretations. But they may both be subjective judgments: Gadamer actually claims that 'the prejudices of an individual, far more than his judgments, constitute the historical reality of his being' (Gadamer, 1976: 245). However, Ricoeur points out that both the statement (or the hermeneutical interpretation) and the emancipated criticism may be regarded as ideological unless it is seen in some form of conjunction or dialogue with the original statement in seeking to discover a creative new meaning.

There are, then, four elements in the process of learning by listening to words, although they may not occur in sequence nor do they necessarily only occur once in the process of seeking to understand:

- hearing;
- giving meaning;
- understanding;
- critical awareness.

But writing leads to text and we also learn from reading: we learn from a text, and it is here that hermeneutics actually began. But hermeneutics, as we have already seen, has become a process of understanding that has now been assumed to be wider than just reading text. Indeed, the historical development of hermeneutics has also shown us how complex the process of understanding text is and, therefore, how difficult is the learning process. Hermeneutics arose from the study of text, and in the first instance many of the texts studied were religious texts. I recall that as a theological student I was introduced to the writings of Schleiermacher, who was one of the earliest scholars to engage in this approach who tried to make the processes of interpretation and understanding a scientific technology, as he endeavoured to discover rules for exegesis. Ricoeur (1981: 45–8) nicely summarised Schleiermacher's position and he (ibid.: 47) highlights one of the major hermeneutical problems in seeking to understand the text:

> Schleiermacher makes this clear: to consider the common language is to forget the writer; whereas to understand the individual author is to forget his language, which is merely passed over. Either we perceive what is common, or we perceive what is peculiar.

This conflict has exercised students of hermeneutics ever since, and we are forced to ask the question about our own reading of text – are we seeking to understand the author's intentions in writing the text or are we actually more concerned with what the text says to us as readers? It may be that both concur, but this is not always the case because text transcends time and cultural change.

Nevertheless, when we read, especially when we engage in studying a text, we are engaged in a hermeneutic exercise and there is a sense that in order to understand the processes of learning from reading we open the whole hermeneutical debate, which we have no intention of doing here. Suffice to note that reading takes us through the same stages – understanding, interpreting and explaining – but we are constantly faced with profound problems in seeking to understand the text – are we understanding or even trying to understand:

- what the writer wished to communicate?
- the context of the writer?
- the actual words/language of the writer?
- the writer's own personality?
- what the text says to us at the time of reading it?
- what more we understand about ourselves as a result of reading the text?

And then we have to interpret each of these in the light of our own understanding, learning and biography and at the same time we have to recognise that the text stands by itself irrespective of the intention of the author. Ricoeur (1981: 161), analysing Dilthey, suggested that to interpret is to appropriate here and now the intention of the text, that is – to learn. But he then examines other approaches before arriving at a paradoxical conclusion that

> reading is the concrete act in which the destiny of the text is fulfilled. It is at the very heart of reading that explanation and interpretation are indefinitely opposed and reconcile.
>
> (ibid.: 164)

But the point is that reading is the destiny and this may not be understanding! Learning is, at this point, a synthesis of these processes, but we are still confronted with the problem of knowledge: what we have internalised is actually a subjective and personal knowledge that has involved a number of these processes and in this sense we also learn more about ourselves as learners. What we have internalised is certainly not objective and absolute knowledge.

Conclusion

In everyday living we learn through the processes of talking, reading and writing – but we also learn by seeing and experiencing the environment. This is a similar hermeneutical process, as we recall, to that suggested by Gadamer: life interprets itself within the cultural framework into which we have been socialised. However, as we have already seen, not all experiences of the environment are capable of a cognitive interpretation – some are best understood from an emotional one, as we discussed above. But understanding text and writer also entails the process of understanding values, and it is to this that we now turn.

Chapter 15

Valuing

Learning morality and values in everyday life is a complex and sometimes, but by no means always, pre-conscious process. Throughout the history of thought the problems of morality and social commitment have existed – morality is often related to the stability and security of the social group of which individuals are members and to which they should be committed by virtue of their membership – such concerns are reflected in the works of early thinkers such as Confucius and Aristotle. But we have also already pointed out that the group can stifle and inhibit change and even inhibit the development of the person, and so there are occasions when it is moral to transgress the group norms; these are actions which have led to a reaction against the group and an emphasis on individualism. Primitive thought and practice endeavoured to overcome this problem by portraying the leader as a reluctant leader who had to be forced to assume leadership. But individual responsibility was probably first discussed by the prophet Jeremiah (Holy Bible) in the eighth century before the Christian era. He claimed that all individuals are responsible for their own acts:

> The fathers have eaten sour grapes, and the children's teeth are set on edge. But everyone shall die for his own sin; every man who eats sour grapes, his teeth shall be set on edge.
>
> (Jeremiah 31:29–30)

Individual responsibility was subsequently emphasised in Judeo-Christian thought – individual salvation, and so on – but the actual word 'individual' is a late-comer to the English language, and in Chinese there is no word at all for individual and the nearest word to individual means 'selfish'. In recent times human/individual rights have been emphasised in the West, even when the individual acts detrimentally to the group's best interests. But we are born not as individuals but in relationship, and it is only as we develop our consciousness and interact with our significant others that we learn to become individuals.

We can see, therefore, that discussion on individual morality and values themselves is a long and complex process. In this chapter we will examine some aspects of it briefly in four parts: first, we will look at the way we begin to learn values and how it leads into family values: second, we will examine the way we learn the basic models of morality; third, we will examine cognitive moral development and relate it to the discussion in the second part; and, finally, we will relate this discussion to private values and public standards.

Part 1: Pre-cognitive and pre-conscious learning of universal value

From the moment of conception the emerging fetus is in a physical relationship with the mother. We are all born in relationship and as small children we are cared for by our mothers, fathers and significant others. In the womb and during our earliest days we are hardly conscious or cognitively aware, but what we experience is a loving relationship. This being loved and cared for is almost universally experienced – it is the earliest value we learn: we learn it through the experience of relationship – or, as Buber (1958) rightly argues, in the beginning is relationship. Self-denying love is learned by experience pre-consciously and pre-cognitively. Our earliest experiences are in an agapeistic relationship (Jarvis, 1997, 2008), and this is the only value that is universal. By this we mean that it is never wrong to be concerned for another person.

However, we have already noted that as we grow and develop as small children we exert our own interests and needs and these bring us into potential conflict with other members of the family and so we develop our individuality: we do this as children still unaware of the value of the loving relationship that we have experienced and most often still are experiencing. But the potential conflict of the individual and the group has already emerged and is as universal as the love itself, but it is dealt with differently in different cultures, the Confucian heritage countries emphasising the family and the group more than the West. This same individualism is reflected in family breakdowns that set children little or no example of family values; nevertheless it has been experienced and learned pre-consciously and pre-cognitively – agapeism is the one value that is universal and almost universally experienced

The philosophical basis of agapeism lies in the Greek language. *Agape* is one of at least three Greek words for 'love': the first is friendship, the second is sexual love and this is the third and it means 'disinterested love', 'concern for the Other'. It is argued here that agapeistic love is the sole moral good – there is never a time when it is wrong to be concerned for the Other. Yet we have to recognise that acting on this concern does not mean that our actions will always result in good since we may act out of either ignorance or forethought and our actions may be subject to unforeseen circumstances. This form of love is disinterested concern, but it does not imply lack of interest, only lack of self-interest. In this sense it is the very antithesis of modern values. It is paradoxically a sense of commitment – to the Other; at the same time it does not deny that we have a self-love, only that in relationship with the Other is not the place to practise it. But nearly all of us have experienced this love from the earliest moments of our lives and because we all experience it in our earliest days it is why we all feel that relationship and even caring for others is fundamental to our humanity.

This value of the group and of duty to the group is also found in the formulations of ethical goodness in moral philosophy, but while we will make reference to the philosophical bases of each, as we have already done with agapeism, we will illustrate how we experience each of these as we grow and develop: they are not far removed from the experiences of everyday lie, although their philosophical formulations are!

Part 2: Learning moral goodness

In this section we will relate our learning experiences to five schools of thought about ethical value: deontological, teleological, intuitive, emotionalism and discourse ethics. It is important to note that all are grounded in either individualism or rationality or both, and these bases tell us something about the nature of modernity itself since they were all formulated after the Enlightenment. Indeed, we find the philosophical basis of this approach in the works of Kant, who specified that: 'I ought never to act in such a way that I could also will that my maxim should become a universal law' (Kant, 1997: 15) and this law should be treated rather like a universal law of nature. Consequently, one basis by which we can judge these arguments is the extent to which they can be universalised.

Deontology

From our earliest days within the family and throughout our primary socialisation we learn that we have a duty to the family, to organisations to which we belong and even to society and humanity. We are expected to conform to the norms and mores of the group and to the laws of wider society. We have a duty to our membership groups and we are expected to be loyal to them: if we are disloyal we suffer forms of punishment and even exclusion from the group by imprisonment, excommunication, and so on. Goodness, then, resides in our duty to the law and ultimately to the group and even humanity itself. Crudely, this is probably the first value that we consciously learn: obedience to the group and to those in authority – it is a value highly emphasised by Confucian heritage cultures, but its weakness are also very apparent in those cultures that emphasise the value of instrumentalism and individualism since we learn that the rules of the group may inhibit change which might lead to social improvement and might also inhibit individual development.

As young children we begin to exert our own will against that of the group: children seek to test the parameters of their life-worlds within which they have freedom to exercise their own wills. Consequently, we see that the idea of duty and loyalty to the group as always being good is neither natural nor universalisable. Having discovered the weaknesses of the deontological position by our own experience rather than through cognitive reasoning, we tend to move to more rationalistic instrumental forms of behaviour in which the emphasis is placed on the end-product of the action rather than obedience to the law itself.

Teleology

The major weakness of the above position is perhaps the strength of this second position – it seems common sense to seek to realise our own desires or wishes, and in its more ethical form it was Bentham (1789) who postulated that the goodness of an act lies in its consequences, so that a good act seeks to produce the greatest amount of happiness for the greatest number of people. As we grow and develop we recognise that this is the ethical aspect to common-sense instrumental rationality. Of course, it is good to try to make the greatest number of people happy. But we also learn that minorities have significance and that in making the greatest number of people happy we may make others unhappy. We also realise that the end does not justify the means, that our motives for acting in certain ways are very important even though the outcome is not always what we desire, that some of the consequences of an action cannot be foretold and that we are not sure when the end-product of an action actually occurs Through the experiences of everyday life, we learn that, although this position appears to be common sense, it is not always right or good – indeed, it certainly cannot be universalised, but there are other approaches to which we might turn.

Intuitionism

We might feel that we do not always have to justify our own behaviour – we just know what it is right. Perhaps the most famous exponent of intuitionism is G.E. Moore (1902), who argued that goodness is goodness and as such it is indefinable: we just know what is good – this is uninferred or immediate knowledge. It could be claimed that revealed knowledge might be regarded as intuitive, although the ramifications of this suggestion take us beyond the scope of this study, which does not, in any case, accept the idea of revealed knowledge. Clearly, this position places subjectivity before objectivity, and this need not be a weakness, but the idea that the situation can be isolated from the whole in both time and space is much more dubious. Yet it might be argued that knowing what is right in a situation is something we all experience: it is as if common sense prevails, but we have already suggested that this does not automatically lead to correct consequences. Moreover, even if I think that I know intuitively what is right, there is no logic in this position to compel me to act upon the intuition. However, a more fundamental problem with this position is that Kohlberg (1976) – as we will see below – has shown quite convincingly that our conception of goodness alters with education and experience, so that what might be intuitive at one stage in development might not be so at another and so intuitionism opens itself to the argument that the intuitive goodness might be a relative concept.

However, I want to argue later in this chapter for a view that our 'intuitions' are learned and they reflect our analysis of the situation that we are in. In this sense, we can see that existential behaviour is also learned behaviour. At the same time, it would be possible and perhaps probable that some of our intuitive goodness relates to our evolutionary history – Dawkins (2006: 240–67) suggests how this might be possible. As I pointed out in the very opening chapter of this book, there is now a real need to examine carefully the relationship between learning and evolution.

Emotivism

As we grow, we come to realise that it is fundamentally difficult to decide upon what is a good action, and at times we might ask in exasperation, 'What is goodness?' The difficulty in tying down the concept of goodness led linguistic philosophers, such as A.J. Ayer (1971), to claim that there is no such thing as goodness, it is merely a sign of approval that we signify about somebody or thing that we like or, conversely, that we dislike. Ayer (ibid.: 146), for instance, wrote:

> Thus, if I say to someone, 'You acted wrongly in stealing that money', I am not stating anything more than if I simply said, 'You stole that money'.

But I am saying that I disapproved of it! Hence I am expressing my emotion. This theory was epitomised by Stevenson's (1944) *Ethics and Language*. Emotivism seeks to combine reason with the affective and provide emotive meaning. It also captures the idea that the emotion might be stronger than the reason. This is what Habermas (1990: 58) calls strategic action rather than communicative action.

In many ways this theory captures the spirit of the times when everything was conveyed by language, but it does have a number of weaknesses: Urmson (1968), for instance, suggested that it confuses emotion and attitudes in an unhelpful manner and that it ultimately leads to the idea that evaluation is based upon non-rational human behaviour, and this is not very satisfactory. But there is another linguistic weakness in Ayer's statement which is implied with the use of the word 'stole' – stealing suggests that the action has contravened some more universal moral position.

All of these four approaches to value all point to the fact that we learn from our experiences the strengths and weaknesses of each of the approaches to moral goodness and that we tend to do it alone. Our final approach, however, suggests that we can learn values in relationship with others through discussion.

Discourse ethics

Habermas claims that 'none of the competing ethical traditions can claim prima facie general validity any longer' (Dews, 1986: 248), and we have shown this to be true, but it does not mean that we have not learned them, and their strengths and weaknesses, through the experiences of living and reflecting upon our experiences. He, therefore, sought to pose another theory that overcomes some of the weaknesses of the previous ones and which also reflects how we learn values in everyday life – through discussion with others. Habermas's theory of discourse ethics emerged naturally from his theory of communicative action although it can also claim its origins in Kantian thought: for Habermas, discourse ethics is about procedure rather than substantive orientations (Habermas, 1990: 122) and we learn through reaching agreement with others. Habermas points to the fact that in discussion with others we can agree on what is good in any situation, but agreement does not mean that we arrive at a universal ethic – only that we might reach a pragmatic agreement in given situations. Habermas actually recognises that the discourse contains within it intuitive and pre-theoretical knowledge that need to be made explicit so that participants are aware of the basis of some of their propositions through a process of rigorous questioning. He is also clear that this discourse is a learning discourse for the participants. While he recognises the significance of conceptual development in the development of morality, he is faced with the problem that not all people may develop their moral conceptual understanding to its highest levels and so it is difficult to locate the moral good in individuals' developmental processes and their dialogue since they may not all be sufficiently developed to enter enlightened moral discourse. Indeed, it is to locate morality in knowledge itself.

One of the main strengths of Habermas's position is that it is through the process of discussion between people that we all learn, and so we can learn our ethics in relation to other people, but one of the weaknesses of such a position is that it can be 'the blind leading the blind', since it is possible for two misguided people to reach an agreement through an apparently rational discussion even though they are both wrong! Clearly, his work is not without its critics: Benhabib (Rasmusen, 1990: 67), for instance, suggests that rational discourse occurs about norms when they are endangered and not when they are taken for granted and so rational discourse might not be a realistic way of reaching a universalisable ethic.

In all the theories that we have examined we can see that we learn our moral values from different aspects of human behaviour: the first in rules, the second in consequences, the third in intuition, the fourth in language and the fifth in discussion and communication. We learn most of them during our early years and we also learn that in some instances one or other approach is right and in others it is wrong. None offers a satisfactory answer to the problem for every situation but each contains more than a semblance of the truth. Each of these approaches relates to our own individual learning experiences in the processes of daily living.

It can thus be seen that as a result of our learning experiences we actually learn the strengths and weaknesses of the fundamental theories of moral goodness. In everyday thought we recognise some of the strengths and weaknesses of each, but we do not systematise these in the ways that moral philosophers do, and so there is a sense in which we tend to 'apply' one or other of the approaches to our situations as seems to befit them. Although this is not the place to debate their universal validity, we can see that each is functional to daily living but we can also see that at the heart of ethics and morality lies relationship with other people and that ethics begins the moment a stranger crosses our paths and we become aware of the stranger's humanity – it is a desire to enter a relationship of care and concern for the sake of the Other. But it is very easy to exercise power in such a relationship since we might do what we think is good for the other without reference to the other's wants or desires: this is a well-intentioned misuse of power in the relationship. Bauman (1993: 124) suggests that:

> [m]oral behaviour is triggered off by the mere presence of the Other as a face: that is, an authority without force. The Other demands without threatening to punish, or promise rewards. The Other cannot do anything to me, neither punish nor reward; it is precisely that the weakness of the Other lays bare my strength, my ability to act, as responsibility.

It is the presence alone that always demands the response of love, or concern (Gaita, 2000). But we might want to ask, 'Why should we be concerned for the Other in this way?' We may find no satisfactory answer to this question and yet from our very earliest existence we find an answer – it is only through the love and concern showed to us that we survived our earliest days and so the answer must lie in the very existence of the Other: we must be concerned for the Other because the Other exists and for no other reason – this is what we experienced – it is the moral worth of humanity. It was in the beginning of our own life that we experienced the love and concern of the significant others for us just because we were born. We learned this pre-consciously and pre-cognitively and so we can begin to see how the universal value of love underlies all the other approaches to moral behaviour. As MacMurray (1979 [1961]: 122) claims:

> To act rightly is . . . to act for the sake of the Other and not for oneself. The Other . . . always remains fully personal; consequently its objectives must be the maintaining of position personal relations between all agents as the bond of community.

Whereas we can see how we learn each of these moral positions during the course of everyday life, we also develop cognitively, and it is during this process that we are able to evaluate these learning experiences more rationally and so we now look at this developmental process.

Part 3: The stages of moral development

Perhaps the most well-known approach to cognitive moral development is that of Kohlberg (1987), whose work was developed from Piaget's (1929) classical analysis of conceptual development in children. However, Kohlberg took Piaget a little further because he did not see each conceptual stage clearly demarcated in the way that Piaget did. We will see in this discussion how each of the stages reflects some of the discussion into which we have already entered. Kohlberg's conceptual stages are shown in Table 15.1.

It is very clear from the outset that there is considerable overlap between Kohlberg's stages of moral development and what we previously described when we examined the way that we experience each of the major schools of moral thought in our process of personal moral development – this development both affects our behaviour and is affected by it. Indeed, it is suggested here that this is a form of lifelong learning since we grow and develop our moral principles throughout our lives in the light of learning from our experiences in everyday living. Kohlberg's stages are not independent of what we learn from doing and reflecting upon what we do. Consequently, it is no surprise that we find considerable similarities between his formulation and our previous discussion. Indeed, when we compare Kohlberg's work with that discussed in the previous section we can see that his level 1, stage 1, heteronomous morality, is very close to the deontological position, i.e. we may obey the laws in order to avoid punishment, and stage 2 approaches the teleological position. Underlying the whole of the conventional level is the idea that it is important to support the group, and this is something that we learn from birth itself but only in this stage do we seek to justify what we have learned pre-consciously. Stage

Table 15.1 Kohlberg's model of moral development

Level 1: Pre-conventional

Stage 1: Heteronomous morality
Sticks by the rules in order to avoid punishment and has an egocentric point of view

Stage 2: Individualism, instrumental purpose and exchange
Right is what is fair, individuals only follow rules when they are in self-interest in order to serve the needs of self, concrete individualism and aware that people's interests conflict

Level 2: Conventional

Stage 3: Mutual interpersonal expectations, relationships and interpersonal conformity
Lives up to what others expect in order to be a good person in the eyes of self and others, puts oneself in the other person's shoes

Stage 4: Social system and conscience
Fulfilling agreed duties and contributing to society in order to keep the system going. Considers individual relationships in terms of place in the social system

Level 3: Principled

Stage 5: Social contract, utility and individual's rights
Upholds relative rules in the interests of impartiality, abides by the rules for the welfare of all and in order to protect people's rights since the actor is a rational individual aware of values and rights

Stage 6: Universal ethical principles
Follows self-chosen ethical principles even when they conflict with laws because they are committed to those principles and because the actors recognise that this is the nature of morality and that people are ends in themselves and should be treated as such

Note
This table has been copied directly from Jarvis (1997: 57) although Habermas (1990: 123–35) gives a slightly more elaborated form.

5, however, seeks to combine the group and the individual, whereas the final stage recognises that we choose our own ethical principles and seek to live by them. Consequently, we are beginning to see how our behaviour is related both to our development and to our social situation, and so in the final part of this chapter we can explore this relationship even further.

Part 4: Private values and public standards

In our model of learning (Figure 2.2) we see that boxes 3, 4 and 5 relate to thought, action and emotion, and we are now in a position to discuss our behaviour in relation to these processes. For instance, we can see that cognitively our values are affected by many processes, including what we have learned earlier in our lives and our moral development. In this sense, we do not merely pass through the stages of moral development and then leave them behind: our decisions about our moral behaviour are inclusive, i.e. we utilise the whole of our learning and decide what is right in the situation. In this sense we do reflect something of the intuitionist position, simply because we have learned from our lives and made cognitive decisions about what is right. In another sense, we have constructed a belief system – a personal ideology – with which we are satisfied and which satisfies our conscience. Such a system, however, may well reflect our own cognitive development and predispositions as a result of our previous learning, so that we may be a leader and seek to step outside the group's norms and mores for the sake of the group, or we may be individually selfish and step outside of them for our own ends. In contrast, we may prefer to fit into the group for fear of punishment, and so on.

But our moral values are affected not only by our cognitions, but also by our emotions: during our upbringing we may have had pleasant experiences or unpleasant ones that affect the way that we both think and feel about situations. Consequently, we may like to feel part of the group and so we conform to it or we may have learned that it is satisfying to achieve ends beyond those of the group and so we are prepared to step outside of it in order to achieve our desires and aspirations. Indeed, as we have developed we may have learned to believe in such issues as human rights and also to feel passionately about them, so that our moral position is also reinforced by our emotions. Commitment to such moral views is always a combination of belief and emotion, and which precedes which, or which is the stronger, is a matter of our own individual development.

Throughout this brief discussion another factor has entered in – our moral behaviour is not only affected by our beliefs and emotions, it is also affected by our social situation. We feel good about being a member of a social group and so we conform to its moral norms. If, as a result of our previous learning, we think the group is wrong but we are committed to it, we may seek to stand outside of its norms but not its structures and reform it from within. But if the group's power elite does not approve of those reforms that we wish to introduce, then we may be forced to leave the group and the group may condemn our views as wrong. Consequently, our moral behaviour is affected by the power of the social structures within which we function and this brings us back to Figure 4.1 – we behave and learn in different situations. If the social structures within which we function are loose, informal and weak we may be able to exert our own moral behaviour without fear of being excommunicated from the group, but, if they are strong, we may be forced to conform more closely to what is expected of us than we would wish or else be forced to leave the group. In social living, however, we are also members of groups and organisations which are themselves elements of society: if society is open and lax the groups may exert their own moral norms irrespective of whether they conform to the norms of the wider society, so that in an open society, such as the UK, different social groups have over the years been given the freedom to do their own thing to such an extent that the power elite is now having problems dealing with them. We can see this in, for instance, teenage gangs and the like. In this we can begin to see how immoral behaviour can occur and be condoned or at least tolerated. But if the social situation has tight procedures then we are forced into a different situation – one suggested in part by Habermas.

In Habermas's discourse ethics, he recognises that there are many different and valid ethical positions – as we do here. His concern was to create a democratic society in which differing viewpoints can be accommodated when there is agreement about the procedures even if there are still differences about the content. In precisely the same way, we can see when we function in a strong society the accepted procedures are laid down by the governing body in the form of laws and rules and we are forced to conform to them or pay the penalty. In a weak society, there is little power to enforce the rules. Hence, democratic behaviour is about agreement of the procedures of social action irrespective of personal values, and so on. If we do not approve either cognitively or emotively, then we pull out of the agreement or, if we stay in, we may well have problems of conscience. Moreover, we continue to learn from our actions so that we may learn to like the relationship or agree with the norms laid down, and so on.

Consequently, when we are placed in situations where we have to evaluate another, we can do so either in terms of the content or in terms of the procedures within which the other has functioned. For instance, when we evaluate an impersonal object, our own likes and dislikes are prevalent but expression of our evaluation may well take the situation into account. For instance, we may dislike certain forms of modern art quite intensely, but within groups that like them or approve of them we may temper our evaluation so that we fit in with the group a little more. But when we evaluate people and their behaviour, we may well be more affected by what we know either about the groups in which they function and have learned or about the ones within which we are functioning, or both.

Now many of the emotive orientations that we have to moral behaviour may have been learned pre-consciously or pre-cognitively, whereas we may be more aware of the actual cognitive positions that we are adopting, whether they be ideological (beliefs) or positions that we have deliberately espoused because we accept the arguments for their correctness. But the significant thing, in terms of Kohlberg's schema, is that we may be choosing from a variety of different learning experiences in the past that reflect different stages in moral development, so that the choice almost appears intuitive in certain situations whereas in others it is more formally structured.

Conclusion

We began this chapter with the claim that agapeism is the universal good – that it is never wrong to be concerned about persons – and that we learned this pre-consciously by experience before we developed conscious selves. Nevertheless it is a principle, and when we seek to practise it we can and often do choose the wrong solutions, if there is a solution at all. Often we live in a world of 'greys' rather than of clear-cut solutions.

The agapeistic principle, however, still underlies the whole debate about learning moral values, and it has not been affected in any way by the remainder of the argument – we also learn about non-universal moral goods that we apply to situations as a result of our daily living, but even all of these are not consciously learned even though they can be categorised though analysis after they have been learned and practised. This is a more existentialist position, but one which relates closely to the philosophical discussion about ethics and moral behaviour. Nevertheless, we can also recognise the complexities of the learning processes that has led us to this position. In the final chapter of Section II, therefore, we move to an idea of positioning – the positions that we adopt in society and the attitudes that we demonstrate.

Chapter 16

Positioning

We all position ourselves in different ways in our social world, and in so doing we present ourselves accordingly (Goffman, 1959), which also affects our perception and our experience, and, therefore, our subsequent learning. According to Reber and Reber (2001), psychologically, 'position' can refer to:

- the location of an object with reference to the point of view of the observer – perception;
- a place in the social class system of a society;
- a point in the dominance hierarchy;
- a region in the life-space where an event occurs;
- a point of view, an attitude.

Consequently, how we perceive our own position in society will be reflected in our attitudes, or personality traits, and in our motivation to act. It will be recalled that in Chapter 8 we explored the ideas of perception, and so our understanding of our position in society will be reflected in our attitudes about it and our intentions to act within it. Consequently, this chapter falls into three main parts: attitudes, intelligence and motivation. Concluding this second section of the book with a part on motivation also points to the fact that we, as persons, actually exist in our acts and that we learn by doing and interaction as much as, if not more than, by being taught.

Part 1: Attitudes

In many a curriculum we used to see that the specific objectives of a course were to learn 'knowledge, skills and attitudes,' with the last idea being discussed in a nebulous and not very rigorous manner. This was partly because we had such a restricted view of learning but also because we were not very sophisticated in our thinking about learning attitudes. Although we did utilise attitude scales in some learning research when we were interested in attitude change, we rarely related this change to learning theory. We all learn attitudes and they affect the way that we perceive our future situations and so they are an important dimension in the learning process. In traditional social science research, attitude has been defined as 'a state of readiness, a tendency to act or react in a certain manner when confronted with certain stimuli' (Oppenheim, 1966: 105). It is in the confrontation with the stimuli that our attitudes become apparent whereas the remainder of the time they are dormant although, in a sense, still present in the person – as part of our personality – a trait, perhaps, as we will mention below. That they do tend to remain dormant points to the fact that there is a tendency for them to be tacit and learned coincidentally – often preconsciously. Attitudes are abstractions although they are real to the person who holds them (ibid.: 106).

At the time when he wrote, Oppenheim (ibid.: 105–19) held that our thinking about attitudes was a little unsystematic, but he argued that some attitudes are more enduring than others, that they vary in intensity, and so on. Nevertheless, he endeavoured to subdivide attitudes into their different dimensions, although not accurately, for the purpose of measuring them, and then aspects of each dimension can be assessed in relation to specific experiences, such as change. However, we can see the need to relate attitude change to learning theory more systematically.

'Attitude', however, as a concept, has been used in a number of different ways. According to Reber and Reber (2001) it is:

- rendering one fit to engage in performance;
- a bodily position or posture;
- a posture that conveys an intended action;
- an intention which has cognitive, affective, evaluative and conative dimensions;
- a response tendency.

Reber and Reber suggest that the final meaning has all but disappeared. I am not entirely convinced about this in practice, although it might have disappeared from personality theory. The dimensions that are included in the fourth meaning depend to a considerable extent on the perspective of the writer, learner, speaker or actor. But we can see that the combination reflects the approach to whole-person learning that underlies this book: we will deal with the first three of these in the first part of this chapter, and conation (disposition for action) is included in the second part. Attitudes, as characteristics, tend to be enduring, although attitude change is a well-known phenomenon and a major element in the learning process. 'Attitudes' relate to an orientation to practical living, both as a response and as an intention, that has cognitive, affective, evaluative and conative dimensions – Reber's and Reber's third, fourth and fifth meanings. Krech *et al.* (1962: 139) effectively combine these different meanings in the following manner:

> As the individual develops, his cognitions, feelings, and action tendencies with respect to various objects in his world become organized into enduring *systems* called attitudes.

In seeing attitudes as systems, Krech *et al.* are emphasising the interrelation of the three different dimensions which may serve many varied functions in our daily living. Indeed, attitudes have been categorised into different types which reflect the domination of one or other of these dimensions: affective attitudes, intellectualised attitudes, action-oriented attitudes and balanced attitudes (Katz and Stotland in Krech *et al.*, 1962: 145).

Wlodkowski (1985: 46), for instance, captures both some of the complexity and the functionality of our attitudes nicely:

> Attitudes are powerful influences on human behavior and learning because they help people to make sense of their world and give clues as to what behavior will be most helpful in dealing with that world. If someone is going to be hostile towards us, it is in our best interest to be careful of that person. Attitudes help us feel safe around things that are initially unknown to us. Attitudes also help us anticipate and cope with recurrent events. They give us guidelines and allow us make our reactions more automatic. This makes life simpler and frees us to cope with the more stressful elements of daily living.

We can see, therefore, that the generation of attitudes assists us in taking for granted our life-world: attitudes underlie our habitual behaviour and are learned as part of our responses to disjuncture.

At the same time, it is significant that in many recent studies of the person and personality the concept of attitudes plays a very small part in the discussion. For instance, Haslam (2007) has three only very brief references in a book on personality, in which he (p. 7) implies that attitude and belief 'concern specific propositions' which are cognitive and which he (pp. 11–12) regards as a dimension of personality that he couples with beliefs, emotions and behaviours. The more common term in personality psychology is personality trait, which Haslam sees as an aspect of the total personality rather than an individual dimension within it, as is attitude. For him (ibid.: 18–19), a personality trait is:

- a relatively enduring characteristic;
- a pattern of behaviour, thought or feeling;
- relative to the person;

- a disposition;
- an aspect of the personality relevant to everyday life.

He (ibid.: 18) defines trait as 'a characteristic form of behaviour, think-ing, or feeling', and this is similar to Reber and Reber's definition of it as 'any enduring characteristic of a person': both of these definitions come close to the fourth definition of attitude suggested by Reber and Reber above. It is easy to merge these two concepts at this point, although per-sonality theory is much wider than the study of attitudes. Although we concede here that attitude and personality traits are not precisely the same concept, both are regarded as aspects of personality, and the wider the definition of attitude, the closer it comes to the definition of a personal-ity trait. Consequently, we will discuss attitude as an aspect of personality and we will examine the phenomenon in relation to learning in the four dimensions of cognition, emotion, evaluation and conation, although, as we pointed out above, the last will occupy us more in the second part of this chapter when we look at motivation.

From this perspective, therefore, there is little difference in our under-standing of attitude and personality trait although the latter points us much more firmly towards the idea that there is an individual person who expresses these attitudes or characteristics whereas a trait is a part of the personality. Significantly, Haslam refers to learning only in relation to cog-nition and emotion, which, surprisingly, he also discusses under cognition. However, our concern is in recognising that attitudes are multidimensional and that we have to recognise that those which might be regarded as ele-ments in the process of construing experience and then transforming it are cognitive, emotive and evaluative, in the first instance, and that in differ-ent situations one or other of these dimensions might predominate. Like many other aspects of the human person, attitudes are rarely learned in their wholeness and neither are they learned in a completely conscious or intended manner. For instance, we may change our emotive orientation towards an object or phenomenon before we change our cognitive one, or we may have our values altered and this affects other dimensions of the attitude. We have also already seen how much of our cognitive learning can be unintended and is often pre-conscious, whereas our emotive and evaluative learning can also be pre-conscious or even unconscious in the first instance but as a characteristic becomes more enduring we may be more conscious of it. Once it is enduring, it is easier to understand it as a personality trait.

Attitudes are also learned in the context of our life-world: we adopt the attitudes held by leading members of our membership group and also those held by out reference groups or 'heroes' (see Krech *et al.*, 1962). Indeed, recognition that this occurs is frequently used by advertisers when they seek to persuade people to change their attitudes and adopt that held by their reference group or heroes. Many advertisements picture crowds adopting specific products or social positions in the hope that we will follow the crowd. Celebrities, especially famous sports personalities, are paid huge sums of money to be seen to be endorsing a commodity in anticipation that we will adopt a positive attitude towards the product and purchase it. In a similar manner, our membership group may function as a reference group and our attitudes are affected by the group so that we learn them and in some cases continue to hold them long after we have left the group.

We see that in modern campaigns to change people's attitudes the cognitive dimension is often coupled with visual experiences and emotive situations since different dimensions of the experience affect the behaviour of different people. Advertisements on television, for example, seek to convey information and affect the emotions and often the values of the viewers: teaching intensive courses on stress situations also seek to touch on the different dimensions of attitudes. We may be more aware of one of the dimensions when we have an experience, for example the informative or the emotive in visual images; the evaluative is less obvious but is still learned pre-consciously. Our attitudes may, however, be affected in all three dimensions by the experience. In other words, the instructor who devises the experience may deliberately include some hidden elements in the programme so that they are learned pre-consciously at the same time as the dominant elements are learned consciously. (This was always the nature of the hidden curriculum, although sometimes the programme designer's own attitudes are hidden in the programme because the designer merely assumed them to be part of the situation.) However, all of these elements are all theoretical until we examine the ensuing behaviour, but, before we act, changes in our attitudes may actually change our motivation to act in a given manner.

Learning attitudes, then, may be conscious or pre-conscious, or a combination of the two. However, we rarely set out to learn an attitude, although certain teachers, in specific situations, advertising, correctional education, and so on, may deliberately design the instruction/information to include the teaching of attitudes in a less obvious fashion. Our attitudes are important dimensions in our orientation to life's problems and our propensity to solve them.

Part 2: Intelligence

It is clear that our intelligence is not really a single factor built into us: Gardner's (1983) theory of multiple intelligences indicates this. Consequently, we are bound to ask what precisely is intelligence and both how it affects our learning and how it is affected by that learning. Early research into intelligence suggested that there were at least two forms of intelligence: fluid intelligence depends upon our own mental fluency whereas crystallised intelligence grows and develops as we acquire new knowledge and skills through learning and life experience. We would expect that the former declines with age whereas the latter would continue to develop for as long as we stay engaged with social living – we will meet disengagement theory in the following chapter. Cattell (1963) developed this distinction, and more recently Craik and Salthouse (2000) have confirmed that this actually does happen as we age.

However, another way of looking at intelligence is suggested by Flynn (2007: 53–4), who suggests that we have six traits that affect our ability to solve problems with cognitive content:

- mental acuity – ability to provide on-the-spot solutions to problems that we have never encountered before;
- habits of the mind – generating new ways of looking at problems and habitualising them;
- attitudes – these lay bare the ability to acquire habits of the mind;
- knowledge and information – the more knowledge possessed, the more problems that can be tackled;
- speed of information processing – the higher the speed, the quicker we can solve problems;
- memory.

He recognises that there are other traits but suggests that these paint a realistic picture allowing for cross-cultural variation although he recognises that others, e.g. Goleman, would argue for a slightly different list and that this list is pre-theoretical. Clearly, the more knowledge that we have generated, the greater will be the ability to solve future problems – which is consistent with the ideas of fluid and crystallised intelligence.

Crystallised intelligence suggests that we can actually learn to become more intelligent as a result of what we have previously learned. If we take this position seriously, we will recognise that we become more intelligent as we age – provided that we utilise our previous experiences in our future actions. But this is not always the case, and we might also require motivation to do this. Nevertheless, the fact that we all have crystallised intelligence is sufficient reason for claiming that we can actually learn to become intelligent.

Part 3: Motivation

We live in our acts, and motivation is the driving force to act: its definition has always been elusive, but 'motivation is a concept which explains why people behave as they do' (Weiner, 1980; cited in Wlodkowski, 1985: 1). Nevertheless, this is a complex phenomenon and, as we have already pointed out, there is no logical connection between *knowing how* and *being able*, i.e. there is no logical connection between knowing and doing. Learned information is an insufficient reason for behaviour, but emotive commitment to a phenomenon or object may be a driving force that makes us act in relation to it. As we pointed out in the first part of this chapter, motivation may be seen as an attitude or a disposition that has a number of dimensions besides the cognitive, such as the emotive, the evaluative and even the belief or ideological dimensions. We learn to want/need/have to do something through a combination of these dimensions. The mere fact that we combine want, need and necessity illustrates the idea that the concept of motivation is an umbrella one to explain a number of driving forces that affect our action, most of which are learned – although there may also be evolutionary forces operating at the same time as the physiological and the social.

From the evolutionary perspective, we have needs that must be satisfied – these are both bodily and safety needs. In fact, they are the bottom two of Maslow's famous hierarchy of needs and as such they are the basic motivators of human living – Halmos (1978) referred to these as primary needs whereas all others are secondary, and in some cases the primary ones can be over-ridden by conscious decisions to fulfil secondary ones; thus, for example, mountaineers will put their lives at risk in order to gain personal fulfilment, and so on. We make conscious efforts to respond to these needs and learn coping mechanisms, which include attitudes, beliefs and actions. These are learned from experience and assessed quite pragmatically. The fact that we can over-ride our basic needs indicates something more about the nature of the person being more than a very sophisticated mechanism.

Tomasello (1999: 72–7) illustrates how we acquire our intentions to act very early in our lives, although he also recognises that our evolutionary inheritance plays its part since he argues that we 'inherit a special ability to identify with conspecifics' (ibid: 77). Throughout this discussion Tomasello is keen to point out that infants act intentionally from the time that they are a few months old and that by, or even before, the time that they are eight to nine months old they can even recognise intentionality in others, that is, they learn from trial and error, observation and experience and then later learn to respond to what they perceive to be the intentions in others. Intention to act – motivation – is learned from very early on in our lives and it is based on the principle of pragmatism. Intentionality, therefore, is not pre-conscious or pre-cognitive but at the same time it is difficult to describe learning intentionality as a conscious process. The act is certainly intentional, but the intention to act has also been learned through imitation and trial and error, and so on. Both needs and intentions underlie our understanding of motivation, but there is more to motivation than this since needs is a more complex concept.

Social needs, such as Halmos's secondary needs and the higher ones in Maslow's hierarchy, generally exhibit themselves in the form of desires

– but not all desires come from internal needs. Advertising is aimed at creating needs (Jarvis, 2008) and so we learn to desire commodities that are advertised. We may learn the desire consciously or subconsciously, and this is part of the skill of advertising since the advertisements often utilise several dimensions of attitudes, such as satisfaction, enjoyment, comfort and so on, in order to create the need in a person. We acquire the motivation to act in a certain manner through learning to desire objects and outcomes.

In precisely the same way, needs are generated through our beliefs and values. Being committed to certain ideologies and forms of behaviour which we have learned previously results in our being motivated to act in accord with the demands of, or needs generated by, our beliefs and values, but the motivation may itself be emotive since it is our commitment to the belief or value that encourages us to act in a certain manner. Action becomes an endeavour to fulfil our desires or, ultimately, our learned needs. Being free to realise our desires brings us back to the social situation in which we live and act. Whereas our actions may fulfil our needs, they may also impinge upon the lives of others, and so it is no wonder that Levinas (1991) regards meeting with the stranger as the beginning of ethics since we have to learn to take the Other's being and needs into account in our own behaviour.

If our behaviour is public, then our motivation may be affected by how we perceive that others view us, or the expectations that they have of us (Goffman, 1959). We may wish to conform, or even to present ourselves in a certain manner, and so our motives to act are guided by our perception of the world. We have learned that there is a certain expectation and we may desire to fulfil it, to present ourselves in an acceptable or even successful manner, and so on. Or we may be controlled internally by our morality and behave in accord with our own demands upon ourselves. The strength of these demands depends on the degree of emotional commitment we have to those moral values. Often the commitment may be weak and so, while we espouse the values in theory, we may fail to do so in practice, and this brings us back to the fundamental difference between theory and practice. In these cases we have learned consciously to act in specific ways but our commitment may not be sufficiently strong to do so, for one reason or another. Behaviour, then, is more than a single intention – it may be the result of conflicting motive, or attitudes, values, beliefs, and so on.

Conclusion

Haslam (2007: 15) suggests that 'the study of personality is distinctive for its focus on individuality and its concern for the person as a functioning whole'. As we draw this section to a close we can see that we have looked at the way that the whole person learns thorough a variety of procedures. In precisely the same way, therefore, we see that the different dimensions of personality are learned, and that learning occurs through our experiences of daily living in different social situations. We have begun to point to the way in which we learn to be persons, but before we reach our conclusion we need to combine these deliberations and we will do so in the final two chapters by first examining the process of becoming and, finally, that of being itself.

Section III

Being and becoming

Chapter 17

Becoming

During the previous part of this study we broke down the concept of experience into its various dimensions and we noted that we learn in each of them; in so doing we have highlighted the complexity of the whole process of learning, and throughout this book we have seen quite clearly that learning is a lifelong process – but our conception of lifelong differs from the two most commonly used ones, work life learning and adult learning. We are concerned about learning throughout the whole of the life cycle and so lifelong learning is effectively lifetime learning: we learn through the whole of our lives and, in a sense, learning is almost synonymous with consciousness. Using the concept of disjuncture we have tried to highlight the points at which learning is most likely to occur in a conscious manner when we can no longer behave in a habitual and taken-for-granted manner, and so we have to learn how to do or think things differently. But we have also suggested that, as we age and have more similar experiences, so our concepts and values change – time and experience within it underlie much of our learning. Both the body and the mind change with lifetime experiences. The body would change quite naturally although our learning can affect it, but our perceptions, cognitions and so on are also changed as a result of ageing. Thus, in this chapter we look at the life cycle and ageing, the life transitions and how we grow and develop, life history and the way in which we learn from our own lives including reminiscence and, finally, achieving our potential – whatever it is.

That we live in time is a truism, and we so often conceptualise time as a linear phenomenon, and this gives rise to the biological understanding of ageing: the body undergoes irreversible changes through the processes of time which will eventually prevent it functioning but, as we are all well aware, modern medicine has delayed this process and genetic engineering might continue this process even further. In this sense, we are moving in a linear direction. However, when we talk about us achieving our potential the process might not be so linear; if it is, do we never achieve our potential or do we achieve it earlier in our lives? Yet, for as long as we are alive, we are always becoming. It is interesting that we employ the term 'life cycle'

– not a linear concept but one that suggests that perhaps we are going nowhere, or that the end of our living is still becoming however long we live and whatever we achieve. We will return to this towards the end of this chapter. Ageing, then, is a complex interplay between the body and the mind in time and the one might 'age' at a completely different rate from the other, and so on.

Part 1: The life cycle and ageing

Over the years many have postulated the idea of life having its various stages:

> All the world's a stage
> And all the men and women merely players;
> They have their exits and their entrances;
> And one man in his time plays many parts,
> His acts being seven ages.
>
> (*As You Like It*, Act 2, Scene 7)

Such a scene might well have inspired Goffman's dramaturgical studies in sociology in seeing the world as a stage in which we all play our different roles, which we have to learn, but the seven ages points us to the different stages in our lifespan. The have been many formulations of the life cycle built on this idea, such as:

Erikson's (1965: 239–61) eight ages of man –

- basic trust versus basic mistrust;
- autonomy versus shame and doubt;
- initiative versus guilt;
- industry versus inferiority;
- identity versus role confusion;
- intimacy versus isolation;
- generality versus stagnation;
- ego integrity versus despair.

Since childhood was the topic of Erikson's work, it is not surprising that the earlier part of life is more fully dealt with here than the later part. His seventh stage appears to cover the whole of adulthood in as much as it is about the fulfilment of 'the need to be needed' through the producing and raising children. But McAdams (2000: 576–89) shows quite clearly that this is also a characteristic that spills over into old age and so it is not entirely age related, and it will be argued below that ego integrity is not only an end-of-life phenomenon. Other formulations, however, have rectified Erikson's emphasis on childhood and adolescence: Levinson and Levinson (1996: 25–6), for instance, offer nine stages after childhood:

- early adult transition (17–22 years old);
- entry life structure for early adulthood (22–28 years old);
- age 30 transition (28–33 years old);
- culminating life structure for early adulthood (33–40 years old);
- mid-life transition (40–45 years old);
- entry life structure for middle adulthood (45–50 years old);
- age 50 transition (50–55 years old);
- culminating life structure for middle adulthood (55–60 years old);
- late life transition (60–65 years old).

Unlike Erikson, Levinson is more concerned with biological age and its relationship to lifestyle, but he also omits the issue of older persons, and this is something that Sheehy (1995) captures, although she also omits the early years and, like Erikson, she is concerned about integrity:

- tryout twenties;
- turbulent thirties;
- flourishing forties;
- flaming fifties;
- serene sixties;
- sage seventies;
- uninhibited eighties;
- nobility of the nineties
- celebratory centenarians.

In these periods she recognises crisis points, which are important learning times, for example when we suddenly realise, when we are in our mid-30s, that we have to take stock of our lives; when we leave our early adulthood behind us and have a mid-life crisis; during the menopause; when we have mortality crises or meaning crises; and so on. Each of these critical points in our lives is a time when we are forced to think about our life and what it means: when we face the situation that we have less time to retirement than we have spent in work; when we ask what have we achieved and what can we achieve; and so on. We will return to the idea of learning from our lives later in this chapter, but it is significant that Sheehy argues that we can choose (learn) how to age. Hudson (1999) adopts a similar life cycle structure to Sheehy's, although he does so within the context of human purpose, to which we will also return later in the chapter.

From the fact that some of the theorists base their understanding on the biological age of the body and social situation of the individual, we can see that even ageing is a conceptually problematic process. Even in the 'maps of life' that we have outlined above, we can see differences, and we have only to look at how life expectancy has changed to recognise that the maps are relative to the age in which we live: but it also means that we may be living with an outdated map in our mind, e.g. expecting to die at 70 when 70 may just be the beginning of old age, and so we actually make mistakes with our life plans. There are numerous theories of ageing (see Moody, 1998). This is not the place to review them all in depth, but it is significant that the social context plays a large role in some of these theories and this is, in turn, related to learning, either directly or indirectly.

Clearly, any theory of ageing is bound to our biological base, although it is increasingly recognised that we can affect our bodies through activity – both physical and mental. It used to be assumed that, however active we were, as we aged we lost some neurons in the brain, but Sheehy (1995: 353), citing established neuroscientists, makes the comment that:

> Brain cells don't die off in annual batches of a hundred thousand, as we believed; rather, they shrink or grow dormant in old age, particularly from lack of stimulation or challenge. But even in an older brain 'sprouting' can take place, in which new neural processes form additional synapses.

Indeed, Blakemore and Frith (2005: 8–9) make the point that the ageing brain can learn, but the extent to which it can learn depends upon how much it is used. Indeed, they are advocates of lifelong learning. Activity can restimulate the brain. Activity theories of ageing appear to presuppose that people seek to perform the same roles and activities throughout life because they have needs and values and that they will continue to do even into their old age. However, activity theory suggests that we can prolong the body's active functioning through physical activity and that this activity also affects the mind since it assists the blood flow through the brain. Another version of this is the continuity theory, which claims that throughout our lives we seek to maintain the same personality, habits and values even as the body changes, and, although it may be true that we are creatures of habit, this does not mean that we are inflexible or that we cannot and do not change as we age. In contrast, a popular theory a few years ago suggested that, as people age, so they seek to disengage from the wider society and build their lives around their own wants and needs irrespective of the wider society. This is understandable in a time of very rapid social change; as we age we find it difficult to keep abreast of all the changes in modern society and so we gradually disengage from some of it and as a result become apparently less relevant to that world. However, such a view of the ageing reflects the relativity of social values: in bygone days the wisdom of the elders was prized and respected, but in modern society the elderly are often construed as not understanding the world, from which they are sometimes estranged. Whereas modern medicine can affect our biological process, it is clear that learning can affect our mental ones and the more we learn and continue to learn and the more we are engaged in the world, the more we can adapt to the changing society and perform our roles and activities within it. Hudson's (1999) study indicated ways in which we can continue to self-renew as we age even to extreme old age. Hudson (ibid.: 202) records the fact that in America there are over a quarter of a million centenarians who live and continue to function in the community in a wide variety of ways.

Part 2: Life transitions

Primitive societies changed very slowly, in fact they were almost static. However, the people who lived in them were far from static: they changed physically and in status in the tribe as they grew and developed. In order to accommodate this change, primitive societies marked these changes with ritual – what van Gennep (1960 [1908]) called *rites de passage* – so that at puberty, marriage, childbirth, and so on, society could adjust to the changes through a ritual process and the individuals could be taught the new responsibilities of their biological age. There were three stages to the ritual: moving from one status through liminality to re-incorporation into society in a new status. Basically, this process involved moving from one set of social structures that inhibited change to another that also demanded conformity – liminality is the transition period in which novitiates were taught their new roles by the elders and priests. It was a time of disjuncture, a time of learning. Liminal periods are always times of learning – times when we try to reconnect with the world but in a different way from that which we have experienced previously. Few of these rituals are still practised in society, but childbirth and naming, marriage and death are three: a fourth one which is widely practised but which we (Jarvis, 2001) have suggested is an incomplete ritual is retirement. At retirement we are ritualised out of our employment and enter a period of liminality, but society has no ritual of re-incorporation and so we are left to learn how to be old and unemployed: retirement can be a time in which we learn to use our freedom actively or one in which we gradually feel disengaged from society. Increasingly in contemporary society, organisations are being established, such as Universities of the Third Age, that help older people to learn to find a full life again.

But in modern society rites of passage do not accompany many of our transitions; every time we move from one status to another, we have to learn what the new role or status demands from us. This is, in part, what Hudson (1999) sees as self-renewal and Sheehy (1995: 357) suggests that, 'The quickest way to learn . . . is to interrupt your everyday, predictable experience. Put yourself on the line'. Life generates many transitions – times when we move homes, times when we change jobs, and so on;

Sheehy suggests that we should create our own. What transitions do is to break down the social structures that contain and restrict us and force us to get away from old habits, etc.; we have the opportunity to learn new things free of many past constraints and so there is a sense in which 'successful' ageing might take the form of a discontinuity theory, although for some who cannot make the crossover to a new way forward, the transition can be a dangerous moment.

The rapid changes in society are such that we often hear people, usually but not always older people, exclaiming that they do not know what the world is coming to these days. Change generates disjuncture and forces us to learn or to disengage from society and seek a world of the familiar in which we are not so challenged to learn new things and, in this sense, this is partly opposed to the modernist theory discussed above. We need not be pushed aside as we age, but we will be unless we continue to learn and keep abreast with the changes with which we are continually confronted, because rapid changes in society mean that life transitions are not rare social occurrences as they were in primitive society, but are more frequent and individual – they are almost, but not quite, everyday occurrences. The rapid changes in society present us with opportunities of learning, exploring new experiences, growing and developing – so that we can see this as a social theory of ageing and as a complement to the modern theory that we discussed above. We are still becoming for as long as we continue to learn and practise what we learn, as many a biography – such as those recorded by Sheehy – illustrates.

Hudson (1999) sees those who respond to the challenges created by modern societies as self-renewing persons who are continuing learners and who refine their capabilities. He (ibid.: 235–41) suggests that they have 10 qualities. They are value driven; are connected to the world around them; require solitude and quiet; pace themselves; have contact with nature; are creative and playful; adapt to change; learn from down times; are always in training; and are future orientated. Not everybody has these qualities in equal amounts, but each of them is positive, and it is their positive nature that is important. Hudson goes on to suggest that there are certain skills that we have to learn if we are to have personal mastery as we age. They revolve around feelings, thinking and doing, which are at the heart of learning, and we have to be positive about each of them. Consequently, we can see that we can continue to grow and develop for as long as we are positively engaged in the world, seeking to learn from it and being flexible within it. However, we need to point out that tolerance need not mean tolerating all of those things that we think are wrong.

Life transitions are not fixed as they were for primitive societies – as society has become more open, they occur more frequently and at different times for different people. However, each transition is a time for growth and development. Hence, the non-formal education and learning that primitive people undertook at periods of life transition are now built into a system of continuing learning and education. New studies, such as Willment's (2008) anthology on mid-life learning, reflect the reality of lifelong learning and becoming. This is also a time of identity change which reflects both the changes in our lives and the processes of becoming – but identity is also personal and not quite so related to life transitions, and so we will deal with this in the final chapter of this book.

Part 3: Life history and learning from our lives

Understanding the way people learn and how they learn from their own lives has given rise to two slightly different but very similar approaches: the study of life history itself and the study of learning that stems from seeking to understand how people learn consciously from their own life experiences (Dominice, 2000; see also the web site for Learning Lives, www.learninglives.org, for a research project that was conducted just before this book was written).

Many older adults write their autobiographies in order to let their children and grandchildren know what it was like in their younger days. However, in doing so they are not only recording events because, as we saw earlier, writing is a creative process and part of what we do when we write our biography is actually learn something more from our own recollections of our lives, and thus learn more about ourselves. Whereas an autobiography may be presented as if it was a factual narrative of the past, it is often much more creative and constructive. Consequently, life histories help us to reflect on the past to try to capture a little more of the reality – in a sense it is retrospective learning.

But in studies of learning from our lives, the focus is always much more specifically on the learning that has occurred. Even then, however, it is clear from Dominice's work that just thinking about the past generates learning experiences for the authors of the stories. Dominice asked his students to write their own educational biography – an account of their own learning (Dominice, 2000: 171) – and then to discuss these in small groups. This demonstrated clearly how significant interpretation is in the process – it is a continuing process of learning as individuals account for the past in terms of the present.

The Learning Lives project is similar in many ways to Dominice's work, although it was not conducted with students but is the result of 528 interviews with 117 people across the age range. This research project was designed to discover what learning meant to the lives of the respondents. Their findings (Strategies for Improving Learning through the Life-Course, 2008: 5) suggest that learning can:

- help people with the processes of routine living;
- help people adjust to changed circumstances;

- provide valuable knowledge or skill for particular purposes;
- contribute to changing self-identity;
- contribute to the achievement of agency.

It is clear that, although this extensive and important research project approaches the conceptualisation of learning that underlies this book, it still seeks to distinguish learning from living in a way that I feel is a little artificial. However, its findings are very important to experiential learning theory generally.

As we age, so the desire to tell our stories stays with us, and even towards the end of our lives many of us reminisce – tell others about our past. In this way we reconstruct our lives. Alheit (1995: 57) cites Kirkegaard: 'Life can only be understood backwards. In the mean time, it has to be lived forwards'. Reminiscence has a number of different functions according to Merriam (1985):

- life satisfaction;
- adaptation to stress;
- cognitive functioning;
- ego integrity.

Merriam (ibid.: 57) further suggests that:

> reminiscence functions as an adaptive mechanism, or facilitates per-
> sonality reorganization in late adulthood. Reminiscence appears to
> play a role in life satisfaction, coping with stress, enhancing cognitive
> functioning, and facilitating the life review process.

Gibson (1995: 4) suggests that:

> reminiscence is one way of pushing back or holding at bay, at least for
> a time, this shrinking world (of a person suffering from dementia).
> We all possess memories, we all have our own unique life history that,
> for good or ill, however it has turned out, is an indissoluble part of
> ourselves, our own unique personhood.

Our memory of who we are and what we have learned stays with us for as long as we can consciously recall it – at this point we have stopped becoming and through the weakness of our bodies and minds we are no longer able to continue learning and growing in the ways that we were doing previously and so we begin to lose those aspects of our being that make us a person.

Part 4: Achieving our human potential

One of the four aims of lifelong learning, according to the European Commission (2001) policy document, is achieving our potential. The assumption is that, whatever our potential, we can achieve it some time in the future through learning. The document, however, lacks any basic theoretical underpinning. There seems to be an idea that time is linear and we progress, or process, through time to an end – as if our potential is finite and we may achieve it at some time or another in the future. It is a lifespan concept rather than a life cycle one, in which we may achieve some of our potential at different stages of our lives – athletes, for instance, usually fulfil some elements of their bodily potential quite early in the lives. But we may have much potential that we have no desire to achieve, even though colleagues and friends bemoan the fact that we do not fulfil their own estimates of us – and this may be because we prefer to do things that we like doing and even to self-actualise.

Self-actualisation can be similar to achieving our potential when, following Maslow's (1968) famous hierarchy, we fulfil all our lower needs and reach the stage of self-actualisation – we have grown and developed and have reached the highest point. But a problem with this approach is that we can self-actualise while fulfilling more basic needs, or even putting at risk basic needs in order to achieve another end – in this sense self-actualisation becomes a motivation to act. For instance, mountaineers may put at risk their need for bodily safety in order to achieve the physical and mental satisfaction of scaling some dangerous peak, and so on. In the same way, it may be that, as we age, so we may get satisfaction by listening to music, talking with friends, or just being with the family, and so on. Satisfaction is not necessarily achieving some potential or other, although it may be that we experience a sense of integrity – which is a dimension of the dilemma that Erikson suggests we all experience at the end of our lives – ego integrity versus despair. For him (Erikson, 1965: 260):

> Although aware of the relativity of all the various life styles which give meaning to human striving, the possessor of integrity is ready to defend the dignity of his own life style against all physical and economic threats. For he knows that the individual life is the accidental coincidence of but one life cycle with but one segment of history; and that for him all human integrity stands or falls with the one style of integrity of which he partakes. The style of integrity developed by his culture or civilization thus becomes the 'patrimony of his soul', the seal of his moral paternity of himself.

Clearly, such a state is one for which most people will strive, but it need not be an end-of-life state: it can be a state that we achieve at a much younger age when we become satisfied with our life choices and so on. It may be that this might be regarded as one of the ends of our own humanity – and fulfilling our potential may also be a matter of fulfilling our human potential, and this we can also do by learning and doing at any age in our lives by being and acting in some way or other.

However, Sheehy (1995) records many stories of people in their sixties who have discovered that achievement results in happiness with their lives – a sense of being at ease with themselves. Much of this happiness comes from finding meaning or purpose in life rather than, in Erikson's words, stagnating. Happiness may be seen by many as achieving our potential, but it may be regarded as an indicator that our needs are being satisfied by our present lifestyle and we are doing the things that we want to do, which may be a sign that we are on the way to achieving both some of our potential and a sense of personal integrity. In this way we begin to achieve our human potential.

Discussing our human potential begs the question about what it means to be human and, although this is a philosophical question that lies beyond the remit of this book, it is also one that underlies the concept of the person, to which we will return in the final chapter. As human beings we have a degree of, but by no means total, freedom to choose to achieve our potential; this makes us different, so we would believe, from other animals. Indeed, Vardy (2003: 41) suggests that human nature is measured in terms of potentialities, and if these potentialities are fulfilled individuals become what they are capable of becoming. In this sense, achieving our potential becomes an interesting moral question since in many cases we choose to achieve our potential – but it may be that we actually miss the opportunity of achieving it when we are presented with it by social position, condition or inclination. Vardy (ibid.: 39–40) suggests five ways in which our potential may fail to be actualised: by being too lazy or too busy to work at it; by choosing to take a lesser pathway; by being so self-centred that we fail to connect properly with the world; by failing to think about what type of person we might become; and by ignoring our moral and spiritual human nature. In a sense, we may be becoming other than what we could become and by so doing fail to achieve a sense of integrity in our lives. But we can see in each of these five points on non-achievement that, in considering our humanity and our human potential, we are concerned with practical living in a social context – or in a real sense 'the primacy of practice' – even in our learning. At the same time, we can begin to see that underlying our becoming is always a moral question about achieving our potential as human beings.

Conclusion

Becoming, then, is about lifelong learning, but at different stages in our lives we have different needs and motivations and, although all learning may be developmental, Hudson (1999) suggests that in the early part of life learning is instrumental – he calls it developmental. He (ibid.: 246) suggests that:

> The central theme of adult learning in the first half of life is to gain knowledge and skills for leading secure, successful, joyous lives. Learning is getting ahead, obtaining certification or licensure, and ensuring successful passage through careers and human systems.

Learning in later life, what he calls transformative learning – although since all learning is transformative this is a misleading term – is more concerned with the development of the self. Since all learning is about the development of the self, we prefer to use more traditional terms such as vocational and non-vocational to describe the difference and to recognise that vocational learning might well decrease after mid-life, but, as the work life expands, so new forms of continuing vocational learning might also be emerging. At the same time, a greater proportion of our learning in later life is non-vocational. However, another difference is that less of our learning in later life is formal and intentional but since we are still engaged with the world in a conscious manner, we are still learning and becoming and perhaps still endeavouring to fulfil our human potential.

Chapter 18

Being

Becoming, as we saw in the previous chapter, carries with it a sense of time, i.e. that time is linear and we continue to develop throughout the whole of our lives. In contrast, being carries with it only a sense of the present: we are or I am at almost any time in our lives. As a concept, 'being' has undergone considerable scrutiny over the years and has several major connotations. In the first place it refers to existence; however, we can say that a stone exists and that it is there in the ground, but it does not have being in the sense that we are implying here, i.e. carrying with it some sense of life. Even then we need to ask whether a cat is in the same sense as we are or I am, and perhaps we answer this in the affirmative. Would we then do so for even lower forms of life? If we would, we can see immediately that we use being in the sense of living existence – it is almost then the equivalent of life itself. This is the implication in Agamben's (1995) use of the term 'bare life', i.e. life before or without any form of enculturation. But we have seen in the early chapters of this book that, since fetuses begin to learn pre-consciously in the womb, there cannot be human life without learning or some form of enculturation. This, though, raises the question of the nature of brain death and being in a vegetative state – questions that lie just beyond the edge of this discussion but will not be pursued any further here.

Being, then, is not about the passing of time, but it is about our human existence at any point throughout the duration of our lives, although we recognise that at various times in our lives aspects of our being change. But despite this change, we still exist – we are throughout our lives. The cells of our body and brain change frequently, but we remain throughout all of these bodily changes, or as Donald (2001: 207) says: 'By the time we are adults, we do not have a single atom of our childhood left. Yet the physical "we" still exists'. It is a different 'physical' being, but what is not different is the feeling that we are still the same person. Our being transcends, but cannot exist without, our physical bodies, but our being is synonymous neither with ourselves nor with the fulfilment of our desires.

Existentialists tend to contrast being, that is human being in some way, with the more basic forms of existence to which we have already pointed.

We can see that there is a sense in which bare life is hardly a viable concept in human terms although it is clearly viable in a scientific sense. Consequently, we can see that being is a fundamental tenet to humanity and that because we are, we think or experience – which is precisely the opposite from Descartes' *cogito ergo sum*. Thus, being precedes knowledge, and this is what we have shown in the earlier chapters of this book – or, rather, being precedes conscious knowledge. This does not mean that the cosmos did not exist before we were conscious of it, only that it existed independently of being known to us or by us. We are obviously part of the universe and a latecomer to it, but only through our being can knowledge exist and in this sense we, as part of the evolutionary process, are the producers of knowledge – knowledge is dependent upon the knowers and this assertion neither demands nor denies the existence of a creative force behind either the universe or humanity.

Nevertheless, human existence is the fundamental underlying our discussion: only through our existence can we know the world, or can the world be known to us and by us. However, this also implies that there is an external and an internal world and that we can know the external and the internal. But that raises another fundamental problem – whereas I can know the external and my own internal understanding of reality, and other people can know their own external world and their own internal world, none of us can know each other's internal world, and so we meet the solipsist argument that we are encapsulated within ourselves. The fact that we can relate to each other and can discuss the external world with each other in a knowledgeable fashion means that our perceptions of that world are almost certainly similar and so we are not imprisoned by the self. But we do have our own perceptions – we are aware of our own life-world and we are aware of ourselves as being aware of our life-worlds in a way which allows us to discuss this awareness and create another awareness, and so on.

Being aware of our experiences and our own life history means that we have choices about our lives, which, as Erikson (1965) noted, can leave us with a sense of integrity or despair as we age, so that we can view each moment of our lives as authentic or inauthentic; that is, that we can utilise our freedom to achieve our potentiality and individuality or we can just fit into society and not really endeavour to transcend the everyday expectations of daily living. In both senses, we respond to the experiences of social living, although our actions and our learning differ: in trying to transcend the everyday and achieve our potential as authentic human beings we are exposed to doing things differently and learning new things, whereas in inauthentic living we tend to repeat experiences – although we can never actually repeat them precisely – go through the same rituals and routines of daily living and in so doing we may learn fewer new things. There is an important distinction in experiential terms between creating or generating an experience and merely having a experience, as Turner (1986: 35) records about Dilthey's (1976 [1914]: 210) work. In both of these cases we are discussing our own actions, our behaviour, and others can see what we do but only infer what we experience. They may draw inferences from our body language, and so on, but they can never be sure of precisely what we experience. When others observe our actions, they see us as players in the social world and, in this sense, we are ascribed a social identity, whereas later in our lives and as a result of our own experiences we gain a sense of self and of individual identity. This is an important distinction that we want to draw in this chapter, and the first two parts of this chapter analyse both of these in terms of learning and being. However, identity is a major problem in itself, and we will not enter the discussion fully here: our concern is to relate it to our learning and personality, and this we do in the third part. Finally, we want to approach the title of this book and ask questions about the nature of the person who exists in society, and this constitutes the final part of this chapter.

Part I: The emergence of individual self-identity

Tomasello (1999) traces the history of the emerging self to a child's joint attention with significant others upon an object or an event from the time when the child is about nine months old: he (ibid.: 61–77) calls this the nine months revolution. He shows that the idea of intentional agents emerges very early in interaction with others, although it is in imitative learning rather than other forms of initiative in the first instance: children 'recognize that they have goals that are clearly separated from behavioural means, at eight or nine months of age, that is how they understand other persons as well.' Imitative bodily learning is the way that children acquire the culture of their social group since they understand others as intentional agents and copy their behaviour. Tomasello (ibid.: 89) describes this process.

> As infants begin to follow and direct the attention of others to outside entities at nine to twelve months of age, it happens on occasion that the other person whose attention the infant is monitoring focuses on the infant herself. The infant then monitors the other person's attention to *her* in a way that was not possible previously . . . She now knows that she is interacting with another intentional agent who perceives her and intends things toward her. When the infant did not understand that others perceive and intend things toward an outside world, there could be no question of how they intended and perceived things toward *me*. After coming to this understanding, the infant can monitor the adult's intentional relation to the world including herself (the 'me' of William James and George Herbert Mead).

Children, then, understand themselves and others as intentional agents and they recognise that others treat them accordingly – they are entities in their own right. Nelson (2007) suggests that it is after this stage in development that children begin to develop autobiographical memories which revolve around this emerging sense of self. In the very early days of childhood the major change in the self is the transition from one 'confined to one experience-based reality to the possibility of many possible realties, represented by others, viewed through media, and imagined alone, made available through social, cultural, and symbolic resources' (ibid.: 184). This results in a uniquely human kind of memory – episodic and autobiographical – and a realisation that our memories of the past differ from our memories of other's experiences that are described to us through language. Nelson suggests that autobiographical memory emerges at the end of the pre-school period and consists of episodic memories of major events that occur in our own lives and in past time.

It is in these early processes that the sense of self emerges – it is, as Nelson (ibid.: 187) suggests, 'coterminous with the beginning of autobiographical memory'. The learning and remembering of these events in early childhood enables children to place themselves in time, but those early social identities which we describe below as being ascribed to the child are not even known to the child because it does not have the conceptual apparatus in these early days to understand them. It is only through interaction with others that children gradually develop a sense of themselves in time: interaction itself is important because children gradually learn about other's intentions and experiences and how to express them and then they can identify with the present and with the community within which they participate. However, the significant thing about autobiographical memory is that once children have developed it they can revisit the past and this allows them to claim that 'I was there': this emerges in the late pre-school years, and then they can talk about their own experience of past events and even future possibilities. Consequently, 'me' becomes an enduring phenomenon, in a sense transcending immediate time but manifesting itself in it, which is built into our memories and learned. Once they can make this distinction, children develop the distinction between their memory and another's memory. Consequently, we can begin to see that with the emergence of the self in autobiographical memory we begin to develop a sense of our own uniqueness.

Here then we can begin to see how conscious but unintended learning occurs, generating memories of past events and a sense of self-continuity. In this sense, identity is dependent upon memories of our previous experiences and, therefore, of our earlier learning.

Part 2: Towards social identity

There are at least two aspects to the process of obtaining social identities and we will deal with them separately: the first is the identities which we are ascribed by those who are external to us and the second is the identities we achieve (learn) by playing our roles in society.

Ascribed identities

It is a truism that we are born into a social world and from the outset members of our life-world identify us in terms of our relationship to our significant others: first we are the child of our parents (John's son or daughter) and then we are named – either in a civic registration or in a secular or religious ritual, or in a combination of these. This is socially recognised in a *rite de passage,* in which the parents are formally and socially recognised as parents. This is our ascribed identity.

During our early childhood, our name is objectively our identifying factor, but during school years most of us join groups, clubs, gangs, and so on: in each of these outsiders label us, e.g. by the name of the school or the group or, as we become widely known, by our personal characteristics. As this process progresses we are achieving an identity which relates to our status or membership within the social group. We may actually wear distinguishing features that display something of our identity, and this is the earliest form we see to present ourselves in everyday life (Goffman, 1959), although as we age this process becomes much more subtle. If we do display our identity in childhood, we are taught how we are expected to behave as a member of that organisation.

We continue to have ascribed social identities as we age, since we are children, teenagers, young adults, older adults, aged, male or female, European or Asian, and so on. The life cycle acts as an ascription process as far as one aspect of our social identity is concerned: we do not achieve this identity, and in some ways it is too broad to be very meaningful, and yet we do meet expressions such as 'that behaviour was unbecoming of an adult', 'older people should not act that way', and even ironic or humorous references, such as Noel Coward's 'Englishmen out in the midday sun', and so on. These are stereotypical images of conformity; ritualising our behaviour and conforming to the institutions of society is part of the lifelong socialisation process displayed in Figure 2.1 – we are always internalising the cultural expectations that affect us.

Later in life, we occupy roles that are based upon our employment or lack of it: we wear uniforms or other symbols to display the occupational roles that we play and people label us by that uniform, if we wear one, or we carry stigma (Goffman, 1963) illustrating that we are members of other categories in society, often those which are eschewed by the greater majority of people. In all of these cases our learning about our identity is reinforced by the way in which others behave towards us in social interaction. However, there is a sense in which an aspect of social identity is conferred upon us simply because we occupy positions in the social structure – it is almost 'objective' and it is almost but not quite independent of the person being identified since it relates to our position in the social structure rather than to us as persons. Indeed, our individual identity emerges in the way that we make the role our own – the unique manner in which we play the role as we habitualise our role performance and manifest our personalities.

Often we are given a social identity before we ourselves identify with it: Camilleri (2009), for instance, discusses how student and novice nurses, once they don the uniform, are seen by others as nurses, even though they themselves cannot immediately identify with that role. In the first instance, then, they know that they are new nurses but they have not yet identified with the role and it takes days, even weeks, before new nurses cease to feel that they are play-acting. This is another part of the learning process, and they certainly do not feel that they are a nurse before they feel that they have the requisite knowledge and can habitualise their behaviour accordingly. Then they actually feel – a sense of knowing – that they are a nurse. Knowing, then, is a product of experience, and knowing who we are depends upon the experiences we have of being ourselves and playing our roles in society.

Occupying a role is a prerequisite for the ascription of a social identity but, even though we are given a social identity, we may not actually feel that we have that identity. Like the nurses, it is very common to hear older people exclaim that they do not feel their age and they do not conform to the stereotypical image of the elderly – they do not identify with the social identity which they are ascribed. Hence, ascribed social identity is but one element in achieving social identity.

Achieved identities

Throughout our lives we play many roles, and in playing them we are doing and learning by doing: as we noted earlier, a great deal of our actions are learned by imitation, trial and error, and discovery learning. However, learning the role performance or competency is only one step in the overall process since, as we habitualise our role performance and take our behaviour for granted, we begin to identify ourselves with our roles and with the acts that we perform and also with the symbols that accompany the roles – for instance, we identify with the uniform, as married people we identify with the ring that we wear, and so on. But we also learn to identify with the social identity which we have been ascribed, and in so doing we feel an integral part of the social world in which the role is performed – we have achieved a social identity. This social identity may relate to race, ethnicity, gender, class, power positions, occupational positions, and so on. The sociological analysis of these differing social identities lies beyond the scope of this book (see Taylor and Spencer, 2004).

Thus, we can see that we learn social identities through a combination of processes: there is external ascription and then internal realisation of the way that we perform our roles. However, we do not identify with our roles until we have learned to combine both the internal and the external and until we can also identify the role performance with the identity that is ascribed to us by the wider society. It is only then that we can begin to relate the social identity with the individual one and claim that 'we are nurses', and so on. But this sense of knowing differs from mere cognition – it is more of a holistic experience in which we play our role in a way which reflects our personality, and so our social identity is related to our sense of self. Hence, we are the role player, and our self is identified with the role and we claim to be a nurse, doctor, and so on. If we ask people about to retire to complete the sentence 'I am (a) . . . ' some 10 times – as I have done very frequently in running pre-retirement education courses – it is extremely rare to find that the occupation of the pre-retiree does not occur in the first three answers. I am my occupation – for many people. We learn to be ourselves and our occupation – we have combined the external with the internal. But none of us plays our occupational role in precisely the same manner – our personalities are far broader and whatever the roles we play our personalities are likely to be apparent. We are separate from our roles and, although we identify ourselves with them, our personalities transcend them – we do things 'our way'.

Part 3: Personality

Whereas I may see myself as a teacher, or some other occupation, so that I can claim to be a teacher, others who know me would distinguish me as a teacher from someone else who is a teacher. What, then, makes our role playing different? Basically, it is because we have different personalities and traits of my personality can be detected in the way that I perform my role. Consequently, the 'I' in 'I am a teacher' is not just a subjective acceptance of my socially prescribed role, it is me actively embracing that role – or, as Husserl argued, I am to be found in my acts. My personality is to be found in the way that I perform my role, as McAdams (2001) clearly shows in his opening chapter.

Personality is a complex concept, and here is not the place to write about personality psychology. Suffice to note that psychologists (Haslam, 2007: 27) claim that personality is structured along five major axes, or dimensions:

- extraversion–intraversion;
- agreeableness–disagreeableness;
- conscientiousness–irresponsibility;
- neuroticism–stability;
- openness to experience–conservatism

Various personality traits find their place along these dimensions and my personality, which is unique to me, is the combination of these traits which I exhibit. In this sense, personality psychology has two major strengths as far as this study is concerned – it is about the whole person and it is about the uniqueness of that person.

When we perform any action, we impose our own personality on the act and we are recognised not only by our physical features but by our personality characteristics. Our identity is not just that we are a teacher but that I am this teacher – the 'I' is the unique me that I have learned from early childhood and which is still with me for as long as I exist as an independent human being. But how I play that role is, in a sense, unique: it has never been played that way before and so I cannot merely repeat past acts – I do something more – I impose myself upon the situation and play my unique role. In this sense, I am continually learning to play my role my way.

But it could be objected that I have previously made the point that, because I can take for granted many of my actions, I have habitualised them, then I need not think about them because I act and it is only in disjunctural situations that I have to think about my actions. This is not an inconsistency in my argument: if I have played my unique role on many occasions in similar situations, I can assume that I will undertake that action in approximately the same way another time – until such a time as a disjunctural situation occurs. Then I have to learn how to play my role afresh – but it is still the same 'I' who learns it and plays it. But herein is one of the major problems – we are no longer free to play that role in any way we wish since there are two sets of constraints. First, we have social identities, which means that we will consider how any new role performance will be perceived by our social life-world and so we will feel constrained to act in accord with the way that we perceive others anticipate that we will act. Second, there is another problem – we have spent a lifetime developing our own personality characteristics and so, even if we could, we are unlikely to produce a different set of personality traits in any new action. My fresh expression is still recognisable as 'me'.

Now there are a multitude of personality traits, and it would be impossible to provide a definitive list – indeed, it would be impossible to provide a definitive list of those that describe us when we act. We may be able to list a number of the major ones, which may well be orientated along one of the five major dimensions, but these personality traits are not hard-wired into the brain, they are learned – and they reflect our individual differences along the lines of our habits, attitudes, beliefs, tastes, emotions, skills, and so on. Significantly, these are the subjects of the chapters in the second section of this book:

- different experiences and different ways of experiencing;
- different perceptions and ways of perceiving;
- our own individual thoughts and different ways of thinking;
- different levels of knowledge and different ways of knowing;
- different beliefs, ideologies and meaning systems;
- different feelings and emotions towards different phenomena;
- different ways of doing things;
- our own life-worlds, interactions with a wide variety of different people and functions within different cultural settings;
- different sets of values;
- different attitudes, intelligences and motivations.

Each of the chapters in the second section of the book shows how we have learned the above characteristics of our personalities, so that our role performance is bound to be individualised. We have all learned to be individuals and we learn to practise our own individual characteristics – each time we act, there is a significant sense in which we are continually learning to be ourselves. But we, ourselves, are more than just the 'cognitive personality'. That personality finds expression only through the use of our body and through speech and, more significantly, our learning of each of these characteristics begins with bodily sensations – we are both body and mind.

But in just the way that we have learned to be different, we have all learned to be persons. In a sense, the term 'person' pulls us back from our individuality and locates us within humanity itself, and so we finally need to ask ourselves what it means to be a human person.

Part 4: On being a person in society

Being a person is more than just playing these different social roles, and we have already implied that there is a self behind the roles, as Goffman (1959) would suggest, and that the role might just be a mask hiding a persona. Or would it be more correct to say that in every role performance, the person in present? After all, this is one of the meanings of 'person' – to be present 'in person'. What, then, is a person? At its broadest, it can mean an individual human being – both body and mind – and immediately this gives rise to a further discussion about what it means to be human (Archer, 2000; Vardy, 2003, *inter alia*). Archer is concerned that persons are agents. Vardy, however, argues that we are human persons when our lives exhibit the moral characteristics of accountability.

However, different cultures have tended to use the term slightly differently (see Carrithers *et al.,* 1985). Charles Taylor (ibid: 257–81), in the same volume of papers, has suggested that we are persons if we are agents acting in the world, aware of ourselves and of having purpose in our actions. But Taylor (ibid.: 261) goes on to say that we must have significances in our lives, i.e. desires, aspirations, feelings, aversions and emotions that make our purpose significant. But persons must also be able to plan for the future and, overall, a person must be a self-interpreting animal: a 'person is an agent who has an understanding of self as an agent' (ibid.: 263). This conception of the self is reflexive – we are self-aware. Taylor (ibid.: 276) summarises his own position thus:

> Being a person cannot be understood simply as exercising a set of capacities I have as an individual, on all fours with my capacity to breathe, walk, and the like. On the contrary, I only acquire this capacity in conversation, to use this as a term of art for human linguistic interchange in general; I acquire it in a certain form in conversation, that of my culture; and I maintain it through continuing interchange. We could put it this way: I become a person and remain one only as an interlocutor.

Relationship is at the heart of Taylor's understanding of an agent who relates to others, and through language we express all those human significances that make us ourselves. But it has been in relationship that we developed all of these human capacities – for 'in the beginning is relationship' claimed Buber (1958). In the very first chapter I cited Buber (1958: 17), who wrote that 'all real living is meeting'. He concluded that this meeting is a present phenomenon between *I* and *Thou*. But he (ibid.: 22) goes even further to claim that 'In the beginning is relationship', and it is 'through the *Thou* that the man becomes *I*'. We can be ourselves, as individual human persons, only in relationship with others as persons – we are all persons in society and we learn to be ourselves as we learn to relate to others and this is, paradoxically, more than just rational, instrumental learning – it is often unconscious and unintended and occurs in what might be seen as a by-product of intentional and instrumental learning.

Conclusion

Husserl said, 'I live *in* my Acts' (cited in Schutz, 1972: 51). I am, therefore I act, but also I act, therefore I am. But action is rarely meaningless, so that underlying action are intention and meaning but, paradoxically we have to learn both meaning and how to do things. Action is therefore not mindless – it is learned. In each role I play I learn not only how to perform the role but I learn to be me – in and through my actions in the wider society. Buber is not wrong to say that in the beginning is relationship – the I–Thou dialogue – but not long after that, within a very few months after life and in the early stages of consciousness, another dialogue is born that is just as important to us as human persons – the I–Me dialogue. I learn to be Me and in the reflective dialogue that occurs in, through and after my every act I continue this dialogue and the ensuing learning process – for it continues throughout my conscious life.

Being demands learning – perhaps being is synonymous with learning – and we all learn to be ourselves as persons in society!

References

Abercrombie, N., Hill, S. and Turner, B. (2000) *Dictionary of Sociology*, 4th edn. London: Penguin.

Agamben, G. (1990) *The Coming Community*. Minneapolis: University of Minnesota Press.

Agamben, G. (1995) *Homer Sacer*. Stanford: Stanford University Press.

Agamben, G. (2004) *The Open*. Stanford: Stanford University Press.

Alheit, P. (1995) Biographical learning: theoretical outline, challenges and contradictions of a new approach to adult education. In Alheit, P., Bron-Wojciechowska, A., Brugger, E. and Dominice, P. (eds) *The Biographical Approach in European Adult Education*. Vienna: Verband Wiener Volksbildung.

Allman, P. (1984) Self help learning and its relevance for learning and development in later life. In Midwinter, E. (ed.) *Mutual Aid Universities*. London: Croom Helm.

Apter, M. (1989) Negativism and the sense of identity. In Breakwell, G. (ed.) *Threatened Identities*. London: John Wiley.

Archer, M. (1988) *Culture and Agency: The Place of Culture in Social Theory*. Cambridge: Cambridge University Press.

Archer, M. (2000) *Being Human*. Cambridge: Cambridge University Press.

Arendt, H. (1958) *The Human Condition*. Chicago: University of Chicago Press.

Argyris, C. and Schön, D. (1974) *Theory in Practice: Increasing Professional Effectiveness*. San Francisco: Jossey-Bass.

Aristotle (1925 edition) *The Nicomachean Ethics*. Oxford: Oxford University Press.

Asch, S. (1952) Effects of group pressure upon the modification and distortion of judgements. In Swanson, G., Newcombe, T.M. and Hartley, E.L. (eds) *Readings in Social Psychology*. New York: Holt, Rinehart and Winston.

Aslanian, C. and Brickell, H. (eds) (1980) Americans in transition: life changes and reasons for adult learning. In *Future Directions for Framing Society*. New York: College Board.

Ayer, A. (1971) *Language, Truth and Logic*. Harmondsworth: Penguin.

Bandura, A. (1973) *Aggression: A Social Learning Analysis*. Englewood Cliffs, NJ: Prentice Hall.

Bandura, A. (1977a) Self-efficacy: toward a unifying theory of behavioral change. *Psychological Review* 84, 191–215.

Bandura, A. (1977b) *Social Learning Theory*. Englewood Cliffs, NJ: Prentice Hall.

Bauer, P., Wenner, J., Dropik, P. and Wewerka, S. (2000) Parameters of remembering and forgetting in the transition from infancy to early childhood. *Monographs of the Society of Research in Child Development* 65 (4 serial no. 263).

Bauman, Z. (1993) *Postmodern Ethics*. Oxford: Blackwell.

Bauman, Z. (2005) *Liquid Life*. Cambridge: Polity Press.

Baumard, F. (1999) *Tacit Knowledge in Organizations*. London: Sage.

Belbin, C. and Belbin, R. (1972) *Problems in Adult Retraining*. London: Heinemann.

Belenky, M., Clinchy, B., Goldberger, N. and Tarule, J. (1986) *Women's Ways of Knowing*. New York: Basic Books.

Bellah, R., Madsen, R., Sullivan, W., Swidle, A. and Tipton, S. (1985) *Habits of the Heart*. Berkeley: University of California Press.

Benner, P. (1984) *From Novice to Expert*. Menlo Park, CA: Addison Wesley.

Bentham, J. (1789) *An Introduction to the Principles of Morals and Legislation*. Republished in a wide variety of editions.

Berger, P. (1969) *The Social Reality of Religion*. London: Faber & Faber.

Berger, P.L. and Luckmann, T. (1966) *The Social Construction of Reality*. London: Penguin.

Bergson, H. (1998 [1911]) *Creative Evolution*. New York: Dover Publications.

Bergson, H. (1999 [1965]) *Duration and Simultaneity*. Manchester: Clinamen Press.

Bergson, H. (2004 [1912]) *Matter and Memory*. New York: Dover Publications.

Biggs, J. (2001) Enhancing learning: a matter of style or approach. In Sternberg, R. and Zhang, L.-F. (eds) *Perspectives on Thinking, Learning and Cognitive Styles*. Mahwah, NJ: Lawrence Erlbaum Associates.

Blackmore, S. (2007) Imitation makes us human. In Pasternak, C. (ed.) *What makes us Human?* Oxford: One World.

Blakemore, S.-J. and Frith, U. (2005) *The Learning Brain*. Oxford: Blackwell Publishing.

Borger, R. and Seaborne, A. (1966) *The Psychology of Learning*. Harmondsworth: Penguin.

Boud, D., Keogh, R. and Walker, D. (eds) (1983) *Reflection: Turning Experience into Learning*. London: Croom Helm.

Bourdieu, P. (1973) Cultural reproduction and social reproduction. In Brown, M. (ed.) *Reproduction in Education, Society and Culture*. London: Sage.

Bourdieu, P. (1992) The purpose of reflexive sociology. In Bourdieu, P. and Wacquant, L. (eds) *An Invitation to Reflexive Sociology*. Cambridge: Polity Press.

Brookfield, S. (1987) *Developing Critical Thinkers*. San Francisco: Jossey-Bass.

Bruner, J. (1990) *Acts of Meaning*. Cambridge, MA: Harvard University Press.

Buber, M. (1958) *I and Thou*. Edinburgh: Clarke.

Camilleri, M. (2009) 'Becoming a nurse', unpublished PhD thesis, University of Surrey, Guildford.

Capps, J. and Capps, D. (eds) (2005) *James and Dewey on Belief and Experience*. Urbana: University of Illinois Press.

Carrithers, M., Collins, S. and Lukes, S. (eds) (1985) *The Category of the Person*. Cambridge: Cambridge University Press.

Cashdown, A. and Whitehead, I. (eds) (1971) *Personality, Growth and Learning*. London: Longman.

Cattell, R. (1963) A theory of fluid and crystallized intelligence: a critical experiment. *Journal of Educational Psychology* 54, 1–22.

Chalmers, D. (1996) *The Conscious Mind*. Oxford: Oxford University Press.

Clark, C. (1997) *Misery and Company: Sympathy in Everyday Life*. Chicago: University of Chicago Press.

Collins English Dictionary (1979) London: Collins.

Collins, R. (1987) Interaction ritual chains. In Alexander, C., Giesen, B., Munch, R. and Smelser, N. (eds) *The Micro–Macro Link*. Berkeley: University of California Press.

Collins, R. (1990) Stratification, emotional energy, and the transient emotions. In Kemper, D. (ed.) *Research Agendas in Sociology of the Emotions*. Albany: State of New York University Press.

Craik, F. and Salthouse, T. (eds) (2000) *The Handbook of Aging and Cognition*, 2nd edn. Mahwah, NJ: Lawrence Erlbaum Associates.

Crane, T. (1992) (ed.) *The Contents of Experience*. Cambridge: Cambridge University Press.

Crawford, J. (2005) *Spiritually Engaged Knowledge*. Aldershot: Ashgate.

Csikszentmihalyi, M. (1990) *Flow: The Psychology of Optimal Experience*. New York: Harper and Row.

Daloz, L., Keen, C., Keen, J. and Parks, S. (1996) *Common Fire*. Boston: Beacon.

Davies, J. (1969) The J-curve of rising expectations and declining satisfaction as a cause of some great revolutions and contained rebellions. In Graham, H. and Gurr, T. (eds) *The History of Violence in America*. New York: Bantam.

Dawkins, R. (1976) *The Selfish Gene*. Oxford: Oxford University Press.

Dawkins, R. (2006) *The God Delusion*. London: Bantam.

Delors, J. (Chair) (1996) *Learning: The Treasure Within*. Paris: UNESCO.

Dennett, C. (1991) *Consciousness Explained*. Boston: Little Brown.

Dennett, D. (1995) *Darwin's Dangerous Idea*. London: Penguin.

Dennett, D. (1999) 'The evolution of culture', Charles Simonyi Lecture, Oxford, 17 February 1999.

Dennett, D. (2006) *Breaking the Spell*. London: Penguin.

Dewey, J. (1922) *Human Conduct and Nature: An Introduction to Social Psychology*. London: George Allen and Unwin.

Dewey, J. (1933) *How We Think*. Boston: D.C. Heath.

Dewey, J. (1991 [1910]) *How We Think*. New York: Prometheus Books.

Dews, J. (ed.) (1986) *Autonomy and Solidarity: Interviews with Jurgen Habermas*. London: Verso.

Dilthey, W. (1976 [1914]) *Selected Writings*. Cambridge: Cambridge University Press.

Dominice, P. (2000) *Learning from our Lives*. San Francisco: Jossey-Bass.

Donald, M. (2001) *A Mind So Rare*. New York: W.W. Norton.

Dreyfus, S. and Dreyfus, H. (1980) 'A five stage model of the mental activities involved in directed skill acquisition', unpublished report, University of California at Berkeley.

Dunbar, R. (2007) Why are humans not just great apes? In Pasternak, C. (ed.) *What Makes Us Human?* Oxford: Oneworld Publications.

Durkheim, E. (1915) *The Elementary Forms of Religious Life*. London: George Allen and Unwin.

Durkheim, E. (1933 [1893]) *The Division of Labor in Society*. New York: Free Press.

Erikson, E. (1965) *Childhood and Society*, revised edition. Harmondsworth: Penguin.

European Commission (2001) *Making a European Area of Lifelong Learning a Reality*. Brussels: European Commission COM (2001) 678 final.

Faure, E. (chair) (1972) *Learning to Be*. Paris: UNESCO.

Feigenbaum, E. and McCorduck, P. (1984) *The Fifth Generation*. New York: Signet.

Feser, E. (2005) *Philosophy of Mind*. Oxford: Oneworld Publications.

Flynn, J. (2007) *What is Intelligence?* Cambridge: Cambridge University Press.

Fowler, J. (1981) *Stages of Faith*. San Francisco: Harper and Row.

Fowler, J. (1996) *Faithful Change*. Nashville: Abingdon Press.

Foucault, M. (1979) *The Will to Knowledge – The History of Sexuality*, Vol. 1. Harmondsworth: Penguin.

Fraser, W. (1995) *Learning from Experience*. Leicester: NIACE.

Freud, S. (1900) *The Interpretation of Dreams*. London: Hogarth Press.

Fromm, E. (1949) *Man for Himself*. London: Routledge.

Gadamer, H.-G. (1976) *Philosophical Hermeneutics*. Berkeley: University of California Press.

Gaita, R. (2000) *A Common Humanity*, 2nd edn. London: Routledge.

Gardner, H. (1983) *Frames of Mind*. New York: Basic Books.

Gardner, H. (2007) *Five Minds for the Future*. Boston, MA: Harvard Business School Press.

Gehlen, A. (1988) *Man: His Nature and Place in the World*. New York: University Press.

Gerhardt, S. (2004) *Why Love Matters*. London: Routledge.

Gibson, F. (1995) Reaching people with dementia through reminiscence work. *Reminiscence* 11, 3–6.

Gibson, J. (1967) *Perceptual Learning and Development*. New York: Appleton Century Crofts.

Gibson, J. (1979) *The Ecological Approach to Visual Perception*. Boston, MA: Houghton Mifflin.

Giddens, A. (1991) *Modernity and Self-Identity*. Cambridge: Polity Press.

Goffman, E. (1959) *The Presentation of Self in Everyday Life*. Harmondsworth; Penguin.

Goffman, E. (1963) *Stigma*. Harmondsworth: Penguin.

Goleman, D. (1995) *Emotional Intelligence*. London: Bloomsbury.

Goleman, D. (1998) *Working with Emotional Intelligence*. New York: Bantam Books.

Goleman, D. (2006) *Social Intelligence*. New York: Bantam Books.

Gordon, P. and Holoyak, K. (1983) Implicit Learning and Generalisation. *Journal of Personality and Social Psychology* 45, 492–500.

Gilhooley, K. (1996) *Thinking: Directed, Undirected and Creative*, 3rd edn. Amsterdam: Academic Press.

Gray, J. (1995) *Enlightenment's Wake*. London: Routledge.

Habermas, J. (1972) *Knowledge and Human Interests*. London: Heinemann.

Habermas, J. (1987) *The Theory of Communicative Action*, Vol. 2. Cambridge: Polity Press.

Habermas, J. (1990) *Moral Consciousness and Communicative Action*. Cambridge: Polity Press.

Halmos, P. (1978) The concept of social problem. In Social Work and Community course DE206 Block 1. Milton Keynes: Open University Press.

Handy, C. (1990) *The Age of Unreason*. London: Anchor Books.

Harlow, H. and Mears, C. (1979) *The Human Model: Primate Perspectives*. Washington: Winston.

Harré, R. (1998) *The Singular Self*. London: Sage.

Haslam, N. (2007) *Introduction to Personality and Intelligence*. London: Sage.

Havighurst, R. (1970) Changing roles and status during the adult life cycle. In Burns, H. (ed.) *Sociological Background to Adult Education*. Syracuse: Syracuse University.

Heidegger, M. (1968) *What is Called Thinking?* New York: Harper and Row.

Heller, A. (1984) *Everyday Life*. London: Routledge and Kegan Paul.

Hilgard, E., Atkinson, R. and Atkinson, R. (1979) *Introduction to Psychology*, 7th edn. New York: Harcourt, Brace, Jovanovich.

Homans, G. (1961) *Social Behavior: Its Elementary Forms*. New York: Harcourt, Brace and World.

Honoré, C. (2004) *In Praise of Slow*. London: Orion.

Hudson, F. (1999) *Mastering the Art of Self-Renewal*, revised edition. San Francisco: Jossey-Bass.

Jackson, M. (2005) *Existential Anthropology*. New York: Berghahn.

James, W. (1963 [1892]) *Psychology*. Greenwich, CT: Fawcett.

James, W. (1960 [1901–02]) *Varieties of Religious Experience*. London: Fontana.

Jarvis, P. (1977) 'Protestant ministers: job satisfaction and role strain in the bureaucratic organisation of the church', unpublished PhD thesis, University of Aston, Birmingham.

Jarvis, P. (1980) Towards a sociological understanding of superstition. *Social Compass*, 27, 285–95.

Jarvis, P. (1987) *Adult Learning in the Social Context*. London: Croom Helm.

Jarvis, P. (1992) *Paradoxes of Learning*. San Francisco: Jossey-Bass.

Jarvis, P. (1997) *Ethics and the Education of Adults in Late Modern Society*. Leicester: NIACE.

Jarvis, P. (1999) *The Practitioner Researcher*. San Francisco: Jossey-Bass.

Jarvis, P. (2001) *Learning in Later Life*. London: Kogan Page.

Jarvis, P. (2006) *Human Learning: Towards a Comprehensive Theory*. London: Routledge.

Jarvis, P. (2007a) 'Andragogy versus pedagogy or from pedagogy to andragogy: a re-assessment of Knowles's dilemma with the development of learning theory', conference presentation, American Adult and Continuing Education Conference, Milwaukee, November 2007.

Jarvis, P. (2007b) *Globalisation, Lifelong Learning and the Learning Society: Sociological Perspectives*. London: Routledge.

Jarvis, P. (2008) *Democracy, Lifelong Learning and the Learning Society: Active Citizenship in a Late Modern Age*. London: Routledge.

Joas, H. (1996) *The Creativity of Action*. Cambridge: Polity Press.

Josso, C. (1991) *Cheminer vers soi (Approaching oneself)*. Lausanne: L'age d'Homme.

Kant, I. (1997) *Groundwork of the Metaphysics of Morals*. Gregor, M. (ed.) Cambridge: Cambridge University Press.

Katz, D. and Stotland, E. (1959) A preliminary statement to the theory of attitude structure and change. In Koch, S. (ed.) *Psychology: a Study of Science*, Vol. 3. New York: McGraw-Hill.

Kelly, G. (1955) *The Psychology of Personal Constructs*. New York: Norton.

Kemper, D. (1987) How many emotions are there? Wedding the social and the autonomic components. *American Journal of Sociology* 93, 263–89.

Kemper, D. (1990) Social relations and emotions: a structural approach. In Kemper, D. (ed.) *Research Agendas in Sociology of the Emotions*. Albany: State of New York University Press.

Kingwell, M. (2000) *The World We Want*. Toronto: Penguin.

Knowles, M. (1970) *The Modern Practice of Adult Education*. Chicago: Association Press.

Knowles, M.S. (1980) *The Modern Practice of Adult Education: From Pedagogy to Andragogy* (revised and updated). Chicago: Association Press.

Kohlberg, L. (1976) Moral stages and moralization. The cognitive developmental approach. In Likona, T. (ed.) *Theory, Research and Social Issues*. New York: Holt, Rinehart and Winston.

Kohlberg, L. (1987) The cognitive development approach to moral education. In Carborne, P. (ed.) *Value Theory and Education*. Malabar: Krieger.

Kolb, D. (1984) *Experiential Learning*. Englewood Cliffs, NJ: Prentice Hall.

Krech, D., Crutchfield, R. and Ballachey, E. (1962) *Individual in Society*. New York: McGraw Hill.

Lacey, A. (1989) *Bergson*. London: Routledge.

Langer, E. (1978) Rethinking the role of thought in social interaction. In Harvey, J., Ickes, W. and Kidd, R. (eds) *New Directions in Attribution Theory*. Hillsdale, NJ: Erlbaum.

Lave, J. and Wenger, E. (1991) *Situated Learning*. Cambridge: Cambridge University Press.

LeDoux, J. (1996) *The Emotional Brain*. New York: Simon and Schuster.

Levinas, E. (1991) *Totality and Infinity*. Dordrecht: Kluwer.

Levinson, D., Darrow, C., Klein, D., Levinson, M. and McKee, B. (1978) *The Seasons of a Man's Life*. New York: Knopf.

Levinson, D. and Levinson, J. (1996) *The Seasons of a Woman's Life*. New York: Ballantine Books.

Locke, J. (1947 edition) *An Essay Concerning Human Understanding* (Everyman Edition). London: Dent.

Luckmann, T. (1967) *Invisible Religion*. London: Macmillan.

Luckmann, T. (1983) *Life-world and Social Realities*. London: Heinemann.

Lyotard, J.-F. (1984) *The Postmodern Condition: A Report on Knowledge*. Manchester: Manchester University Press.

Mace, W. (1974) Gibson's Strategy for Perceiving in Shaw, R. and Brandsford, J. (1974) (eds) *Perceiving, Acting and Knowing*. Hillsdale NJ: Erlbaum

McAdams, D. (2001) *The Person*, 3rd edn. Fort Worth: Harcourt.

McGrath, A. (2007) *The Dawkins Delusion*. London: SPCK.

MacMurray, J. (1979 [1961]) *Persons in Relation*. Atlantic Highlands, NJ: Humanities Press.

Manheimer, R. (1999) *A Map to the End of Time*. New York: W.W. Norton.

Maquarrie, J. (1973) *Existentialism*. Harmondsworth: Penguin.

Marton, F. and Booth, S. (1997) *Learning and Awareness*. Mahwah, NJ: Lawrence Erlbaum Associates.

Marton, F. and Saljo, R. (1984) Approaches to learning. In Marton, F., Hounsell, D. and Entwistle, N. (eds) *The Experience of Learning*. Edinburgh: Scottish Academic Press.

Maslin, K.T. (2001) *An Introduction to the Philosophy of Mind*. Cambridge: Polity Press.

Maslow, A. (1968) *Towards a Psychology of Being*, 2nd edn. New York: Van Nostrand Co.

Mead, G. (1934) In C. Morris (ed.) *Mind, Self and Society from the Standpoint of a Social Behaviorist*. Chicago: University of Chicago Press.

Mead, G. (1938) *The Philosophy of the Act*. Chicago: Chicago University Press.

Merleau-Ponty, M. (1962) *Phenomenology of Perception*. London: Routledge.

Merriam, S. (1985) Reminiscence and life-review; the potential for educational intervention. In Sharron, R. and Lumsden, B. (eds) *Introduction to Educational Gerontology*, 2nd edn. Washington: Hemisphere.

Merton, R. (1968) *Social Theory and Social Structure* (enlarged edition). New York: Free Press.

Mezirow, J. (1991) *Transformative Dimensions of Adult Learning*. San Francisco: Jossey-Bass.

Mezirow, J. (2000) Learning to think like an adult. In Mezirow, J. and Associates (eds) *Learning as Transformation*. San Francisco: Jossey-Bass.

Moody, H. (1998) *Aging: Concepts and Controversies*. Thousand Oaks, CA: Pine Forge.

Moon, J. (1999) *Reflection in Learning and Professional Development*. London: Kogan Page.

Moore, G. (1902) *Principia Ethica*. Cambridge: Cambridge University Press.

Moser, P., Mulder, D. and Trout, J. (1998) *The Theory of Knowledge*. New York: Oxford University Press.

Nelson, K. (2007) *Young Minds in Social Worlds*. Cambridge, MA: Harvard University Press.

Newman, M. (2006) *Teaching Defiance*. San Francisco: Jossey-Bass.

Newman, M. (2008) The 'self' in self-development: a rationalist meditates. *Adult Education Quarterly* 58, 284–98.

Nisbett, R. (2005) *The Geography of Thought*. London: Nicholas Brearley.

Nisbett, R. and Ross, L. (1980) *Human Inferences*. Englewood Cliffs, NJ: Prentice Hall.

Noonan, H. (2003) *Personal Identity*, 2nd edn. London: Routledge.

Nussbaum, M. (1986) *The Fragility of Goodness*. Cambridge: Cambridge University Press.

Nyiri, J. (1988) Tradition and practical knowledge. In Nyiri, J. and Smith, B. (eds) *Practical Knowledge: Outlines of a Theory of Traditions and Skills*. London: Croom Helm.

Oakeshott, M. (1933) *Experience and its Modes*. Cambridge: Cambridge University Press.

OECD (2007a) *Understanding the Social Outcomes of Learning*. Paris: Organisation for Economic Cooperation and Development.

OECD (2007b) *Understanding the Brain: The Birth of a Learning Science*. Paris: Organisation for Economic Cooperation and Development.

Ogden, T. (1986) *The Matrix of the Mind*. Northvale, NJ: Jason Aronson.

Oppenheim, A. (1966) *Questionnaire Design and Attitude Measurement*. London: Heinemann.

Ormrod, J. (1995) *Human Learning*, 2nd edn. Columbus, OH: Merrill.

O'Sullivan, E. (1999) *Transformative Learning*. Toronto: University of Toronto Press, and London: Zed Books.

Otto, R. (1959 [1917]) *The Idea of the Holy*. Harmondsworth: Penguin.

Pasternak, C. (ed.) (2007) *What Makes Us Human?* Oxford: Oneworld Publications.

Pavlov, I. (1927) *Conditioned Reflexes*. New York: Oxford University Press.

Piaget, J. (1929) *The Child's Conception of the World*. London: Routledge and Kegan Paul.

Pinker, S. (1999) *How the Mind Works*. Harmondsworth: Penguin.

Plutchik, R. (1962) *The Emotions: Facts, Theories and a New Model*. New York: Random House.

Plutchik, R. (1980) *Emotion: A Psychoevolutionary Synthesis*. New York: Harper and Row.

Plutchik, E. (2002) *Emotions and Life: Perspectives from Psychology, Biology and Evolution*. Washington DC: American Psychological Association.

Polanyi, M. (1962) *Personal Knowledge*, revised edition. London: Routledge and Kegan Paul.

Polanyi, M. (1967) *The Tacit Dimension*. London: Routledge and Kegan Paul.

Polkinghorne, D. (1988) *Narrative Knowing and the Human Sciences*. New York: State University of New York Press.

Rasmusen, D. (1990) *Reading Habermas*. Oxford: Basil Blackwell.

Reber, A. (1967) Implicit learning of artificial grammars. *Journal of Verbal Learning and Verbal Behavior* 6, 317–327.

Reber, A. and Reber, E. (eds) (2001) *Dictionary of Psychology*, 3rd edn. Harmondsworth: Penguin.

Ricoeur, P. (1981) *Paul Ricoeur: Hermeneutics and the Human Sciences*. Cambridge: Cambridge University Press.

Ricoeur, P. (1984) *Time and Narrative* (3 vols). Chicago: University of Chicago Press.

Ricoeur, P. (1986) *Fallible Man*. New York: Fordham University Press.

Ricoeur, P. (1995) *Figuring the Sacred*. Minneapolis: Fortress Press.

Riegel, K. (1973) Dialectical operations: the final period of cognitive development. *Human Development* 16, 315–24.

Riesman, D. (1950) *The Lonely Crowd*. New Haven: Yale University Press.

Robertson, R. (1978) *Meaning and Change*. Oxford: Basil Blackwell.

Rogers, C. (1961) *On Becoming a Person*. London: Constable.

Rogers, C. and Freiberg, H.J. (1994) *Freedom to Learn*, 3rd edn. New York: Merrill.

Rogers, C.R. (1983) *Freedom to Learn for the 80s*. New York: Merrill-Macmillan.

Rose, D. (2006) *Consciousness: Philosophical, Psychological and Neural Theories.* Oxford: Oxford University Press.

Ryle, G. (1945) Knowing how and knowing that. *Proceedings of the Aristotelian Society* 46, 1–16.

Scheler, M. (1980 [1926]) *Problems of a Sociology of Knowledge.* London: Routledge and Kegan Paul.

Schön, D. (1983) *The Reflective Practitioner.* New York: Basic Books.

Schutz, A. (1967) *The Phenomenology of the Social World.* London: Heinemann.

Schutz, A. (1972) *The Phenomenology of the Social World.* London: Heinemann.

Schutz, A. and Luckmann, T. (1974) The *Structures of the Lifeworld.* London: Heinemann.

Sheehy, G. (1995) *New Passages.* Toronto: Random House of Canada.

Simmel, G. (1971) The metropolis and mental life. In Thompson, K. and Tunstall, J. (eds) (1971) *Sociological Perspectives* Harmondsworth: Penguin.

Skinner, B. (1968) *The Technology of Teaching.* New York: Appleton Century Crofts.

Speake, J. (1984) *A Dictionary of Philosophy.* London: Pan Books.

Starbuck, W. and Milliken, F. (1988) Filters hamper our perception. In Hambrick, D. (ed) *The Executive Effect.* Greenwich, CT: JAI Press.

Stern, W. (1938) *General Psychology from a Personalistic Standpoint.* New York: Macmillan.

Sternberg, R. (1997) *Thinking Styles.* Cambridge: Cambridge University Press.

Stevenson, C. (1944) *Ethics and Language.* New Haven, CT: Yale University Press.

Taylor, G. and Spencer, S. (eds) (2004) *Social Identities: Multidisciplinary Approaches.* London: Routledge.

Thorndike, E. and Rock, R. (1934) Learning without awareness of what is being learned. *Journal of Experimental Psychology* 1, 1–19.

Tomasello, M. (1999) *The Cultural Origins of Human Cognition.* Cambridge, MA: Harvard University Press.

Tompkins, S. (1981) The quest for primary motives: biography or autobiography of an idea. *Journal of Personality and Social Psychology* 41, 306–329.

Tremlin, T. (2006) *Minds and Gods.* Oxford: Oxford University Press.

Tuomi, I. (1999) *Corporate Knowledge: Theory and Practice of Intelligent Organizations.* Helsinki: Metaxis.

Turner, J. (2000) *On the Origins of Human Emotions: A Sociological Enquiry into the Evolution of the Human Affect.* Stanford: Stanford University Press.

Turner, J. and Stets, J. (2005) *The Sociology of Emotions.* Cambridge: Cambridge University Press.

Turner, V. (1969) *The Ritual Process.* Harmondsworth: Penguin.

Turner, V. (1986) Dewey, Dilthey and drama. In Turner, V. and Bruner, E. (eds) *The Anthropology of Experience.* Urbana: University of Illinois Press.

Uleman, J. and Bargh, J. (1989) *Unintended Thought.* New York: Guildford.

Urmson, J. (1968) *The Emotive Theory of Ethics.* London: Hutchinson.

Vardy, P. (2003) *Being Human.* London: Darton, Longman and Todd.

van Gennep, A. (1960 [1908]) *The Rites of Passage.* London: Routledge and Kegan Paul.

Vernon, M. (2007) *After Atheism.* Basingstoke: Palgrave.

Von Rad, G. (1961) *Genesis.* London: SCM.

Vygotsky, L. (1978) *Mind in Society,* Cambridge, MA: Harvard University Press.

Wallis, G. (1926) *The Art of Thought.* London: Jonathan Cape.

Weber, M. (1930) *The Protestant Ethic and the Spirit of Capitalism.* London: Unwin.

Weil, S. and McGill, I. (eds) (1989) *Making Sense of Experiential Learning.* Buckingham: Society for Research into Higher Education and Open University Press.

Weiner, B. (1980) *Human Motivation.* New York: Holt, Reinhart and Winston.

West, L. (1996) *Beyond Fragments, Adults, Motivation and Higher Education: A Biographical Analysis.* London: Taylor & Francis.

West, L. (2001) *Doctors on the Edge: General Practitioners, Health and Learning in the Inner-City.* London: FABooks.

West, L. (2007) An auto/biographical imagination and the radical challenge of families and their learning. In West, L., Alheit, P., Anderson, A. and Merrill, B. (eds) *The Uses of Biographical and Life History Methods in the Study of Adult and Lifelong Learning: European Perspectives.* Munich: Peter Lang.

Wexler, B. (2006) *Brain and Culture.* Cambridge, MA: Bradford Books, MIT.

Williamson, B. (1998) *Lifeworlds and Learning.* Leicester: NIACE.

Willment, J.-A. (ed.) (2008) *Learners in Midlife.* Calgary: Detselig.

Witkin, H. (1971) Psychological differentiations. In Cashdown, A. and Whitehead, I. (eds) *Personality, Growth and Learning.* London: Longman.

Wlodkowski, R. (1985) *Enhancing Adult Motivation to Learn.* San Francisco: Jossey-Bass.

Index

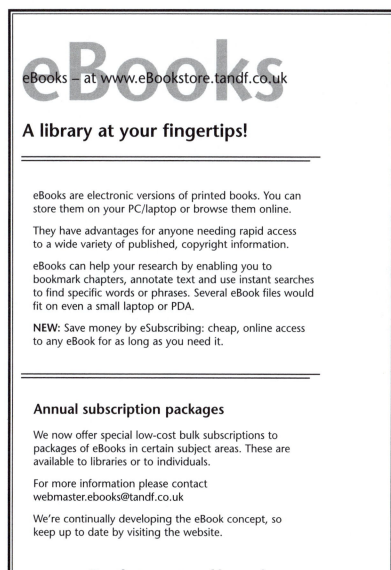